PERFORMANCE
Breakthroughs

FOR **Adolescents**
WITH **Learning Disabilities**
OR **ADD**

**How to Help Students Succeed in the
Regular Education Classroom**

Geraldine Markel AND **Judith Greenbaum**

Research Press
2612 North Mattis Avenue
Champaign, Illinois 61821

*To the students who dealt with confusion, frustration, anger,
and depression, but who still managed, through hard work,
to make breakthroughs, as well as to their counterparts,
those students who dropped out of school
before we could help them*

*To the parents who, lacking information and skills,
were often misunderstood, frustrated, and angry,
but who advocated staunchly for their children's education
and were willing to put aside past grievances*

*To the teachers who struggled daily with the many problems
all students bring to school, with changing system requirements,
and with dwindling resources, but who still managed
to care enough to persevere and change course
when needed to help their students succeed*

Contents

Figures

1

Introduction

When I got the paper back I almost started to cry. The paper looked like it was smeared with blood. Even though the teacher wrote "good ideas," the only thing I saw was all those red circles telling me how dumb I was.

—Twelfth-grade student

I hate being with other people. I hate being made fun of by kids. And sometimes teachers make me feel stupied. They do that by pointting me out in class and only showing me what to do in front of the holl class and after that saying do you understand know? The only reason I'm in school is my very best friend and family tell me that all those people don't under stand my needs and feelings, And I'm the same as everyone else.

—Tenth-grade student
(excerpt from a self-report questionnaire)

I read a lot. Everybody say I'm very smart. They don't know why I'm having problems in school. The teachers say I'm lazy, but I'm not. They tell me to pay attention, but I still can't understand what they are saying sometimes. I'm really worried because my parents want me to go to college.

—Seventh-grade student

School is a student's life, and for students with learning problems like the ones just described, life can be hard. Indeed, nearly all students with learning problems have at some point felt inadequate and incompetent. School has always been difficult for them. They suffer from chronic failure. Almost all of them have problems with self-esteem and stress. It may be difficult to look at students who appear so unattractive, annoying—even defiant—and see promise. It takes a special teacher to be willing to try to work with such students to help them learn.

1

Research has begun to help us realize such students' true potential and to develop effective strategies for helping them achieve in school and beyond. It is now clear that educators can foster real performance breakthroughs for students with learning problems. They can guide these young people to attain goals that would just a few years ago have been considered out of reach.

A breakthrough is an accomplishment, an achievement, or some progress that is beyond the realm of expectation. It is something that visibly—and perhaps dramatically—changes the way an individual or group behaves. A performance breakthrough means putting everything together, using one's potential, and doing one's best on demand.

"I focused and finished the math quiz. I got them all right! I never knew it could be that way." These are the comments of a tearful eleventh grader who had finished the previous semester with a 2.2 grade point average and had just experienced a performance breakthrough, a powerful, singular experience that provides vision and motivation.

A breakthrough can occur over a month or two, a semester, or a year or more. Following are some of the breakthroughs classroom teachers can foster:

Improvement in test scores

Improved skills in such areas as time management
and problem solving

Maintenance of passing grades or better while the
student confronts new or increased challenges

Reduced stress and irritability

Increased class participation

Reduced tardiness and absenteeism

Timely completion of assignments

Increased self-esteem

Willingness to persist and confront challenges

Over longer periods, the following types of breakthroughs are possible:

Significantly improved grades in one course
or in several courses

Integration of new skills in a variety of academic
and home situations

Fewer relapses and performance plateaus,
as well as shorter rebound time

Improved ability to predict consequences

Improved ability to plan proactively to avoid
or prevent crises

Commitment to stay in school

Return to school or completion of education
through an alternative means

Growth in school or at work

Enjoyment of more positive social or work-related
experiences

Significant shift toward more positive or more
productive life choices

For students at risk, breakthroughs may involve personal interactions with a number of professionals. At different points in the
process, these professionals may be teachers, coaches, role models,
therapists, visionaries, and advocates. Every professional can play a
part in the breakthrough process. One father of an adolescent with
learning and attention problems described it this way:

> It's not unlike Michelangelo's *David.* While I have never
> seen the statue, friends have told me that they stood
> before it and cried. When people asked Michelangelo
> how he was able to carve such a perfect David, he had
> a simple response: "The perfect David was already in the
> stone," he replied. "All I had to do was chip away at
> everything that wasn't David."

As educators, we need to keep in mind the metaphor of Michelangelo's
David. Like the "perfect David," the motivated, capable student is
already inside every child. Our task is to chip away everything that
is not a part of that fully realized learner.

Anyone can make a breakthrough—break away from negative
thoughts and expectations that impede progress, break out of old

habits that interfere with academic success, and break down barriers to learning and behavior management. Teachers can help students with learning problems or differences make breakthroughs when they help students take control of their behaviors. Students can and do discover hidden talents, employ underused strengths, develop unrealized potential, and access untapped spirit. The ultimate breakthrough is acceptance of oneself as a whole person with the capacity to learn and improve: "I am who I am because of all of me—both the gifts and the glitches."

The question, then, is not whether performance breakthroughs can occur, but how to ensure that more and more students experience them earlier and in more areas of their lives. This book presents an integrative model that teachers at the middle school and high school levels can use to encourage performance breakthroughs for students with learning and attention problems. Intended primarily as an instructional guide for classroom teachers, the book will also be useful for a variety of other professionals, including special education teachers, counselors, psychologists, social workers, school administrators, and anyone else who works with at-risk youth. The strategies and techniques discussed here will also enhance the learning of all students.

This introductory chapter sets the stage by describing how learning difficulties, attention problems, and adolescence challenge students. It also gives an overview of the legislation through which services are provided for students with learning difficulties and attention problems.

The next two chapters present a framework for understanding the instructional process and systems affecting the student with learning problems. Specifically, chapter 2 discusses the roles of various professionals, presents the components of an integrative approach, and suggests core steps in instruction. Chapter 3 presents two case studies to contrast the features of productive and unproductive systems.

Often no one realizes the depth to which a student's problems have evolved until the student is in a full-blown academic crisis. Chapter 4 discusses a systematic problem-solving process for crisis intervention, describing the context in which crisis occurs and spelling out strategies for communication and collaboration among a crisis manager, parents, teachers, and the student.

Chapter 5 presents an overview of assessment issues. Specifically discussed are the purposes of assessment, the referral process, components of a comprehensive assessment, members of the assessment team, the role of the classroom teacher, and the assessment process itself.

Program planning is the focus of chapter 6. The Individualized Education Program, or IEP, is offered as a model for program planning that can be effective whether or not students are eligible for special education services. The chapter also outlines the steps in program planning, discusses the importance of motivation and reinforcement, and examines ways to balance conflicting philosophies, instructional needs, and system demands.

Chapter 7 discusses self-management skills for students with learning difficulties and attention problems. The role of the classroom teacher in integrating self-management strategies into the content area classroom is described, as are specific self-management strategies and skills: self-observation, self-contracting, self-evaluation, self-recognition and reward, time management, and others.

In chapters 8 through 12, classroom teachers will find information to help students develop their skills in specific areas: reading (chapter 8), listening and note taking (chapter 9), preparing for and taking tests (chapter 10), academic writing (chapter 11), and homework (chapter 12). These chapters offer a strong rationale for the content area teacher's providing direct instruction in these particular skills; each chapter describes specific strategies teachers can use and outlines the instructional process whereby these strategies can best be taught.

Finally, chapter 13 underscores important principles brought out in the preceding chapters and presents some closing thoughts on ways to foster performance breakthroughs.

Throughout the book, case examples are used to illustrate educational problems and their solutions. Some case examples combine the experiences of several students. The students whose stories have been chosen represent diversity in gender, race, and socioeconomic status. All of them were having difficulties in school. All were in regular education classes; many were receiving special education support. Although they were of average or above-average intelligence, many were failing courses. Despite their problems, these students achieved breakthroughs in learning.

Based on real-life experience, the case examples allow us to better understand the problems confronting these young people and the adults in their lives. Quoted speech and dialogues are used throughout the book for the same reason; the actual words students, parents, and teachers say to one another communicate depth of feeling, range of needs, and quality of support better than any description.

UNDERSTANDING LEARNING AND ATTENTION PROBLEMS

The terms *learning disability* and *Attention Deficit Disorder* are defined by educational law and the medical or mental health profession. The definitions of these terms have undergone many changes over the years and no doubt will continue to evolve as data are collected. In this book we use the term *learning problem* broadly, to suggest both a specific learning disability and a learning problem that does not meet the formal criteria for a learning disability. When a specific learning disability is meant, we have used that term. The most recent version of the *Diagnostic and Statistical Manual of Mental Disorders* (DSM-IV; American Psychiatric Association, 1995) identifies the diagnostic category Attention-Deficit/Hyperactivity Disorder. Although this is the most up-to-date terminology for mental health practitioners, in this book we employ the general term *attention problem* and use the specific term *Attention Deficit Disorder,* or *ADD,* because they reflect more common usage among educators.

Not all students with learning problems meet the criteria for learning disabilities. Not all students with attention problems meet the criteria for ADD. However, students with learning disabilities generally exhibit learning problems, attention problems, or both. Of students diagnosed with learning disabilities, up to 80% have secondary problems in attention. Of students who have ADD, 20 to 50% also have learning disabilities (Barkley, 1990; Silver, 1992).

Learning problems may be just learning differences, according to Levine (1993), part of the continuum of human behavior. Most of us have learning or attention problems at some time in our lives. Successful educational interventions for students begin with a clear understanding of the specific learning differences or problems they face (Blalock, 1981; Levine, 1993).

Learning Disabilities

A learning disability is defined by special education law as, first, a severe discrepancy between a student's intellectual ability and his or her achievement in one or more areas, such as oral expression, listening comprehension, written expression, basic reading skills, reading comprehension, mathematics calculation, or mathematics reasoning. The second part of this legal definition involves the "exclusionary clause." This part states that the severe discrepancy cannot be due to visual, hearing, or motor handicap; mental retardation; emotional disturbance; autism; or environmental, cultural, or economic disadvantage. Students must meet both parts of the definition if they are to qualify for services under special education law. Five percent of the school age population are currently receiving services under special education law (Ayers, 1994). There are estimates that up to 20% of the school age population have learning disabilities (Tucker, Stevens, & Ysseldyke, 1983).

The presence of a learning disability can also be inferred in ways other than by the presence of a severe discrepancy between ability and achievement. For example, medical doctors look for hard or soft signs of neurological conditions, such as seizures or developmental delays. Psychologists look for discrepancies in subtest scores on tests like the Wechsler Intelligence Scale for Children (WISC-III; Wechsler, 1991). For example, two students may have the same global score of 110 on the WISC-III (this would be considered in the high-average range). However, one student may have a high verbal score and a low performance score, whereas for the other student the situation might be reversed. If we look at the subtest scores, we might find a similar variation of high and low scores. Large discrepancies among subtest scores or between verbal and performance scores are interpreted by some professionals to mean that a student has learning disabilities. The student has strengths and weaknesses that would be hidden if only the global score were considered.

Speech and language problems are often the earliest signs of a learning disability. Preschoolers with expressive or receptive language problems are at high risk for learning disabilities. Learning disabilities per se may not be discovered until a student enters second or third grade and is not learning to read or write as expected. Sometimes a bright student can compensate so well that learning disabilities are not discovered until that student enters middle or high school or even college.

In order to understand learning disabilities it is useful to break down learning into four steps (Silver, 1992): input, organization (integration), memory, and output. Information must be received and understood (input), organized, stored (memory), and used (output) in order for it to be learned. Obviously, these four steps are related. A fifth problem, slow rate of processing, is also a factor.

Students with *input problems* have difficulty receiving information. They may have problems with listening comprehension or reading comprehension. In addition, they may have difficulty understanding information presented in a particular manner but often can understand information presented in an alternate form. Many of the students we see in class who are not following directions have auditory input problems. Students with dyslexia have visual input problems.

Students with *organizational problems* have difficulty sequencing and categorizing new information, relating new information to old, relating parts to the whole, or finding main ideas. They have difficulty with the organizational aspects of listening comprehension and reading comprehension. Because they have problems organizing information, they have difficulty with learning and retention. They might do well on multiple-choice questions but do poorly on essay questions. They may lose their homework, often be unprepared for class, and have time management problems.

Students with *memory problems* can often participate very well in class discussions but do poorly on tests. They seem to learn the material and then forget it, especially where cumulative knowledge is necessary for problem solving (Hagen, 1984; Hagen & Barclay, 1982). They may study very hard but have little to show for it, therefore appearing "lazy." With short-term memory problems, students have difficulty remembering spelling, multiplication tables, and instructions, whether auditory or visual.

Students with *output problems* can understand the information presented but have difficulty expressing that understanding in oral or written form. Orally, they may use circumlocution to express an idea because they can't find the words they want. These students often do poorly on essay tests and/or have difficulty answering questions in class. They can appear "dumb"—as if they don't understand what they have just read or heard in class.

Students with a *slow rate of processing* need significantly more time to understand new information. They may or may not need repetition. What they need is time—time to organize their ideas and formulate their responses. If responses are demanded quickly, these students may appear not to know the information. They have trouble responding to questions in class and taking timed tests.

Because many items on intelligence tests are timed, the IQ scores of students with a slow processing speed may be depressed and are not an accurate reflection of their ability.

It is important to distinguish between learning disabilities and other causes of low achievement in order to design an appropriate program for the student. The student with learning disabilities has by definition at least average intelligence. Many are very bright, and a certain percentage are gifted. They do have difficulties in one or more areas but generally can deal with information on a high level if it is presented appropriately (Fox, Brody, & Tobin, 1983; Silverman, 1989; Suter & Wolf, 1987). "Slow learners," on the other hand, have borderline intelligence and need information presented at a slower pace and at a lower level of difficulty. "Underachievers" are generally bright but have problems with motivation and/or self-esteem (Whitmore, 1980). Often they are perfectionists. Students who are emotionally disturbed have low achievement because their emotional problems often interfere with daily functioning. Many students with emotional impairment have underlying learning disabilities. Some students with learning disabilities have secondary emotional impairments due to frustration, chronic failure, depression, and low self-esteem.

Attention Deficit Disorder

In the classroom, students with attention problems constitute a diverse group. Some students may have received a formal diagnosis of ADD, either with or without hyperactivity. Often, however, attention problems are undetected or misdiagnosed.

There is great variation in type, degree, and manifestation of attention problems, although all can result in poor or inconsistent day-to-day academic performance, regardless of ability. The complexity and inconsistency of these problems baffle and frustrate adults and peers alike (Baren, 1994a, 1994b). At the same time, students with attention difficulties may be unaware of the impact of these problems on themselves, their schoolwork, their families, and their friends. Such students often think of themselves as "crazy."

In general, students with attention difficulties exhibit problems in focus and maintenance of attention, distractibility, impulsivity, hyperactivity, and other areas. Of course, no single student exhibits all these behaviors, nor are these behaviors symptomatic of problems per se. Some of these behaviors are part of the normal developmental process and as such may signal a temporary developmental delay in an older student. Some are merely normal personality traits—part of what makes everyone unique and interesting.

Focus and maintenance of attention

In and out of the classroom, students with attention problems may have difficulty focusing and maintaining attention. They often cannot attend to important information while ignoring or screening out irrelevant or unimportant information. They have short attention spans, especially for boring or repetitive tasks. A related problem is erratic focus; students report that they feel as though they are on an attention roller coaster because their attention varies so widely. They miss information and then expend enormous energy attempting to concentrate or to conceal their difficulties. When they do concentrate, they tire easily. In addition, they may allocate inappropriate amounts of time to some tasks and fail to finish other things, have difficulty listening, and be generally forgetful. Such students often lose materials necessary for academic work and forget instructions, plans, and promises.

Distractibility

Students with attention problems may be highly distractible. They often daydream. They may experience excessive, interfering thought patterns whereby their minds race and their thoughts jump from one thing to another. Extraneous auditory or visual stimuli are highly distracting to them. In addition, many such students are generally inconsistent in their behavior; they frequently change their minds and may say one thing yet do another.

Impulsivity

Students with impulsivity problems have difficulty controlling their behavior or delaying gratification. They are unable to stop and think before acting or wait for their turn. They blurt out answers to questions or make inappropriate remarks, find organizing time and tasks very difficult, and take a long time to "settle down" in class. They put off starting their homework and make decisions quickly, without anticipating the consequences. Impulsivity is also expressed in the form of speaking out inappropriately (without considering the impact of the expression), making careless errors, and being impatient and easily frustrated. They may exhibit extreme irritability, sometimes acting explosively, yet at the same time they can be friendly, charming, and loyal. Finally, such students have trouble being satisfied and may often feel bored. As a result, they may take needless risks.

Hyperactivity

Hyperactivity is another characteristic of attention difficulty, although it may or may not be present. Students fidget, jiggle, tap their feet—generally being restless and moving around unnecessarily. They exhibit movement that is not needed to complete a task, or they talk excessively. They ask nonessential questions, make unnecessary spontaneous remarks, interrupt, and request repetition of previously explained directions (Robin, 1990).

Although hyperactivity generally becomes less of a problem during adolescence, impulsivity may become a much greater problem, manifesting itself in risky behavior, family conflict, and rebelliousness and truancy in school (Robin, 1990).

Other complications

Students with attention problems often seem to ignore rules and may refuse to shift activities if they are involved in a preferred activity. They may be unable to stop their inappropriate behavior or their response to inappropriate stimuli. In general, they have a tendency to seek immediate rewards and find it difficult to modulate their activities or emotions. Their behavior sometimes gets out of hand. They can, and teachers fear that they will, incite minor riots. They are quick to arouse and slow to calm down. In general, they are deficient in self-regulation. Many of these students cannot read social cues and signals, and therefore interact inappropriately in social situations. Often they lack the time or patience to review their work and fail to see the relevance of doing so.

Diagnosing Attention Deficit Disorder

The diagnosis of ADD usually involves the direct observation of student behavior in different situations by trained personnel, parent questionnaires and rating scales, teacher rating scales, student interviews, psychoeducational assessment, academic performance data, and medical examination (Conners, 1989a, 1989b; Goyette,

Conners, & Ulrich, 1978; Ullman, Sleator, & Sprague, 1991). The criteria for eligibility established in the DSM-IV (American Psychiatric Association, 1995) include the presence of either inattention or hyperactivity-impulsivity, onset no later than 7 years of age, presence of symptoms in two or more situations, and clinically significant distress or impairment in social, academic, or occupational functioning.

Kaufman's (1979) grouping of subtests on the WISC-III can yield a measurement Kaufman calls "freedom from distractibility." Additional testing by neuropsychologists can also be used to assess impulsivity (Greenberg & Waldman, 1993; Weber, 1988). Often, however, ADD is deduced largely from observations of student behavior (Maag & Reid, 1994).

Differential diagnosis is very important because ADD can coexist with, as well as mask, other problems. A student who is rarely on task in class may be having trouble understanding verbal directions. Although this student may appear to have ADD, he or she may actually have learning disabilities. A student who has trouble focusing on a repetitive task and often seems to be a million miles away may appear to have ADD. Actually, the student may be gifted and bored.

Many of the symptoms of ADD can be confused with emotional impairment, resulting in the view that the student is "crazy." The distinction can be important because it dictates the treatment or remediation of the disorder. Students with an emotional impairment primarily need a therapeutic environment; students with ADD primarily need to learn new skills. Some students with ADD have developed a secondary emotional problem due to frustration, chronic failure, or difficulty with interpersonal relationships. They may need supplemental therapy in addition to new skills.

Last, the behavioral problems of students with ADD are often attributed to unstructured or unstable home environments. This may or may not be the case. The focus for the teacher is that even students from such environments can learn appropriate academic and social skills.

Effects of attention problems on learning

Regardless of the etiology of attention problems, their effects can be devastating to learning and academic performance. Attention problems may seriously interfere with cognitive processing. To process information, students need to focus attention. They need the ability to sustain alertness, stay flexible, and withhold inappropriate responses.

Inattention or lack of sustained attention interferes with searching for relevant details, planning, sequencing tasks, remembering strategies, using information, reproducing visual information, and self-correcting. All of these processes are important to successful learning.

In addition to their negative effects on learning, attention problems have a counterproductive impact on teacher attitudes and social interactions. Students with attention problems are often seen staring into space or engaging in horseplay with other students when they should be working. In addition, students with attention problems often interrupt others (including the teacher) when they are talking and bother the teacher and other students with constant jiggling or tapping. Their behavior persists despite reprimands. These problems are compounded when students trivialize the effects of their behavior by saying things like "What's the big deal?" or "I didn't think you would care so much."

Students with attention deficits, with or without hyperactivity, are often perceived by others as socially insensitive, stubborn, or lazy. Self-esteem suffers as a result of chronic failure and the negative attitudes of others. In turn, motivation to learn is reduced, and negative behavior is increased. In brief, a negative cycle ensues.

Punishing such students or ignoring their problems tends to intensify their difficulties, but successful interventions are possible. The earlier attention problems can be identified and managed, the better. Students will perform better academically and socially, have greater self-esteem, and be spared the added emotional problems that arise from chronic failure and scorn. It is also likely to be easier to work with a younger student who has fewer bad habits than to work with an older student who is defensive and uncooperative, and whose patterns are more entrenched.

THE DEMANDS OF ADOLESCENCE

In addition to specific learning disabilities and attention problems, students with learning problems will display all the difficulties associated with their developmental stage. Adolescence is a time of rapid change and risk taking, with both positive and negative outcomes.

The goals of adolescence are independence, autonomy, and self-determination. Adolescence is an opportune period for intervention: Even though young people are experimenting with independence, parents, teachers, and schools can make an indelible mark on their lives.

Adolescence is also a time when students experience challenges to self-esteem as they struggle to adjust to emerging sexuality, changing social role definitions, cognitive development, and increased academic demands. School transitions from the elementary to the secondary level occur just when there is a decline in students' motivation to learn and perform in school and an upswing in peer influence. Such transitions can place particular stress on students with learning problems.

When students move into the middle school, they face school populations that may be triple those of the elementary school. High schools are often two to three times as large as middle schools. A secondary school student may have five to seven different teachers, to whose personalities, teaching styles, course requirements, rules, and routines he or she must adjust. At a time when students most need strong personal relationships and a sense of belonging in order to feel motivated, teachers become less and less knowable, and students feel more and more anonymous (Eccles & Midgely, 1989).

These unfamiliar pressures can be overwhelming for students with learning and attention difficulties. In addition to the challenge of improving their basic academic or behavioral skills, middle and junior high school students face increased demands on their time management and organizing skills, self-management and coping skills, and ability to work independently. Reading, writing, and listening tasks become more complex. Meeting these challenges while coping with the physical and emotional changes of adolescence can seem an insurmountable task for at-risk students.

Mercer and Mercer (1993) discuss eight demands placed on secondary school students:

Gaining information from print materials

Gaining information from lectures

Demonstrating knowledge through tests

Expressing information in writing

Working independently

Demonstrating a broad set of cognitive and metacognitive strategies

Interacting appropriately

Demonstrating motivation to learn

Students with learning and attention problems can have problems in all of these areas. It is not surprising that one-third to one-half of students with learning disabilities or ADD drop out of school (Levine, Zigmond, & Birch, 1983) and that they are more prone to substance abuse and juvenile delinquency. The way the school handles the challenges of secondary school and adolescence can quite literally determine the course of a student's life.

THE LEGISLATIVE CONTEXT

The vision of free and appropriate schooling for all children with disabilities in the United States is outlined in two legislative mandates—specifically, Section 504 of the Rehabilitation Act of 1973 and the Individuals with Disabilities Education Act (IDEA) of 1990 (formerly the Education of the Handicapped Act of 1975).

Under both IDEA and Section 504, students with learning disabilities and ADD are placed in regular educational programs, when appropriate. IDEA mandates that students with disabilities be educated in the "least restrictive environment," and Section 504 ensures the access of students with disabilities to all educational programs offered by the school. Generally, students with learning disabilities or ADD spend most of their time in the regular education classroom.

One of the major differences between the two laws is the amount of support offered to the student. Under Section 504, the support that students receive is generally within what regular education programming can provide. This means that "reasonable" programming accommodations must be made by teachers, and regular education support personnel such as counselors, librarians, aides, and volunteers can be used for program support. Under IDEA, special education teachers and teacher consultants, as well as social workers, can be used to support the student's program. These staff members can provide direct services to students or consultative services to the teachers of those students.

Perhaps the primary difference between the two laws concerns their eligibility requirements. IDEA has much more stringent requirements than Section 504 for learning disabilities, specifying the need for a "severe discrepancy" between ability and achievement. Section 504 essentially states that anyone who thinks he or she has a handicap that interferes with learning, and whom others think has such a handicap, is eligible. Many students with learning disabilities and ADD who are not eligible for services under IDEA are eligible under Section 504.

At present, ADD is not a separate category under IDEA. Under IDEA, students with ADD must qualify for services under the categories of learning disabilities, health impairment, or emotional impairment.

Both laws specify that an educational program must be developed for the eligible student by a committee convened specifically for that purpose. Under IDEA that program is called an Individual Education Program (IEP), and the committee is called the Individual Education Program Committee (IEPC). Under both laws, the parents of the student are involved in the development of the educational program.

Under IDEA and Section 504, "reasonable" accommodations for all eligible students are determined by the IEPC or the Section 504 planning team, respectively. Regular education teachers are responsible for making any necessary classroom accommodations. Such accommodations may involve one or more of the following (Mercer & Mercer, 1993):

Methods of instruction

Methods of presentation

Student grouping arrangements

Reinforcement systems

Classroom rules

Types of materials

Test-taking conditions and methods

Grading practices

Because the provisions of IDEA and Section 504 are interpreted differently by different states—and even by different school districts within a state—the process of obtaining services for an individual student can be difficult. A range of educational services for students with learning disabilities or ADD can be invoked under Section 504, but many parents, teachers, and school administrators are still unaware of this fact.

SUMMARY AND CONCLUSIONS

Before effective instruction for students with learning problems is possible, it is first necessary to have a clear picture of the nature and extent of learning disabilities and attention problems, as well as of the demands of adolescence. Legislation, as well as social, economic, and educational realities, affect the delivery of services, as do the attitudes of the educators who provide them. Society needs the contributions of all its citizens. We cannot afford to write off 20 to 35% of the student population who are at risk for school failure (Frymier, 1989; Helge, 1989a, 1989b). We need to adopt a vision of the best possible performance for *all* students, including those with learning and attention problems. Given current technologies for teaching and learning, it is well within reason for us to strive to achieve this vision.

2

Understanding the Instructional Process

As a result of research, we know more than ever before about ways to help students who have learning and attention difficulties. Successful educational programs for students with learning problems hinge on a systematic integrative approach, one that can help structure the provision of services and information in a coherent way. The model described in this chapter will help the regular classroom teacher create successful learning experiences for all students; it is especially useful for students with learning disabilities, ADD, other learning or behavior problems, or problems related to learning English as a second language.

Although a number of professionals will likely be involved in the integrative approach, in our view the role of the classroom teacher is critical. Before discussing the components of the integrative approach and the core steps in the instructional process, then, it is important to examine the various roles of the classroom teacher, as well as those of other professionals.

TEACHER ROLES

Given adequate support from the larger system and access to appropriate resources, a single teacher can help students with learning disabilities and attention problems achieve performance breakthroughs. In the process, the teacher assumes myriad roles. These are roles that most teachers currently assume in an intuitive fashion. We are suggesting a more deliberate and systematic assumption of roles and a broader range of roles.

Classroom manager

The teacher organizes the classroom environment, establishes optimal conditions for learning, sets a positive tone, and fosters student interest. As classroom manager, the teacher is responsible for establishing rules and helping students develop self-management skills and good work habits. Other management functions include keeping records to monitor progress toward instructional goals and using classroom data and feedback on performance to make decisions about instruction.

Group facilitator

The teacher encourages positive interpersonal relationships through small- and large-group interaction and helps students with differing abilities progress in the classroom environment. The teacher raises issues and stimulates discussion; models negotiation, conflict resolution, decision making, and problem solving; and focuses on the collaboration and mutual support that help students to help themselves and one another.

Coach

In the role of coach, the teacher focuses on goals, action, and results. As coach, the teacher helps students to improve thinking and self-management strategies (Garmston & Linder, 1993). The coach expects continual improvement in the academic performance of all students, who are viewed as team players in the academic game. As in any game, the teacher as coach helps students build on their strengths and remedy their weaknesses. The coach gets the best group effort by individualizing and helping students attain their personal best, closely aligns practice and rehearsal to targeted academic behaviors, and, by creating team spirit, helps students support one another.

Champion

Students are more easily involved when a teacher is genuinely interested in them and will champion their cause. They need to know that the teacher accepts them, understands their strengths and weaknesses, and can reassure them that their learning difficulties are not character flaws but rather problems to be solved through collaboration.

The teacher as champion believes in the student and encourages and publicizes student progress. In the role of champion, the teacher intervenes on the student's behalf in difficult situations with other teachers, providing information and training.

As champion, the teacher also proposes role models for students—for instance, famous inventors, sports heroes, or other students who have struggled and succeeded. As appropriate, the teacher may occasionally share personal experiences that were embarrassing or challenging and explain how he or she confronted failure and/or embarrassment.

Detective

Learning disabilities and attention problems bring with them complexities and contradictions. This is baffling for students, parents, teachers, and employers alike. How does one understand the student who can answer a complicated math problem but cannot explain or show how it was done? How is it possible that a student who can read and speak well cannot learn a foreign language?

The teacher as detective helps students find the conditions under which they can and cannot learn or perform in order to design an environment that will maximize learning. This detective work entails gathering information about students' learning styles, interests, strengths, and weaknesses, as well as experimenting with ways to spark motivation and enhance thinking strategies. The teacher also searches outside the classroom for additional resources that can help students learn.

Team member

The teacher participates actively with other professionals to make sure that IEPs and 504 plans are implemented and that positive outcomes are attained. In addition, the teacher forms partnerships with students and parents, encouraging them to take active roles in learning, goal setting, and problem solving. The teacher identifies and suggests referrals and resources that are appropriate for students. As team member, the teacher helps facilitate students' transition from one academic level to another and/or to the work setting.

OTHER PROFESSIONAL ROLES

Surrounding the teacher are other professionals who can provide specialized support as needed. Benefits to the student multiply when teams of concerned professionals collaborate in planning the educational program (Sprick, Sprick, & Garrison, 1993; Wood, 1992). Some of the professionals involved in working together on the student's behalf include the following.

Special education teacher consultants

Because they have specialized knowledge and skills relating to learning disabilities and ADD, special education teacher consultants offer training and resources to classroom teachers who have students with these disabilities. A special education teacher consultant can help in a variety of ways—by providing the classroom teacher with information and materials, by team teaching with the classroom teacher and giving special help to students who need it, and by providing intensive instruction, either in or out of the classroom, to students with severe difficulties. One of the most important services the teacher consultant can offer is explaining the nature of individual students' learning disabilities and/or attention deficits.

The teacher consultant can help the classroom teacher translate information from IEPs and 504 plans into instructional activities for specific students. In addition, the teacher consultant may screen and observe for learning or attention problems. However, because they are paid with special education funds, teacher consultants can work only with students who are eligible for special education services.

School social workers

School social workers are trained to intervene and manage crises, identify mental health resources, and make referrals. They can teach students coping, self-awareness, and social skills. Some social workers conduct small-group sessions to help students develop skills in managing difficult situations, resolving conflicts, and averting crises. Social workers may also screen for emotional problems and/or provide therapy for individual students.

Usually, social workers are paid out of special education funds and are therefore unavailable to work with students who are ineligible for special education services. In some cases, arrangements may be made so they can serve regular education students.

School counselors

School counselors are available to serve all students in the school. At the secondary level, school counselors have three main responsibilities: assisting students and parents with academic and vocational decisions and program planning, consulting with students about school adjustment problems, and communicating with parents, teachers, and administrators about students (Benjamin & Waltz, 1989).

Counselors see students periodically and can provide documented information on past successes, current strengths, and possible vulnerabilities. The counselor is often the one person in the school who follows a student's progress over several years. Because counselors can provide a schoolwide, districtwide, and community perspective, they can help students and their parents avoid pitfalls and develop realistic plans for the future.

For a student with learning disabilities or ADD, counselors can provide a needed anchor and support, as well as coordinate necessary special services. Counselors can also help with transitions from elementary to middle or junior high school, to high school, and on to postsecondary education or the work world.

The extremely important counseling role does not need to be assumed by only one person. Parts of it can be assumed by other professionals—for example, the homeroom teacher, assistant principal, or community liaison. A community liaison is often a member of an ethnic minority group who can serve as a link between that group and the school system. The main functions of the liaison are to ensure and enhance communication, prevent problems, and solve difficulties.

School administrators

The school administrator plays a number of roles in the education of students with learning problems, the primary one being leader and visionary. In this role, the administrator energizes the school staff to explore new educational options for students in order to help them learn. As system manager, the administrator ensures the delivery of support services to students and their teachers in a timely fashion. Also in this role, the administrator assures adequate functioning of the system and arranges for resources to meet student needs, as outlined in IEPs and 504 plans. In both the visionary and system manager roles, the administrator provides for staff training in new and emerging educational programs, methodologies, and philosophies.

The administrator serves as decision maker when necessary and facilitates decision making by staff members. The administrator also facilitates the team approach to planning and problem solving by allocating time and resources to teamwork. In difficult situations, the administrator serves as a liaison between teachers and families, keeping the lines of communication open. Most important, the administrator keeps everyone's attention focused on the support of student learning.

School psychologists

Traditionally, the school psychologist is called upon only to assess students with possible disabilities. This is a time-consuming procedure for the few psychologists in each district. School psychologists rarely have time for meetings and consultation. However, because of their expertise, they can play a significant role in the design and monitoring of instructional and behavior management plans for individual students. For this reason, every effort should be made to involve school psychologists in the planning process.

Speech and language pathologists

Speech and language pathologists in school systems have traditionally concentrated on the diagnosis and treatment of speech problems (e.g., articulation). As evidence increases of the underlying role of language problems in learning disabilities, the expertise of speech and language pathologists has become more critical to diagnostic and instructional efforts. Their role can be expanded to include team teaching with a learning disabilities teacher or language arts or reading teacher. They can also design appropriate instructional programs for students with language-based learning problems.

Other school-based professionals

Other school-based professionals include the librarian or media specialist, curriculum coordinator, reading specialist, and school nurse. Their roles include gathering additional information about the student, participating on problem-solving teams, and providing consultation to the classroom teacher. Physical education teachers or coaches, vocational teachers or consultants, or others in the school with whom the student identifies can also be valuable.

External consultants

Either the family or the school can engage a consultant from outside the school system to provide expertise otherwise unavailable within the school or the family. External consultants can include diagnosticians, mediators, experienced educators, neuropsychologists, physicians, therapists, and family advocates, among others. In their diverse roles they can provide additional information for the purpose of assessment, instruction, or problem solving, as well as new perspectives on and interpretations of existing information and/or legal mandates. They can suggest new teaching methods and techniques and instruct school personnel in their use. They can provide advice and counseling for parents and students and help solve difficult parent-school problems.

AN INTEGRATIVE MODEL

As educators, we know a great deal about how to help most, if not all, students learn. The research is there; the theoretical framework is there (Ellis, 1993; Hughes & Smith, 1990; Wong, 1992, 1993). It is clear that there is not just one way all students learn (e.g., auditory or visual) or just one methodology that works for all students (e.g., whole language or phonics). Many teachers use several different approaches to help students with learning problems succeed in school, but this job has often been lonely, somewhat piecemeal, and insufficient to ensure success. We know that many teachers and school administrators would do more if they had additional information, support, and resources.

Educators must incorporate a greater range of methodologies, teaching styles, and administrative arrangements into their instructional repertoires in order to meet the needs of all students in the regular classroom, including those with learning problems. Teachers need to embrace and apply this new knowledge, and school systems need to support and reinforce teachers who incorporate it into the instructional process.

A systematic, integrative model can translate the latest research in education and psychology into practical strategies for the classroom teacher (Deshler, Schumaker, & Lenz, 1984; Schunk & Zimmerman, 1994; Scruggs & Mastropieri, 1993; Zimmerman, Greenberg, & Weinstein, 1994). An approach such as this takes creativity, courage, and commitment. It requires some retooling on everyone's part, but it is much less costly than student failure and teacher frustration.

The model is based on three assumptions that, although not new, are sometimes forgotten amidst the demands and pressures educators confront daily:

1. All students can learn.

2. Students can learn productive behaviors to replace unproductive learning habits.

3. The teacher's responsibility for each student and for the group is to arrange the learning environment, instructional activities, and behavioral consequences to maximize learning.

The model integrates the following specific components into classroom practice:

1. A systems approach

2. Teamwork

3. Student involvement

4. Motivation and student interest

5. Individualization

6. A problem-solving approach

7. Positive expectations

8. A focus on thinking strategies

9. A focus on self-management skills

10. Communication and collaboration with parents

A Systems Approach

The purpose of a systems approach is to coordinate the progress of the individual student with that of all the other students and to ensure continual improvement based on observable results. As chapter 3 shows in greater detail, learning problems do not exist solely within the student (Levine, 1993). Learning problems are also related to conditions and consequences in the learning environment— the classroom and the school. It is necessary to focus on both the student and the learning environment, with the twin goals of analyzing student performance in terms of strengths and weaknesses and modifying the learning environment to overcome or minimize the weaknesses and help the student learn (Bandura, 1977, 1986; Hendrickson, 1992; Maag & Reid, 1994).

A systems approach to the instructional process emphasizes the alignment of the individual student's goals and objectives with those of the class and the curriculum. In addition, short-term educational goals and objectives are organized so they build toward the student's long-term goals.

A systems approach also emphasizes the coordination of goals and objectives across courses and grade levels. Having similar goals in each class and grade assures adequate practice and generalizability of thinking and self-management skills, as well as mastery of specific skills (reading, writing, note-taking, etc.).

Last, a systems approach offers support to the classroom teacher in the form of consultation and planning time (National Joint Committee on Learning Disabilities, 1987), and it offers the opportunity for a team approach to problem solving.

Teamwork

Students' attainment of academic and behavioral goals depends in large measure on teamwork at school and at home. If everyone in the student's life joins together, the instructional program has a good chance for success.

A team approach can yield creative solutions because it brings diverse viewpoints to bear on the problem and promotes greater accuracy as a result of the pooling of information. Teamwork has the added advantage of ensuring better communication between home and school and between teachers of different courses and at different grade levels. As a result, it promotes continuity between short- and long-term goals.

A variety of teams form to provide services to students with learning difficulties—for example, problem-solving teams, multidisciplinary evaluation teams, and instructional teams. At minimum, a team should include those who know the student and those who are responsible for implementing the student's educational plan.

When working as a team, it is necessary to identify persons responsible for individual tasks and activities within the educational plan. For example, the administrator has responsibility for allocating the necessary resources, including teacher training and team planning time; the counselor serves as case manager and ensures that each teacher understands the student's difficulties and the need for the accommodations listed in the IEP or 504 plan; the case manager and parents are responsible for monitoring the implementation of the plan; the student is responsible for completing the work as modified in a timely fashion.

Student Involvement

Student involvement in educational decisions such as goal setting is important for several reasons. Shared goal setting can enhance student motivation to achieve. Direction, effort, and persistence are brought into play when students commit themselves to strive for goals that are meaningful to them. In addition, involvement in educational decisions gives students a sense of control over their learning and their lives. Having a sense of control reduces anxiety and helps students take on a more adult role. Teachers can guide students in the goal-setting process and thus assure that the goals selected are both worthwhile and attainable. They can encourage students to set educational and/or behavioral goals for themselves, select educational activities, solve problems, and participate in instructional decisions.

As part of the goal-setting process, students can monitor their own progress and use feedback to modify their original goals. These are skills they will need to function effectively as adults. In this way, involvement in educational decisions helps prepare students for independent learning and problem solving.

Motivation and Student Interest

A primary responsibility of the teacher is to tap into student motivation. Motivation is the key to learning. In fact, a strong motivation to learn can go a long way toward overcoming learning problems (Carbo, Dunn, & Dunn, 1991). Because a student's interests are intrinsically motivating, teachers can use them to help overcome student weaknesses. Because success or the expectation of success can be strongly motivating, teachers should design success experiences for students. For tasks that carry little intrinsic motivation, rewards and reinforcement can provide preliminary success experiences that in turn can set the stage for more intrinsic motivation. Learning formats that include games, humor, curiosity, and creativity are naturally motivating. Short term or long term, without motivation students will not learn. It is the teacher's responsibility to create a motivating environment.

Individualization

Individualizing the instructional process can have a profound effect on a student's ability to learn. For example, research indicates that different students have distinct learning styles (e.g., visual, auditory, tactile) and often do best when new material is presented in their preferred modality (Carbo et al., 1991). This is especially true of students with learning disabilities and ADD, who may have varied strengths and weaknesses in visual, auditory, or tactile/motor areas.

Some students learn best in small groups because they benefit from social support. However, some students with ADD are too easily distracted to learn in groups and do best alone. In order to be effective, teachers must anticipate and respond to individual differences in learning and attention. Some students need more time to process information, and others need less time. Designing and using multiple instructional strategies can improve teaching and learning success (Alberto & Troutman, 1986; De Bono, 1989; Fantuzzo & Atkins, 1992; Kolb, 1976; Lazear, 1991; McCarthy, 1990).

Individualization provides the type and degree of instruction and support required for the student to enjoy observable success while at the same time presenting increasingly difficult challenges. Optimal conditions vary from student to student, from content to content, and from context to context. Variables to consider include instructional methods, groupings, tasks, time, materials, test-taking and other learning environments, grading practices, types and frequencies of reinforcement, and interaction with teachers and peers.

Individualization does not mean using a different teaching technique for each student in a class. Rather, it means having available a repertoire of strategies and methods for students with differing learning styles, strengths, and weaknesses.

A Problem-Solving Approach

A problem-solving approach involves both a process and an attitude. On the one hand, the problem-solving process is a systematic set of steps that includes identifying the performance problem, collecting data, generating solutions, developing and implementing an action plan, monitoring progress, and using feedback to improve student learning. On the other hand, the problem-solving approach is based on a "can do" attitude—that is, the teacher expects and is committed to solve student performance problems.

The teacher must fully understand a student's particular learning or attention problem to develop strategies to prevent, circumvent, or overcome it. The question is, How can we improve student performance? Problem-solving or diagnostic strategies can be integrated into teaching activities. The teacher collects and analyzes evidence of student progress at various points in the problem-solving process.

Problem solving is best done as a team effort. Students can be asked about their performance problems; parents are brought into the equation. If necessary, the teacher can refer a student to a psychologist for more in-depth or supplemental information.

Positive Expectations

Teachers who expect that all students can learn and improve successfully influence students and their work. Teachers who have high expectations tend to treat their students in a subtly different way and thus generate positive results (Grayson & Martin, 1985; Kerman, Kimball, & Martin, 1980; Rosenthal & Jacobson, 1968). Conversely, students of teachers with low or negative expectations tend to fulfill those expectations. Because students with learning difficulties often think of themselves as failures and believe they can't learn, it is important for teachers to communicate positive expectations.

It is equally important for teachers to demonstrate their acceptance of all aspects of student performance while encouraging students to attempt difficult tasks and reach higher than they have before. Positive expectations can be for short-term progress as well as for long-term growth and development. Teachers can provide the vision and the "push" to help students develop positive expectations for themselves.

Thinking Strategies

Students with learning problems usually have ineffective thinking strategies and often need direct instruction in these skills. The teacher instructs students in ways to use strategies for thinking (cognitive strategies) and for thinking about thinking (metacognitive strategies) and provides opportunities for students to use these strategies. The use of cognitive and metacognitive strategies can greatly improve academic performance in all content area courses. For example, students can learn how to generate questions that will help them improve their reading comprehension, solve math problems, and organize term papers. (Chapters 8 through 12 include suggestions for applying cognitive and metacognitive strategies in specific content and skill areas.)

Self-Management Skills

Self-management, the topic of chapter 7, is important in every phase of the learning process and is a major goal of the integrative model. A self-managed student is an effective learner, and the classroom in which students are encouraged to take responsibility for their own learning provides the optimal environment for both teacher and student. Self-management techniques are especially important for students with ADD, who need to learn how to focus and stay on task in situations where their interest is low and opportunities for distraction are great.

Self-managed behavior includes setting goals, making positive self-statements, visually rehearsing, monitoring performance, and providing self-reinforcement. Any one of these approaches is useful; the cumulative effect of combined approaches can be even more powerful.

Integrating the teaching of thinking strategies and self-management skills with content instruction gives students the tools for greater productivity and long-term improvement in performance (Bos & Anders, 1992; Ellis, 1993; Schumaker & Deshler, 1992; Short & Weissberg-Benchell, 1989). The desired long-term outcome is the ability to function independently when conditions are not optimal, when situations are unpredictable and tasks demand change, when problems are complicated and ill defined, and when solutions depend on inventiveness, improvisation, discussion, and negotiation.

Communication and Collaboration with Parents

Although parent communication and involvement has been a goal of schools and school systems for many years, the definition of parent involvement varies widely. True communication and collaboration between parent and teacher can occur only if communication flows in two directions and only if both have similar expectations for the instructional process and share equal status as team members. Both parent and teacher may need some help to achieve this goal (Greenbaum, 1990a, 1990b; Greenbaum & Markel, 1992; Markel & Greenbaum, 1985).

When teachers invite parents to become members of a team and help them become actively involved in their child's education, everyone benefits. However, it is important to note that, for a variety of reasons, some parents cannot become involved. If so, teachers must accept this reality in a nonjudgmental fashion and proceed to meet their own responsibilities.

CORE STEPS IN THE INSTRUCTIONAL PROCESS

The teacher helps students to learn information, think critically, regulate their own thinking processes, and solve problems. To achieve these goals, the teacher provides direct instruction, models learning and self-management strategies, and provides guided practice and encouragement. Record keeping helps both teacher and students monitor progress toward instructional goals; instructional decisions are based on performance data.

More specifically, the teacher engages in the following core steps:

1. Setting the stage
2. Collecting information
3. Analyzing tasks
4. Setting goals
5. Teaching and modeling specific strategies
6. Providing guided practice, feedback, and reinforcement
7. Monitoring progress and making adjustments

These core steps can be applied in different subject matter contexts (e.g., science, social studies, language arts). Core steps are described in detail in subsequent chapters on reading (chapter 8), listening and note taking (chapter 9), preparing for and taking tests (chapter 10), academic writing (chapter 11), and homework (chapter 12). The process they reflect is research based and known to be beneficial for all students, not just those with learning disabilities or ADD (Bandura, 1986; Becker, Engelman, & Thomas, 1971; Gagne, 1985; Graham & Harris, 1992; Hudson, Lignugaris-Kraft, & Miller, 1993; Meichenbaum, 1977; Palincsar & Brown, 1984; Short & Weissberg-Benchell, 1989; Sulzer-Azaroff & Mayer, 1986). The steps can be adapted for use in various classroom settings, in large or small groups, or with individual students.

Setting the Stage

The learning process needs a beginning to focus students on the task at hand and to create a readiness to learn. To set the stage, the teacher opens a dialogue with the students and establishes rapport. When working with a class, the teacher involves and motivates students by activating their prior knowledge of the subject matter and trying to make the new information relevant to their lives. Teacher and students identify interests or expectations and discuss potential benefits and outcomes of learning within the particular content area.

The teacher strives to develop a personal relationship with each student, especially those students who are experiencing learning problems. When working individually with a student who has learning problems, the teacher offers a new perspective on the student as a learner, provides an opportunity for a new beginning, and elicits the student's collaboration. In doing so, the teacher must be aware of the stressors in the student's life relating to the learning difficulties (e.g., chronic failure or peer rejection).

As a part of this initial step, the teacher provides empathy, support, hope, and encouragement, setting positive and realistic expectations for learning and achievement.

Collecting Information

The teacher collects information on existing knowledge and skills to get a general idea of an entire class's entering proficiency with the course materials and subject matter. This information can be collected through a formal pretest or through more informal means. Either way, this baseline information allows the teacher to make data-based instructional decisions. In addition, such information can help the teacher identify learning styles in order to choose strategies that will accommodate individual differences. The teacher can then review an individual student's performance in relation to that of the class and integrate the findings with information available from diagnostic evaluations, portfolios, parent and student reports, and interviews.

Given the constraints under which teachers operate, the aim is to collect the most relevant information with the least amount of effort. The teacher can save time and energy by involving students in the process and by using class materials as a basis for informal assessment (Kern, Childs, Dunlap, Clarke, & Falk, 1994). (Assessment of individual students with documented learning problems is the subject of chapter 5.)

Information on classroom performance can directly benefit individual students by facilitating self-management. If students are expected to assume responsibility for their own learning, they need to be aware of their entering skill levels—both strengths and weaknesses. With this knowledge, they are better able to select goals, consider strategies, and manage time.

Analyzing Tasks

To make instructional decisions, the teacher analyzes tasks in relation to student characteristics, including entry-level skills, learning style, interests, strengths, and weaknesses. Tasks also must be analyzed in terms of the learning activities required for completion and the conditions under which students must perform the task. For individualized instruction, task components and sequence, materials, mode of response, and available time can be altered in ways that make the most of student characteristics. Students with learning problems will benefit when an assignment is broken down into smaller tasks or components.

Individualized checklists can guide students as they work independently or attempt to create their own best conditions for learning or performance. Checklists can enumerate step-by-step procedures for learning, thinking, or managing behavior; items to include in developing a product; aspects of a product to verify or evaluate; and so forth.

Setting Goals

Goals and objectives specify the purpose of classroom learning activities and help to regulate both teacher and student behavior. Goals may be academic or nonacademic (e.g., cognitive, affective, interpersonal, sensory, motor); they should be written in measurable, learner-based terms.

Goals can include long-term, "big picture" goals, annual IEP and 504 plan goals, and short-term instructional objectives. Big picture goals reflect student values and project students into the future as self-directed learners, collaborative workers, and complex thinkers. Annual IEP and 504 plan goals identify skills and behaviors to be achieved over a single year, whereas shorter term objectives form the basis for student progress toward annual goals. Teachers, parents, and students can maintain perspective when they keep in mind and balance short- and long-term goals.

In brief, goals form the basis for instructional activities and help keep things on track. Feedback is then collected on progress toward goals and used to modify instruction.

Teaching and Modeling Specific Strategies

Direct instruction ensures that the learning of both content and thinking strategies is not left to chance. Using direct instruction, the teacher provides students with course content, cognitive strategies, metacognitive strategies, and self-management skills to use with course content. Students learn how to apply cognitive strategies (e.g., generating questions, organizing information, and remembering) to specific academic tasks—reading, writing, listening and note taking, test taking—in particular content areas. Students also learn to use metacognitive strategies. For example, when previewing a reading assignment or preparing for a test, students learn to think ahead. During the reading or writing process, students learn to think while doing the work, selecting appropriate strategies. When reviewing, students learn to think back, revise, or edit their work. Finally, students learn a wide variety of self-management behaviors. These include setting goals, making positive self-statements, visually rehearsing, monitoring performance, and reinforcing progress.

In addition to direct instruction, teachers model or demonstrate the use of thinking strategies to learn new information. Modeling results in a change in behavior when a person observes and imitates the behavior of the model. By imitating teacher behavior, students master the step-by-step processes they need to understand content, solve problems, or complete assignments. Repeated demonstrations by the teacher under increasingly complex conditions are often necessary.

Providing Guided Practice, Feedback, and Reinforcement

Confucius is reputed to have said, "What I hear, I forget; what I see, I remember; but what I do, I understand." Guided practice follows modeling because modeling alone does not guarantee improved performance. Like athletes or performers, students need to practice performing on demand under time constraints and pressures similar to those they will encounter in real situations. Especially with regard to testing, they need to deal with distractions in the classroom environment, cope with uncertainties about test items, and increase their concentration regardless of the time of day or length of testing.

Feedback is information about performance that lets students know which aspects to maintain and which to improve or adjust. Feedback also clarifies aspects of student performance that interfere with completion or mastery of tasks. Students as well as teachers require feedback on progress toward goals. Teachers are responsible for establishing feedback systems for students. The teacher provides examples (and "nonexamples") of acceptable work and pinpoints how student performance differs from the model. Without such examples, students do not understand what should or should not be done. Useful feedback provides students with information about what they did well, the reasons why, and subsequent steps for improvement. When feedback is prompt, direct, specific, and accurate, it can be a powerful influence on behavior. Unless students are shown how to use feedback, however, it is likely to be ignored. The teacher discusses and demonstrates how to incorporate feedback to revise current work and plan for future improvement. Therefore, feedback can be used to encourage continual improvement.

Over 35 years of research support the principle that positive reinforcement results in behavior changes (Ayllon & Azrin, 1968; Baer, Wolf, & Risley, 1968; Bijou & Sturges, 1959). To increase desired academic performance, the teacher uses informal and formal methods to reinforce both effort and progress. The reinforcement system is tied to progress toward goals and objectives; reinforcing small steps leads to continual improvement. The reinforcement system should be based on the values of both teacher and student and should be consistent, predictable, and fair (Downing, Moran, Myles, & Ormsbee, 1991; Sprick et al., 1993).

Informal reinforcers include praise, attention, smiles, and physical proximity. More formal reinforcers include rewards or incentives, points, awards, and public recognition. Public recognition can have a powerful effect and can include displays of work on bulletin boards, letters to parents, honor roll certificates, "I did a good job!" buttons, photographs of students at work, and opportunities to share interests and hobbies with the class.

The completion of a task in and of itself often functions as a rein-forcer because it is a concrete product of hard work. One way to help students recognize their own progress is to have them compare their old work to more recent assignments or tests. In doing so, the teacher models and prompts students to recognize their efforts as a means of developing self-motivation. The long-term goal is for students to learn to modify their behavior and develop their own self-reinforce-ment methods.

Monitoring Progress and Making Adjustments

Monitoring progress over time is necessary to evaluate outcomes and structure adjustments. Indicators of student progress can come from work samples, student-teacher contracts, systematic observations, and individualized projects with recorded milestones of progress (Herman, 1992; Herman, Aschbacker, & Winters, 1992).

In addition to having teachers monitor student progress, students can be encouraged to monitor their own progress—for example, main-taining a graphic display of material learned, goals reached, and so forth in individual portfolios. A continuing record of progress helps both teachers and students recognize improvement. Besides provid-ing evidence of success, such a record highlights the conditions and consequences that affect class performance.

Adjustments are always necessary. Information on group and individual performance enables the teacher to determine whether goals and objectives have been met and to assess the cause-and-effect relationships between different instructional techniques and activities and student progress and performance. The teacher can then adjust instructional and management strategies accordingly.

SUMMARY AND CONCLUSIONS

Many professionals are involved in the delivery of educational ser-vices to students with learning and attention difficulties: teachers, school counselors and social workers, special education teachers and consultants, administrators, and so forth. An integrative model can help structure the provision of these services. By emphasizing specific areas such as teamwork, feedback, motivation, positive expec-tations, and the like, the integrative model allows teachers and others to use their professional skills in the most efficient manner. The teacher's role in this process is critical.

Following certain core steps in the instructional process will likewise guide the successful educational plan. The results of effective planning and instruction for students with learning and attention problems include greater achievement and improved ability to learn new skills and information, along with an increased sense of control, self-esteem, and optimism. The integrative model helps all students learn and increases the chance of performance breakthroughs for students with learning and attention problems.

3

Understanding the Classroom and Larger System

One teacher working alone can make a difference in the life of students with learning problems; an entire system working in concert can have a profound effect, not only on students with learning or attention problems, but on all students. While we are focusing on the individual student, we also need to look at the larger system—the entire learning environment—to diagnose system problems and make modifications if necessary.

A major purpose of a systems approach is to help all students, not just students with problems. What is learned in investigating and solving one student's problems can be used for other students with similar problems in other classrooms throughout the system. Another critical purpose of a systems approach is to ensure support for the classroom teacher from other parts of the system. Although teachers control major aspects of students' education, we need to examine the influences of the larger system, which can enhance or interfere with teachers' instructional efforts.

A systems view is an organized way of addressing a problem by looking at the interrelated elements that form a complex picture. The focus of a systems approach is on student performance—the results of instruction. Student progress is used as feedback to modify the larger system.

As the case examples described in this chapter show, a productive system is characterized by the involvement of many individuals, communication among all concerned, flexibility, and long-term strategic planning. In contrast, an unproductive system tends to be characterized by an autocratic style of teaching and administration and by "quick fix" solutions to the problems of students with learning or attention difficulties. Although individual students may be helped for a short period of time, what is learned is not maintained or generalized to other students and teachers in the system.

THE CLASSROOM SYSTEM

The classroom is an independent and adaptable instructional system that is, at the same time, embedded within and interacting with other systems. Each teacher is a manager of this classroom system, which helps students continually improve. The components of the classroom system include the teacher, the students, the environment, the instructional process (including tasks, materials, and instructional activities), the outcomes relative to short- and long-term goals and objectives, and ongoing feedback that the teacher uses to adjust instruction.

The teacher

In addition to expertise, the teacher contributes his or her own interests, values, and special talents to the classroom system. The teacher's main job is to determine how best to capitalize on students' strengths, remedy or circumvent their weaknesses or vulnerabilities, and respond to their interests and styles so that learning is relevant and interesting.

The teacher engages in dynamic, personalized interactions with the students, both individually and in groups. In the short term, the teacher helps all students learn and improve their performance. Over the long term, the teacher helps students manage themselves in terms of feelings, behavior, and problem solving.

The students

Each student—with his or her own strengths, needs, and interests—is also an element of the classroom system. Students interact with other students and with the teacher. Students are involved in setting educational goals, making educational decisions, monitoring learning, and solving problems. The teacher helps them utilize their strengths to manage difficulties that inhibit progress and precipitate performance breakdowns.

The classroom environment

In a productive classroom system, the environment is arranged to support the progress of all students, regardless of learning styles, strengths, or weaknesses. There is a balance between structure and flexibility; creative thinking and analytic problem solving; paper-and-pencil and hands-on activities, and independent, large-, and small-group work. A positive climate prevails, with respect for individual differences. The assumption is that what is helpful and effective for a student with learning or attention difficulties is helpful for other students as well.

The instructional process

The instructional process encompasses all elements involved in instruction for all students in the class, whether or not they have learning disabilities or attention difficulties. These elements include tasks and activities, methods, materials, classroom organization, rules and routines, and evaluation and assessment. The teacher manages the instructional process to meet students' individual needs. Individual students with severe learning problems may receive intensive help from specialists in order to reach their goals.

Outcomes

Outcomes are measured for the individual student, the class as a whole, and the school. Both long- and short-term outcomes are considered. The purpose of measuring outcomes is to provide and document information that can be used for continual improvement of individual student performance and the performance of the class as a whole.

Individual student outcomes are measured by such means as student portfolios and projects and curriculum-based mastery tests. Some of these outcomes can be aggregated and used as classroom outcomes. Aggregate data such as drop-out rates, graduation rates, and college and work-force entry rates are collected as feedback for the school or system as a whole.

Feedback

Feedback is obtained both within and outside the classroom system. Inside the classroom, the teacher collects information about progress toward instructional goals. The teacher asks: What is working and what is not? What are the next steps? and Do particular students need help? The teacher also attempts to ascertain to what degree lessons learned in the classroom are helpful in other classrooms or school situations. Feedback about outcomes indicates whether changes should be made in the classroom system and suggests the direction and magnitude of any such changes.

As manager of the classroom system, the teacher must continually fine-tune the system to be responsive to all students. A kind of dual focus is required: The teacher solves one problem or helps one student at a time while striving for improvement of the instructional system as a whole.

THE LARGER SYSTEM: TWO CASE EXAMPLES

Following are two case examples, one illustrating a system that is functioning well and the other showing a system that is nonproductive. Nathan's case illustrates a system that is essentially sound. The people in both the classroom and the larger system (including the parents) work well together as a team, and the larger system supports innovation and consultation. Myles' situation illustrates what can go wrong in a system if there are attitudinal barriers in addition to a lack of support from the larger system.

Nathan: All Systems Go

At age 12, Nathan is a year behind in school. He is in Mr. Chapman's fifth-grade class. Nathan sits in the first row. On the chalkboard directly in front of him, Mr. Chapman has carefully printed the day's schedule. It is 9:45, time for the spelling pretest. Mr. Chapman reminds the students to sharpen their pencils.

As Mr. Chapman dictates the words, Nathan writes slowly, with great effort. He completes the first word just in time for the second. He starts writing the second word, erases it, then writes again. He is still writing by the time Mr. Chapman dictates the third word. When Nathan finishes the second word, he looks up questioningly. Mr. Chapman asks, "Would you like me to repeat the word?" Nathan nods yes. The teacher reminds the class that they can ask him to repeat a word at any time.

As the test goes on, Nathan gets more and more out of sync with Mr. Chapman's dictation, and his writing becomes more erratic. Mr. Chapman quietly repeats the words to Nathan, but Nathan cannot keep up. Finally, he gives up. He stares at the door, distracted by a sound outside. Mr. Chapman touches him on the shoulder and points to the spelling paper. Nathan tries to get back on task.

Mr. Chapman finishes the dictation and tells the class to check their tests against their spelling books. Nathan has anticipated this direction by a few seconds and is already busily correcting his test. Looking dejected, he comments under his breath that he has only three words right; he has come close with some other words. Nathan's paper starts out very neat but ends in chaos.

It is recess time, and Mr. Chapman quietly reminds the class that five students must remain in their seats until they finish their work with math fractions from the previous day. Nathan is one of the five. The others finish quickly, and Nathan looks on unhappily as each of them leaves. He turns resolutely back to the task and painstakingly completes the assignment. In one motion he jumps up, hands the paper in, grabs his coat, and runs outside.

Reading follows recess. Mr. Chapman calls first on a girl who reads several paragraphs fluently and with understanding. Nathan is not looking at the book. The second student, a boy, also reads well. Next Mr. Chapman calls on Nathan. Nathan asks, "Where are we?" Mr. Chapman shows him the place.

Nathan reads the first few words clearly, then stumbles. A few students softly prompt him. He repeats the word and picks up the thread, then stumbles again. His reading is dysfluent and expressionless. Words are omitted and mispronounced. After three sentences Mr. Chapman thanks Nathan and turns to the next student. Nathan heaves a sigh of relief.

The student

Nathan is of average to high-average intelligence and has learning disabilities. Specifically, his psychological reports indicate problems with visual tracking, visual memory, and visual motor integration. Although he is in the fifth grade, Nathan has problems in decoding and reads at a third-grade level; he has severe writing problems related to both written expressive language problems and fine motor difficulties. Because of the severe discrepancy between his ability and achievement, he is eligible for special education services under IDEA. It takes him a long time to complete his work. His particular interest is science, a passion he shares with his father.

The teacher

Mr. Chapman is a classroom teacher who has positive expectations of all students, who is flexible and willing to try new techniques to help students learn, and who feels responsible for educating all the students in the class. Even though by Mr. Chapman's own admission he knows little about learning disabilities, he is an intelligent and sensitive teacher who likes Nathan and feels that the boy belongs in his class.

Although Nathan is getting intensive reading instruction from the special education teacher consultant, Mr. Chapman would like to do more to help Nathan in class. He is concerned because Nathan is very hard on himself when he makes mistakes. Nathan rarely feels successful and tends to isolate himself. In such cases, the possibility of depression is great. Next year Nathan will be in middle school, and Mr. Chapman is worried that Nathan will not do well there. Mr. Chapman expresses his concern to the special education teacher consultant and asks for help locating some high-interest, low-vocabulary books on science, Nathan's area of special interest.

The special education teacher consultant

The special education teacher consultant discusses Nathan's strengths and weaknesses with Mr. Chapman, reviews the boy's IEP, and makes some suggestions. She explains that Nathan cannot write and do something else at the same time, especially under time constraints, and advises letting him focus on listening or reading and excusing him from associated writing tasks. Mr. Chapman agrees to keep Nathan's writing assignments short. He mentions that Nathan has been using a tape recorder for book reports and creative writing assignments.

The teacher consultant also suggests allowing Nathan to use a calculator for multiplication. Mr. Chapman asks, "Shouldn't Nathan be required to learn the multiplication tables? He's smart enough." The teacher consultant replies, "The time and effort Nathan would have to expend to do that is too great. Other tasks, such as reading and understanding word problems and solving problems, are more important. Nathan has several weaknesses. We cannot address all of them at once. We must prioritize their importance to Nathan, and we must leave some time in his life for developing his strengths and having fun." Mr. Chapman says he understands.

The teacher consultant also mentions recess and asks whether Nathan often spends the recess period making up the previous day's math work. Mr. Chapman says, "I'm sorry to say, all the time." The consultant relates that problem to Nathan's writing difficulties and suggests decreasing the number of math problems Nathan must complete in class. That way he can finish in the time allotted and participate in recess.

Mr. Chapman and the teacher consultant meet periodically to discuss other techniques that might help Nathan, and students like him, be more successful in class. Nathan's parents begin meeting with Mr. Chapman and the teacher consultant to develop a plan that will prepare Nathan for the coming transition to middle school.

The school system

In Nathan's case, the system is productive. It supports teacher consultation and teamwork, teacher growth, and school improvement. There is an alignment between educational goals, teacher attitudes and styles, and instructional processes.

The organization of elementary schools generally allows teachers to get to know their students well, supports teacher flexibility and innovation, and facilitates cooperation between classroom teachers and special education teacher consultants. However, the secondary school environment may be considerably less friendly. Mr. Chapman's concern about Nathan's transition to middle school is well founded. In a few months Nathan will be in a school almost three times the size of his present one. With four or more teachers, it will be much harder for Nathan to form the kind of supportive personal relationship he has with Mr. Chapman. The teachers will have different and unfamiliar teaching styles and requirements. Several of the teachers will give lectures, and Nathan will have to begin taking notes in class. The course content will be more challenging, the reading level will be higher, and the writing assignments will be longer and more complex. As he enters sixth grade, Nathan will still be almost two grades behind in reading and will still be writing very slowly and painstakingly. Although his self-esteem might have improved through the efforts of his parents and Mr. Chapman, it will be shaken again when he confronts greater challenges.

Nathan will not succeed in middle school without direct, intense, and ongoing support from the system. He will need a special education teacher consultant's help to improve his reading skills and catch up on any class work he doesn't finish in the allotted time. He will require classroom accommodations for his reading and writing problems. Nathan's classroom teachers will need to reinforce his motivation to learn in the face of increased challenges. He will need help in developing his self-management skills and broadening his repertoire of cognitive strategies. The system will need to support the special education teacher consultant's coordination of activities with classroom teachers. There must be a commitment on the part of all Nathan's teachers to consider his learning problems when designing instruction and to avoid "blaming the victim" when plans do not work out.

Myles: All Systems Stalled

Myles enters the classroom walking backwards, talking loudly to two other boys. He continues to talk as the bell rings and the three boys take their seats. Myles throws his bookbag on the floor at his feet. Over the din, the teacher tells the class to take out their books. Myles peers in his bookbag, rummages around, and raises his hand. Without being called on, he tells the teacher that he thinks he has left his book in his locker and asks permission to go and get it. The teacher says yes. Several other students stand up and go out to get their books. The teacher begins the lesson. Myles is the last student to return to his seat with his book. He interrupts the teacher to ask what page they are on.

The student

Myles is an eighth grader of high-average intelligence who has ADD and some auditory processing problems. His grades range from an A in math to an F in language arts. He is getting a D in science, although the science teacher says his class participation is excellent. He rarely hands in any homework. Myles is not eligible for special education services under IDEA because a severe discrepancy does not exist between his ability and his achievement; however, because his ADD interferes with his learning, he is eligible to receive support and accommodations in the regular classroom under Section 504 of the Rehabilitation Act.

Myles has some hyperactivity associated with his ADD, along with distractibility and impulsivity. His teachers report that he has a hard time getting on task. He can't sit still; he touches, pats, and pokes other students. He loses his homework assignments. He blurts out answers in class, and he talks back to his teachers. He fools around with other students in the hallway and often gets to class late. In short, except in math class, teachers find his behavior difficult to manage.

Medication helps control many of Myles' behaviors, but he often forgets to take it. As with other students who have ADD, the issue of medication complicates Myles' situation. Myles is refusing to take his medication at school because he doesn't want to be perceived as "different" from the other kids. In fact, he often rebels against taking his medication at home because he sees it as a form of control by his parents. Myles' attitude is not unique: It is important to understand that it is common for adolescents to refuse medication, even though medication helps them. This challenging situation requires patience and skill on the part of teachers and parents alike.

The school system

Although the state's department of education has distributed guidelines to each school district regarding procedures under Section 504, the school system is just beginning to develop a plan for implementation. The district has few procedures in place, and lines of administrative responsibility are unclear. Few people know what is required, who is responsible, or where to go for help. This chaotic situation contributes significantly to the problems surrounding Myles.

The family

Myles' mother has been meeting with school personnel for the past 9 months in order to secure accommodations for Myles under Section 504, without success. No plan has been written or accepted. She has met four times with the principal and Myles' teachers. She has paid Myles' private therapist to accompany her to several of the meetings in order to explain Myles' ADD to school staff and to suggest appropriate educational strategies. She has contacted the district's Section 504 coordinator.

A month prior to the beginning of the school semester, a 504 plan for Myles has still not been written or implemented; Myles' mother is anxious to have one in place before the new school year begins. She hopes that a good plan will help Myles manage his impulsivity, attention problems, and hyperactivity—and avoid some associated academic problems.

At the mother's insistence, an additional 504 planning meeting is held 2 weeks before the start of school and attended by Myles' mother and stepfather, the school principal, the district's Section 504 coordinator, the assistant director for pupil personnel services, and a volunteer advocate from a parent support group, invited by the family. A plan based on information collected the previous year is discussed. The accommodations are accepted as "reasonable" (the criterion for accommodations under Section 504) by the school administrators.

The teachers and the principal

The principal gives the plan to Myles' new teachers and promises to schedule and attend a meeting of parents and teachers to discuss the plan and fine-tune it. Working from the plan, each teacher is to arrange specific accommodations for Myles, to go into effect as soon as possible. Unfortunately, the teachers refuse to go along with the plan. Instead, they write a report detailing their view of Myles' behavior. In their report, they question Myles' need for accommodations, which they consider a "crutch" for a boy who is academically talented. They express their concern that Myles is manipulating them and his mother and that his behavior problems represent a fight for control against the adult world. They add that Myles needs discipline, not accommodations, and that he can control himself if he wants to. The teachers' report does not mention ADD or its effects on Myles' classroom performance. Rather, it includes the suggestion that his inconsistent performance is a motivation problem rather than a symptom of an attention deficit disorder. The school's principal expresses her unwillingness to pressure the teachers to put the plan into effect.

The Office of Civil Rights

Myles' mother, extremely upset, calls the Office of Civil Rights in late September to file a grievance against the school district. She accuses the district of "undue delays" in the preparation and implementation of a 504 plan, which have resulted in "great unfairness" to Myles.

Over time, Myles' situation deteriorates from difficult to impossible. At the end of the first month of school, Myles is suspended repeatedly from his language arts class for being insubordinate. By the middle of the second month, he is having trouble in a second class. He is also having trouble in the hallway in the time between classes due to horseplay that gets out of control. The suspensions increase. At the middle of the semester, the teacher of an elective class that Myles has chosen refuses to let him take the class, saying— although she has not met him—that she knows he does not belong in the class.

Myles' mother files a further grievance with the Office of Civil Rights, charging the school with "a pattern of exclusion" against Myles. She is contemplating a lawsuit. Myles, his mother, his teachers, and the principal have become increasingly angry and desperate. Myles is constantly being suspended for various behavioral infractions: He makes noise during class, he curses, he runs in the hall, he challenges teacher directives. Several teachers have now refused to allow him in class.

The associate superintendent and the teachers' union

At this point Myles' mother and the parent advocate request that the associate superintendent intervene to mediate the problem. That official invites the teachers, principal, Section 504 director, parents, therapist, and advocate to a meeting. The teachers do not attend but send a union representative. Is this now a union issue? Although suspicious of the union representative's intent, the parents give their permission for him to sit in on the meeting.

Once again, Myles' therapist spends considerable time explaining the effects of ADD on Myles' behavior and making recommendations for the instructional program. These recommendations detail which behaviors require positive reinforcement (e.g., getting on task), which need sanctions and negative consequences (e.g., cursing), and which can best be ignored (e.g., jiggling). The therapist states that Myles' current escalated behavior does not stem from emotional disturbance but rather is a response to the negative expectations of the adults around him and an inappropriate educational program.

At the end of the meeting the associate superintendent tells Myles' mother and stepfather that he will meet with the teachers and principal the following week to discuss the situation with them. However, before he can do that, the principal suspends Myles for running in the hallway and fiddling with the photocopy machine in her office after he had repeatedly been told to stop.

Examining the system problems

What is wrong with this system? Myles' language arts teacher is one of the best and most experienced teachers in the district, the recipient of many teaching awards. Another of Myles' teachers has won several human relations awards. Myles' mother is intelligent and involved. Myles has a concerned stepfather and a loving father whom he sees frequently. Myles is a friendly, intelligent student with a desire to go on to college. He has a good group of friends.

Theoretically, the individuals in this system should be able to work together as a team. However, in a highly charged situation, even competent and well-intentioned professionals can lose their perspective, and the situation can get out of control. Intelligent, motivated people can inadvertently become part of the problem.

Adolescents are often given to power struggles and defiance of authority, and Myles is no exception. His disruptive behavior may have begun with impulsivity, distractibility, and mild hyperactivity, but it has escalated into defiance, largely because of the increasingly volatile situation. If this situation progresses, the adults in Myles' life risk losing him to drugs or delinquency at the very time they could be having a positive impact on him.

The most important attitudinal barrier in Myles' situation is the classroom teachers' belief that he can control his behavior and that they do not have the responsibility to modify their teaching to ensure that all students learn in spite of difficult behavior or learning problems. In addition, there is no incentive for teachers to change these beliefs or modify their instruction.

Unfortunately, Myles' story is replayed in school districts throughout the country whenever a student with learning disabilities or ADD is placed in a regular education class without clear delineation of teacher responsibilities under IDEA and Section 504, a written plan that could help prevent or overcome problems, well-defined lines of administrative responsibility, and awareness of the nature of learning disabilities and ADD and appropriate methodologies.

The System's Impact on Students

In Nathan's case, the system is characterized by a commitment to helping the student learn and strong support for teacher consultation. Nathan's family is a welcome part of the system. They are involved with his education and supportive of both Nathan and his teacher. There is healthy give and take between home and school.

Nathan's teacher, Mr. Chapman, plays a pivotal role in the system. Although unfamiliar with special education strategies, he is competent, creative, and willing to learn. He asks for help when he needs it, and the system provides it. The special education teacher consultant is available to consult with the teacher to solve student performance problems and to provide the student with intensive help if necessary.

The outcome for Nathan is performance and progress, with the likelihood of his moving actively toward long-term goals. The teacher and special education teacher consultant feel successful and motivated; the student feels competent and hopeful.

In Myles' case, the conditions are quite different: Both the classroom system and the larger system are unproductive and out of control. From the beginning, there has been a lack of understanding of the nature of ADD, commitment on the part of teachers, and leadership on the part of the principal. There has been no planning and no consideration of long-term goals. The teachers neither ask for nor accept any information on ADD or help in planning for Myles. Although the associate superintendent is involved, the problem is not seen as a systems problem; rather, it is seen as Myles' problem.

The situation is characterized by conflicting and competing demands, values, short-term goals, and consequences (Keeney & Raiffa, 1976; Quinn, 1988). Significant disharmony exists between Myles and his teachers, between the family and the school, and between the teachers and Myles' therapist. Everyone except the therapist is suffering from severe stress.

Accommodations are not being made to address Myles' difficulties and disabilities. Instead, the focus is on Myles' negative behavior. There are no positive consequences to reward Myles' effort and progress. In fact, the teachers and the administration believe the difficulties will be relieved if the student is suspended or transferred. Thus far, the outcome for Myles is poor academic performance and worsening behavior. It appears likely that the situation will deteriorate further and that there will be long-term negative effects in the future.

Myles has been learning some very negative lessons—how to make his teachers lose control, how to spend the day doing what he pleases by being suspended, and how some adults can behave both inappropriately and unfairly. He is beginning to feel crazy. In fact, school personnel have suggested an evaluation for emotional impairment. Myles' teachers, family, and Myles himself cannot begin planning or moving toward educational goals because he is suspended so frequently.

In comparing the stories of Nathan and Myles, we find good news and bad news. The good news is that even inexperienced, well-intentioned classroom teachers who are flexible and open to new ideas can help students with learning disabilities succeed in a supportive school environment. The bad news is that even experienced, talented teachers can inadvertently make problems worse. System support can make good teachers more effective, as in Nathan's case. Even though Mr. Chapman had been providing Nathan with a good program, the program became better with system support. In a difficult situation such as Myles', a lack of system support can undermine the planning and implementation of an appropriate educational plan and result in irreparable harm to a student.

Both Nathan's and Myles' teachers need system support in order to plan appropriate educational programs. Nathan needs to increase his reading skills and self-esteem. The teacher, special education teacher consultant, and parents need to continue to work together to monitor Nathan's program, preparing him to enter middle school.

In Myles' case the most pressing need is for crisis management (see chapter 4). A 504 plan must be written that spells out Myles' strengths and needs, educational goals and objectives, and necessary accommodations. Teacher consultation and planning time needs to be built into Myles' program. To get and stay on task, Myles needs to learn self-management skills to help him control his impulsivity and distractibility. He needs to learn the conditions under which he works most productively. He also needs to be challenged academically. Because Myles has been successful in math, the math teacher can serve as a resource to other teachers, and that class can function as a model for what works for Myles.

CHARACTERISTICS OF UNPRODUCTIVE VERSUS PRODUCTIVE SYSTEMS

A systems approach aims to bring all parts of the system into alignment to support agreed-upon goals. This means that individual responsibilities, lines of communication and authority, methodologies, goals and objectives, necessary resources, feedback and evaluation measures, and appeal procedures are carefully specified and disseminated.

As more and more students with learning problems are placed in regular classrooms, the teacher's job becomes increasingly complicated. In order to carry out IEPs and 504 plans, teachers need the support of a well-functioning system. Figure 3.1 contrasts the characteristics of an unproductive, chaotic system with those of a productive, continually improving system.

A well-functioning system can help teachers fully utilize system resources to solve problems. Teachers have time to integrate short-term with long-term student goals and base instructional decisions upon data, evidence, and information about student progress. The system facilitates proactive rather than reactive measures and helps school personnel prevent crises rather than having to spend valuable time on crisis management. The system both supports teachers and helps students more fully develop their potential. Systematic responses can be developed for particular problems; these approaches prove helpful for other students with similar problems.

Figure 3.1   System Characteristics

THE LARGER SYSTEM

Unproductive, Chaotic System	Productive, Continually Improving System
The system does not support efforts toward performance breakthroughs.	The system recognizes and rewards teachers who teach toward individual needs and foster breakthroughs.
The system seeks to maintain the status quo.	The system seeks improvement and supports the risk and discomfort of change.
Strategies are reactive; there is little strategic planning.	Strategies are proactive; strategic planning is used.
Objectives for the student are short term; the system is static (i.e., the school "rests on its laurels").	Goals are lifelong; the school is a learning organization.
Planning and decision making are done primarily by administrators.	Students, parents, and the community are involved in planning and decision making.
There is little communication or cooperation among professionals.	Multidisciplinary and cross-functional teams cooperate in diagnosis and instruction.

Figure 3.1   *(continued)*

THE CLASSROOM SYSTEM

Unproductive, Chaotic System	Productive, Continually Improving System
The focus is on a "quick fix" for classroom problems and for remediating student deficits.	The focus is on preventing problems while addressing deficits and maximizing student strengths and interests.
The teacher, the student, the system, and/or the family is blamed.	Personal responsibility and commitment ("I am the system") are stressed.
Instruction emphasizes rote and recall learning.	Instruction emphasizes authentic learning, critical thinking, learning of skills.
Curriculum is lockstep and test driven.	Curriculum decisions utilize feedback on student performance.
Assessment relies on teacher-made or standardized tests.	Assessment vehicles include portfolios, observations, projects, and criterion or mastery tasks.
Teaching techniques and classroom organization are based on a single philosophy or theoretical approach.	Teaching techniques and classroom organization reflect thoughtful integration of philosophies and research.
The teacher rewards only achievement, individual initiative, and competition.	The teacher rewards effort, improvement, and group accomplishment.
Teaching is based on a single (verbal) view of intelligence.	Teaching takes account of multiple intelligences.
The teacher does not consider different learning styles.	Teaching incorporates a variety of strategies based on students' learning styles.
The teacher controls all aspects of classroom life.	Students are active, self-managed learners involved in setting educational goals.

Teachers benefit when the system provides leadership in school restructuring and innovative education; a clear statement of school philosophy and educational goals; clear lines of communication and authority; support for inservice training, collaboration, and consultation; and recognition and rewards for increasing student performance. More specifically, teachers and students benefit when the system provides an unambiguous directive regarding the responsibility of the classroom teacher to educate students with learning disabilities and ADD and follows through by allocating the personnel and resources to do so.

SUMMARY AND CONCLUSIONS

The assistant superintendent called a 3-week moratorium during which Myles attended classes half days and careful planning was to begin by the teachers, administrators, the parents, and the family's advocate. At the end of the 3 weeks Myles was to resume a full program of carefully selected classes. However, none of this ever happened. The 3-week moratorium stretched into 6 weeks because the principal was too busy to start the ball rolling. Classes could not be found for Myles because most were already filled, teachers did not want him, or he did not have the prerequisites. Myles gave up and refused to go to school. Myles' mother went ahead with a lawsuit.

Nathan continued to progress in Mr. Chapman's class. The special education teacher consultant located some high-interest, low-vocabulary science books for Nathan as well as some books on tape for him to listen to and read simultaneously. Mr. Chapman found these useful for other students in the class. Nathan made plans to go to a summer camp for youngsters with learning disabilities so he could meet peers who shared some of his problems, learn more about coping with his disabilities, and improve his reading skills. Planning for his transition to middle school continued.

Using a systems approach will help ensure that the Nathans and Myleses of this country have a good chance to learn the skills they need to succeed in school—and in life. Teachers and other school personnel who are willing to make changes both in the larger system and in the classroom system can provide the best educational opportunities to a diverse population of students, both with and without learning disabilities and ADD.

4

Crisis Intervention

When long-term stresses and unmet needs increase to an intolerable point, the student with learning problems can reach a crisis. The crisis situation creates anxiety, disturbs interpersonal relationships, and often results in maladaptive behavior for all concerned—student, teachers, administrators, and parents.

Often teachers are not aware that a chronic difficulty a student has been having has deepened into a crisis. Unless a student is disruptive or acting out, it is easy to overlook a crisis or the gradual worsening of events that led to the crisis. Nathan, the fifth grader we met in chapter 3, tends to internalize his problems, becoming quieter and quieter in school. If Nathan's academic needs are not met in middle school, he may become depressed. Although he and his family might be in crisis, the school itself will not experience a crisis. Myles, the troubled eighth grader also introduced in chapter 3, could not be ignored because he was becoming more and more disruptive in school. His situation illustrates the way a crisis may look from the point of view of the school: The teachers are frustrated and angry, the principal and teachers feel they are spending an inordinate amount of time on the student, other students' learning is being disrupted—and they are in turn becoming disruptive—other parents begin to complain to the principal about the situation, and the involvement of the teachers' union and the Office of Civil Rights means additional school meetings and reports.

When for whatever reason the system is not working for the student with learning difficulties, immediate crisis intervention is necessary to help mediate the needs of school staff, parents, and student. Crisis intervention is a systematic problem-solving process based on principles of negotiation (Fisher, Ury, & Patton, 1991), conflict resolution (Greenbaum & Markel, 1992), and behavioral intervention (Krumboltz & Thoresen, 1969). Specifically, the process involves identifying the critical issues and how these issues relate to school survival and instilling the belief that something constructive can be done to control the chaos. The latter can involve the analysis of student strengths and factors that have contributed to the student's prior success, as well as activation of emergency measures such as time-out (in this context, a moratorium on any actions). The process also involves employing problem-solving strategies to stop further deterioration and begin the coping process. This often includes getting students (as well as their parents and teachers) out of the past and refocusing them on the present and immediate future. The outcomes of crisis intervention are containment, a reduction of stress, interruption of maladaptive behaviors, and a rebound during which performance improves.

Teachers can learn to recognize a crisis situation early enough to prevent lasting damage to the student. Few crises erupt suddenly, without warning. It is important not to brush small problems under the rug. Teachers can learn to read the early warning signals that presage student crises. Some of these are chronic failure, withdrawal, absenteeism, defiance, refusal, procrastination, and perfectionism.

It is important that teachers, students, and their families become aware that students can recover from a crisis and from failure. Often a crisis gets worse because the people involved believe that nothing can be done to resolve it.

Teachers can reach out to students and families to prevent or ameliorate crises. Clear, respectful, meaningful communication between school and home can often prevent crises. Teachers must take the initiative in working with students and families and in clearly communicating their expectations. Many crises are triggered by unnecessary blame, shame, and misunderstanding.

When teachers find themselves in a situation that seems out of control they can, and are encouraged to, ask for help from other professionals. Similarly, parents can seek help from others during a crisis. Resources for parents are available (e.g., Anderson, Chitwood, & Hayden, 1990; Markel & Greenbaum, 1985). Consultants, whether internal or external to the school system, can help resolve crises. The purpose of consultation is to bring in clinical or technical expertise that is otherwise unavailable in order to defuse a highly charged situation. The consultant can provide an objective, neutral point of view, mediate disputes, and help negotiate compromises.

The consultant outside the school system is in a unique position to encourage all parties to work together because he or she generally has no hidden agenda and no vested interest in the system. As a result, the outside consultant is usually free to express frank, professional opinions. External consultants are commonly educational psychologists, social workers, university professors of education or related fields, or retired school administrators. A consultant who is part of the school system, on the other hand, understands the culture of the system and knows the barriers to and opportunities for change. He or she also has immediate access to the system's internal networks. Within the school system, the following people may be called upon to function in the role of crisis consultant: ombudsperson, community liaison, equity specialist, administrator (e.g., an assistant superintendent), or school social worker. An experienced teacher can also fill this role.

The remainder of this chapter illustrates the process used by a consultant to interrupt the downward spiral of events affecting the student with learning problems. This process provides a model for teachers to better identify, deal with, and perhaps prevent crises.

THE CONTEXT OF CRISIS

In a crisis situation, the consultant is likely dealing with longstanding, complicated, and highly charged issues, as well as with interactions occurring among parents, student, and school. Parents, student, and school professionals alike tend to personalize crisis situations. All may engage in faulty thinking and blame either themselves or others for the problems. For example, when the student is getting poor grades, the parents may think:

> I am inadequate. I caused this problem by not
> doing enough.

> The teacher doesn't like my child.

> The teacher is taking out his or her dislike for me
> on my child.

> My child is deliberately provoking the teacher.

> My child is lazy (or crazy or dumb).

Often parents wonder how the situation could have gotten to this point and why the school did not notice the evolving problem. They may feel that the school let them down by not knowing how to help the child and/or not listening more carefully to the parents' concerns. When parents voice such concerns to the consultant, the consultant explains that the child may have been too young for school staff to really understand what was happening or that in the past much less information was available about ADD or learning disabilities. The consultant also empathizes with the parents and apologizes on behalf of any professionals who have been unable to meet the student's needs.

Teachers may think:

I am inadequate. I must be a poor teacher.

The parents don't care about their child.

The parents don't care about education.

The student is deliberately provoking me.

The student is lazy (or crazy or dumb).

The student may think:

I'm no good.

The teacher hates me.

My parents don't understand me.

The teacher is stupid.

Schoolwork is hard or boring.

I'm lazy (or crazy or dumb).

The consultant empathizes with each person involved without blaming or criticizing others: "I can imagine how difficult that must be" or "I can appreciate how frustrated you must have felt." The consultant then attempts to explain each person's differing perspectives and fears while trying to focus on the real problems instead of on personalities. In reality, everyone involved may have worked very hard to solve the problems. However, they may have been unaware of the student's unique needs and strengths. They may have lacked information or skills. Their attempts may not have been systematic. Finally, they may have been discouraged by repeated failure.

One of the crisis consultant's main objectives is to clarify the perceptions and increase the awareness of all participants. Some new beliefs, attitudes, and expectations the consultant fosters are as follows:

Everyone involved shares the common goal of wanting the student to succeed in school, and everyone will feel better when the student progresses.

All persons, even adolescents with learning and attention problems, can have better control over their own lives and can learn positive techniques for coping and learning.

The parents care about the child's education.

The student wants to learn.

The teacher cares about the student but is sometimes exasperated or overworked.

The teacher wants to be successful with the student.

The student is unhappy and needs support, structure, and success experiences.

The student cannot control a significant portion of his or her negative behavior at this point.

The school environment can be arranged so that the student can learn new skills.

Additional objectives of the crisis consultant are as follows:

Separating out the problems between the adults and putting some (i.e., anger) on hold to deal with later

Maintaining the focus of all parties on the student

Negotiating an agreement between parent and teacher about which problems to tackle first

Explaining the student's needs and strengths to all participants

Explaining the need of adolescents for increasing independence based on their current level of maturity

Helping both parent and teacher empower the student by encouraging him or her to set educational goals and help make educational decisions

Keeping track of progress toward goals and objectives

CASE EXAMPLE: A STUDENT IN CRISIS

Although the crisis intervention process varies according to the situation, the case of Kyle, a quiet, stocky 16-year-old boy in tenth grade, illustrates the main principles involved.

Two years ago Kyle was diagnosed with learning disabilities and ADD, but his problems began much earlier. As a baby Kyle had sleep problems, with his mother reporting that "he never slept." When he was 4, his preschool teacher noted that he had difficulty attending to verbal instructions, memorizing his address and telephone number, and understanding time concepts. His language development was somewhat delayed, and he began speech therapy in first grade.

It became increasingly evident that Kyle was having difficulty regulating his activity level and that he had problems with impulse control and attention. He began fighting with his peers. In third grade he was classified as emotionally impaired; in fourth grade he was placed in a self-contained classroom for emotionally impaired students.

At the end of Kyle's fourth-grade year, the family moved and Kyle changed schools. Until that point, his family, his friends, and the school had been calling him Daren—his first name. When he started at the new school he asked that everyone call him by his middle name, Kyle, because he wanted to start over. He was well aware that he had severe difficulties.

In sixth grade, although Kyle scored in the average range on an intelligence test, he did not have severe discrepancies between his ability and achievement. He was not considered eligible for services for learning disabilities at the time. He did continue receiving services for his emotional impairment; these focused on increasing positive social interactions and decreasing negative behaviors. In the classroom, he continued to be quite distractible. He also had trouble retaining learned material. By this time he was quite frustrated with school, and his self-confidence and self-esteem were very low.

At the end of Kyle's eighth-grade year, intensive testing made clear that he had both learning disabilities and ADD. After medical evaluation, he was placed on the psychostimulant drug Ritalin (which helped his attention problems and hyperactivity considerably) and given the support of a learning disabilities teacher consultant. He was placed in regular education classes, where he continued to have substantial academic difficulty. There were no accommodations written for the regular classroom teachers and little communication between the teacher consultant and regular education teachers.

By the middle of his tenth-grade year, Kyle was in trouble both in school and in the community. In school he was uncooperative and failed to complete or hand in homework assignments. He was absent or tardy so many times that he was suspended from school for truancy. His considerable errors in judgment were getting him in trouble with the police. School and home were also at logger-heads. School personnel saw Kyle primarily as a troublemaker, lazy and unmotivated. They believed that he was involved with alcohol or drugs. The parents felt that Kyle could learn but that the school was deliberately doing nothing to help him. They feared that he would either drop out of school or be expelled and were worried about his poor choice of friends and his apparent lack of judgment. Kyle no longer wanted to go to school. At this point, the situation became a crisis.

THE CRISIS INTERVENTION PROCESS

The crisis intervention process next described provides a basic frame-work for intervention; adaptations are made according to the circum-stances. The process is adjusted depending on the maturity of the student, but the long-term goals for all students are the same: student self-management and the prevention of future crises. For Kyle, addi-tional long-term goals included high school graduation and the acquisition of work skills.

The time required to complete the process will vary depending on the circumstances, but it should be accomplished as quickly as possible—generally, within a matter of weeks or months. To help defuse the crisis, the consultant may meet several times with par-ents, student, and school staff and/or other support personnel. The order and number of these meetings will vary according to who makes the initial contact and other specific factors in the situation. However, the general goals of the intervention process remain the same: to identify and prioritize critical issues and determine how they relate to the student's school survival, collect information on the student's strengths and vulnerabilities, gain commitment from all parties involved in the crisis, develop strategies to stop further deterioration and initiate recovery, and make systematic plans for the time following the crisis.

Worried parents, a teacher, or another school professional may be the first to identify the situation as a crisis and request the help of a consultant, either inside or outside the school system. If parents initiate the contact with the consultant, one of the consultant's first steps will be to schedule an immediate meeting with the parents to gather information, discuss problems and concerns, and notify them of their rights under educational law as well as about any interim measures that might be taken. If a teacher or another school professional initiates contact with a consultant, then one of the consultant's first steps will be to meet with teachers to gather information and discuss concerns. Regardless of who initiates the process, the goal is to meet with all concerned parties as soon as possible. Unfortunately, many schools wait until parents threaten a hearing or lawsuit before responding to the crisis.

In Kyle's case, the parents began the process by seeking the services of an educational consultant outside of the school system. The following description of the intervention process therefore reflects this scenario.

Initial Contacts with Parents

When parents hire a consultant, the consultant works with the parents and student throughout the crisis intervention process. When the school provides or hires the consultant, he or she may work with the teacher, student, and parents. In both situations the parents act as the student's advocate in school.

When a student is in crisis, ongoing, multiple problems have escalated to a stage parents often view as catastrophic. Parents may feel that their child is at risk of being expelled, dropping out, or being lost to delinquency or drugs. This sense of imminent danger triggers high emotions and a great deal of urgency. Parents may not know what actually is happening to the student in school, how to handle the situation, or what the short- and long-term impact will be. They may feel overwhelmed by the cumulative pressures of trying to cope over time. Like anyone in crisis, parents need much patience and understanding.

Whether initial contacts with parents are conducted in person or by telephone, the consultant's goals are to gain insight into their view of the situation, to identify and categorize the problems expressed, and to provide support.

Eliciting parents' view of the situation

The consultant encourages parents to describe the problem in as much detail as possible. At first, parents will likely vent their feelings in an unstructured manner. This is often necessary to clear the air and prepare the way for communication. Emotional release can lead to a willingness to focus in a more objective fashion and to move on to problem definition and problem solving. Along with hostile feelings and verbal attacks, many salient concerns are often reported within the first few minutes. The skilled professional is able to separate important issues and move ahead.

In their first meeting with the consultant, Kyle's parents expressed their frustration with the situation. Kyle's father was very angry. He could not understand why the teachers and principal could not help Kyle. The father also felt that the school was treating him and his wife poorly because they were not well educated or wealthy. Kyle's mother was also extremely frustrated and upset. She had read a great deal about learning disabilities and ADD and had offered many suggestions to Kyle's classroom teachers. She felt that Kyle's regular education teachers did not understand his problems or their effects on his learning and behavior, but were taking their problems with her and her husband out on Kyle. The consultant allowed Kyle's parents to express their frustrations freely for several minutes, then interrupted and focused their attention on problem identification.

Identifying problems and negotiating a time-out

To become more familiar with the student's situation, the consultant reviews any written information the parents may have concerning the student's school progress. This information may come from a variety of sources, including psychological reports, IEPs, student work samples, and teacher reports. If additional evaluations are warranted, the consultant arranges for these to be done.

Once the parents have presented their concerns, the consultant clearly identifies the problems expressed and, with the parents, categorizes them in terms of their relative importance to the student, the teacher, and the parents; their short- or long-term impact; and the ease or difficulty of their likely solution.

In Kyle's case, the problems began in infancy and increased, despite some intervention, throughout childhood and adolescence. Kyle's early learning problems in school had been attributed to emotional disturbance and were hence left untreated. These untreated learning problems led to behavior problems that increased in intensity as Kyle was growing up. His behavior problems in turn affected both his family and his teachers.

Although Kyle is of average intelligence, he has difficulty with reading, writing (spelling and grammar), remembering oral instructions, distractibility, and organization. His reading skills are better than his auditory processing skills. He has such difficulty with handwriting that he cannot take usable notes during a lecture situation. Kyle's previously untreated learning disabilities and ADD can no longer be ignored. They are the underlying cause of the crisis, which was exacerbated by adolescence and the increasing demands of school.

At this point, the consultant may recommend an emergency time-out on all planned action, such as school conferences or placement decisions. To facilitate this moratorium, he or she offers to contact teachers and school administration to request the postponement. This is in fact what the consultant in Kyle's case did.

Providing support

The consultant assures the parents that he or she will help them work to solve their problems. In the process, the consultant often needs to validate the parents' point of view. Parents tend to feel less knowledgeable than educators, and they are often apologetic when expressing their opinions and feelings about their child's educational program. The consultant reassures the parents that in some ways they know more about the child than anyone else and that their opinions and feelings are an important part of the equation. The consultant commends the parents for their involvement in the child's education and reinforces the notion of teamwork: "The student can recover from this situation with our help. We can be a team; I will help you work with the school."

Contact with Student and Parents Together

After the parents have discussed the consultant's role with the student, the consultant meets with both the parents and the student. The main goals of this meeting are to solicit the student's support for interven tion, to obtain the student's view of the situation, to help the student understand the problem and situation, to negotiate a time-out with the student, and to provide support.

Soliciting the student's involvement and commitment

The consultant asks the parents to lay groundwork for a meeting with both parents and student, to be scheduled as soon as possible. Kyle's parents explained the situation to him in the following way:

> We have met with a consultant and described what's happening. The consultant has a lot of experience helping students like you, and we trust and respect her. Now we want you to meet with us to talk about your view of the situation and how we can help you in school. We hope this is OK.

Without the student's involvement and commitment, the intervention will fail. Parents and the consultant need to make special efforts to secure this involvement. The important thing is to connect with the student "at the gut level" and to develop trust and hope.

In Kyle's case, the consultant asked Kyle for his permission to intervene:

> You know your parents have been very concerned about what's happening to you at school, and I know you are concerned also. I've helped other students like you— I hope you will let me help you. I think I can help you make things work better at school. Is it OK for me to get involved?

> We need your help to figure out what's going on and what to do about it. Think of yourself as a detective— watch yourself, ask yourself questions, and give me your opinion.

Eliciting the student's view of the situation

The consultant asks the student to describe the situation and poses probing questions when necessary. The consultant then restates the problems to be sure that he or she understands the student's perspective.

Although few students will be able to interpret or analyze the whole situation, with support most students can identify their own problems. Students as young as age 10 have the capacity to describe their difficulties. A student that age may report that "The teacher picks on me" and, with assistance, describe his or her part in the situation (e.g., "I jump up and bother the other kids"; "I don't do my homework, and the teacher gets angry.")

Students can even suggest strategies to cope with the problems, although they cannot tell you why they do certain things. Kyle was very aware of his problems: He said he had a hard time understanding what his teachers wanted of him. He described himself as "fading out" while the teacher was talking and then making a "smart remark" when confronted with his inattention. He described himself as "losing everything," including money, his keys, and his homework assignments.

Helping the student understand the problem and situation

After collecting information about the problem from a variety of sources—including psychological reports, IEPs, student work samples, teacher reports, and descriptions by the parents and student—the consultant meets with the student, with or without the parents, to identify discrepancies between different versions of the problem as described by the student, teacher, and parents. The consultant also explains and interprets the actions of teacher and parents, and clears up misunderstandings and personalizations (e.g., "The teacher hates me").

Most important, the consultant provides the student with information about his or her specific strengths and learning problems. The consultant may ask the student to complete a self-report questionnaire; such a questionnaire can help the student identify strengths, weaknesses, feelings, and interests (Levine, 1986).

After asking the student's permission to share the information from this meeting with the parents, the consultant helps them understand what is happening in school. The consultant suggests alternative explanations for others' actions and begins to focus the parents and student away from strong negative feelings and toward a more objective description of the problem. The consultant may say to the parents, for example:

> I know how angry you are at what the teacher said to you, but let's not deal with that right now. I promise to deal with that later. Now let's focus on this particular problem so that we can solve it together.

Negotiating a time-out with the student

Often during crisis situations, it is necessary to call a time-out in order to slow the negative momentum and open the way for change. For example, the consultant explained the need for a time-out to Kyle in the following way:

> You might think of the school year up to now as a ball game you are losing. You've struck out almost every time you've come up to bat. But now we want to end that ball game and start a new one that you have a chance of winning. Let's call time-out, and as a start I'll try to convince your English teacher that you'll give the new game your best shot. I'm going to ask your teacher to "forgive and forget" your past absences and missing homework this one time. I'm going to ask you to try to do some things differently to give us time to work things out and to show your teacher that you're trying.

The actions that seem to bring students the most benefit at this stage include attending class regularly, completing homework promptly, being respectful to teachers, and refraining from fighting with other students or other disruptive actions. The consultant tries to secure a 2-week commitment to those actions, then intercedes with school staff on the student's behalf.

Providing support

Support is essential for parents and student alike. The consultant not only empathizes with the student's feelings and respects his or her point of view, but also gives reassurance that something can be done to improve the situation.

The consultant for Kyle and his family underscored the idea that Kyle was not alone:

> Your parents and I are going to help you. Your job is to concentrate on your work. Your parents and I will talk to the school about the problems. When something comes up, we will handle it. Some jobs are best done by adults. For instance, if a teacher says something to you that makes you angry, you can say to yourself, "I don't have to deal with this now—my parents will handle it. I need

to concentrate on my schoolwork." We won't decide anything without your involvement and approval. You'll be in
on the decision-making process. It will take time to come
up with a plan and work out the difficulties. We'll try
some things, and if they don't work we'll try other things
until we get it right.

Initial Contacts with School Staff

The consultant's main goals in initial contacts with school staff are to
explain the consultant role, to elicit their view of the situation, to present a preliminary analysis of problems and patterns, to negotiate a
time-out, to outline steps toward improvement, and, once again, to provide support. As with the student, no intervention can be successful without the involvement and commitment of the persons who
implement the plan.

Explaining the consultant role

Following the guidelines of the Family Educational Rights and
Privacy Act (Public Law 93–380), the consultant gives the school
copies of release of information forms that the parents have signed
in order to permit the school to share information with the consultant.
In addition, the consultant takes care to explain his or her role in the
process. For example, the consultant for Kyle and his parents explained
her role in the following way:

We all share the same goal: to improve the student's success
in school. My role is to try to increase student success by
helping the parents help the student and by working with
the school. I believe that the best educational programs
are those with which the parents, student, and teachers
all agree and are all involved. I have experience in integrating
the efforts of home and school and think I can be helpful
to everyone in this situation.

Eliciting school staff's view of the situation

The consultant relays the parents' deep concern and lets the school
staff know that the parents feel the student is in crisis. The consultant then elicits their view of the situation, listening carefully and
summarizing. Consultant and school personnel review all available

information together to ensure that the emerging picture is complete from the school's point of view.

The consultant summarizes his or her understanding of the different perspectives in the situation: the parents', the student's, and the school's. In an effort to reconcile divergent views, the consultant explains and interprets the student's and parents' points of view to school staff and tries to clear up any misunderstandings. The consultant calls attention to aspects of the problem about which everyone seems to agree as well as aspects about which disagreement exists.

In Kyle's case, teachers and principals were surprised to learn that there was a crisis because Kyle was performing as they expected. For example, the math teacher felt that algebra was too difficult for Kyle. The English teacher thought Kyle was unmotivated because he didn't hand in his homework. Although the learning disabilities teacher consultant was aware of Kyle's strengths and weaknesses, no system existed for communicating this information to his regular education teachers.

Presenting a preliminary analysis of learning problems

At this point, the consultant shares new information about the student with teachers and actively involves them in problem solving. Specifically, the consultant discusses the student's strengths and learning and attention difficulties, providing examples of both. Together the consultant and the teachers brainstorm alternative ways to tap into the student's strengths and manage his or her weaknesses.

If teachers or other school staff perceive the student's negative behaviors as deliberate, the consultant may stress the need to distinguish what the student "can't do" from what he or she "won't do." This takes the form of reinterpreting the student's behaviors as manifestations of specific learning problems. In doing so, the consultant defines learning disabilities or ADD in terms of observable classroom behaviors and discrepancies—for example, "The student is inconsistent. She can do some things on one day but cannot do them on another day. This is typical of students with ADD and is not under the student's control at this time." Inconsistency is frustrating for students and mystifying to teachers.

The consultant may also emphasize the role of motivation and interest in holding focus, sustaining attention, and overcoming deficits: "If he's particularly interested in a topic, he will be able to focus his attention on it for a relatively long time and do a fairly presentable job" or "Because she wants to play basketball so much, she is able to a large extent to overcome her poor eye-hand coordination to sink baskets."

Negotiating a time-out with school staff

Whenever a time-out is negotiated with a student, the consultant negotiates a time-out with school staff. (In a very difficult case, the consultant may actually be suggesting a "cease fire.") Depending on the situation, a time-out may be necessary with a single teacher or with more than one teacher. The purpose is to stop the escalation of hostilities and prevent the problem from spreading.

If, for example, a student has failed to turn in homework for the past month and has been generally disruptive in class, the consultant would assure the teacher that the student has agreed to try (with parental support) to manage these behaviors for the next few weeks. In exchange, the consultant would then ask the teacher to reduce pressure on the student while the problem is being worked out by granting some form of amnesty for the incomplete homework assignments and past disruptiveness. Other ways in which a teacher might help include excusing past absences or tardiness, reinforcing the student for behaviors that he or she is trying to improve, and minimizing negative comments. Most of these strategies were included in the time-out negotiated for Kyle.

The consultant attempts to allay any concerns teachers may have about the fairness of amnesty for one particular student by stressing that the ultimate goal of the amnesty is to get the student back on track so that he or she is able to fulfill the same requirements fulfilled by others in the class. The consultant also emphasizes the ideas that amnesty is a temporary response to a crisis situation and that some accommodations will always be necessary given the nature of the student's disability. If the student has missed critical learning experiences, he or she may need to engage a tutor, attend summer school, or drop and repeat the course.

Outlining steps toward improvement

The consultant first shares information from the student, parents, and other professionals with the school staff, then asks the teachers to think about the student's classroom performance in light of this new information.

At this point the school staff begin generating solutions to problems, with the consultant offering additional suggestions. For example, in Kyle's case the staff was encouraged to generate a list of strategies that took into account Kyle's fourth-grade reading level and his high distractibility.

The consultant suggests ways to individualize the classroom experience to help the student succeed. For example:

> We've discussed how Kyle's reading and attention problems
> affect his test performance, especially under timed
> conditions. This negatively impacts his science grades.
> It is interesting to note that at home Kyle can take apart
> and repair a small engine, but at school he can't pass a
> science test dealing with the same material. Obviously, he
> understands more about the topic than most students in
> the class. Would you consider allowing this student to
> demonstrate his knowledge by doing a project instead
> of taking a test?

The consultant also attempts to elicit suggestions concerning some important short-term measures: The first of these concerns ways to monitor student progress so small steps can be reinforced. This is especially important during a crisis situation, when students are learning new behaviors. Because communication is crucial during and immediately after a crisis, the consultant also sets up a system of daily or weekly home-school communication, if one does not already exist. Finally, the consultant encourages school staff to track the student's positive behaviors and to anticipate a certain number of setbacks.

When the consultant says, "Let's start to work on a plan," school staff may be understandably wary. The teacher in whose class the student is experiencing difficulty may respond, "I've tried this already. Why will things be different this time?" The answer is that all the participants will contribute to the plan and cooperate on strategies and solutions: The student is involved and committed to learning, the parents are ready to support and encourage the student, and a systematic team approach will be used for problem solving and planning.

Providing support

Teachers need ongoing support to maintain commitment to the preliminary plan and to continue long-term problem solving. The consultant empathizes with school personnel by acknowledging the hard work ahead. The consultant offers the assurance that this time the teacher or teachers are not alone, reinforcing the idea that the student, the parents, and the consultant will all be involved in developing a new plan and making it work.

The consultant's support for school staff also involves increasing access to other resources. For example, if the student needs tutoring or outside counseling, the consultant and the parents can arrange it. The consultant can also help arrange for additional testing and evaluation, if necessary.

Postcrisis Planning

With the immediate crisis past, the student, parents, and teacher can turn their attention to program planning. School administration and special education staff may be involved as well. Depending on the success of the crisis intervention and the degree to which everyone concerned is able to work together, the consultant may or may not continue in the process, helping to guide program planning and facilitate communication.

The educational planning team may need more than one meeting to devise a comprehensive plan. However, much of the work will already have been done in the crisis intervention phase. What remains is to formalize the tentative procedures already in place.

The main task for the consultant at this point is to follow through with the student, parents, and school staff. Follow-through is the transition stage between short-term crisis intervention and longer term program planning and implementation.

Following through with student and parents

In follow-up contacts with the student and parents, the consultant continues to consolidate information about the situation, provide information as needed about learning problems, clarify the student's particular learning style and requirements, and offer support. He or she also monitors the agreement between student and school staff and helps all those involved work together as a team and make necessary adjustments.

Providing ongoing information about and examples of learning problems. Because most students and/or parents have an incomplete understanding of the impact of learning difficulties on academic performance, the consultant frequently needs to review and interpret information about learning or attention problems.

To help gauge the student's level of awareness and create a context to provide the student with practical information, the consultant might ask questions such as these:

Do you know any other kids who have problems
similar to yours?

Do you know other kids who are taking medication
like yours?

Would you like to meet an older student who has had
experiences similar to yours?

What are your worst fears about this situation? Perhaps
I can tell you how other students worked things out.

Clarifying the student's learning preferences and requirements. Throughout the process the consultant engages the student in an examination of his or her learning patterns, asking, for example, "Do you know the ways you learn best? For example, some students remember things they hear better than things they read. Do you work best alone or in a group?" To help elicit information, the student can be offered one or more checklists to complete with a teacher or at home (e.g., Bleuer, 1987; Levine, 1986). This information leads to practical suggestions concerning class work and homework methods. It also often suggests the need for further diagnostic testing.

The consultant working with Kyle and his parents asked him to fill out several checklists. On one checklist he completed himself, Kyle checked the following statements as being "most like me":

I learn better when I study alone.

Having assignment directions written on the board
makes them easier to understand.

I like to do things like simple repairs or crafts
with my hands.

Spelling and grammar rules make it hard for me
to say what I want in writing.

Although Kyle preferred written instructions to oral ones, he knew that he had some difficulty with visual memory. (This observation was borne out by the results of assessments.) He checked this statement: "I remember things I hear better than things I read." All of Kyle's responses were considered in designing educational strategies and accommodations for him.

Identifying strengths and successes. Within the context of the student's individual learning profile and needs, the consultant helps the student and parents identify the student's personal strengths and recall his or her successes. Because neither the student nor the parents are likely to be accustomed to thinking about the student's strengths, this idea is repeated throughout the consultation process. The consultant might initiate the topic in the following way:

Consultant: What are some of your special strengths?

Student: (Pauses.) Well . . . I don't know.

Consultant: You look healthy and attractive. That's a start. Can you think of something else?

Student: I can't think of anything.

Consultant: How about something you do? Do you like to draw?

If the list of strengths is short, the consultant advises the family to help add to it. They can come up with answers to the following kinds of questions and statements: "What do I like best about _____?" "When was I most proud of him/her?" and "I really appreciated it when _____ helped me _____."

Following through with school staff

In following through with school staff, the consultant's main goals are to maintain student progress and shift the responsibility for further progress to the school staff. First, the consultant recognizes the efforts of the staff during the crisis and congratulates them on the student's improvements. The consultant stresses the need to continue to monitor the situation and work through setbacks. He or she asks, "What do you think has made the difference in this situation?" "What lessons have we learned?" and "What are the first things you would do if and when another situation like this occurs?" Finally, the consultant helps the school staff generalize what they have learned to other students in the school who might be at risk.

Results of a Systematic Approach to Crisis Intervention

Some crises are resolved—some are not. The crisis faced by Myles and his family, detailed in chapter 3, was not resolved for a very long time. In Kyle's situation, a systematic crisis intervention process could be implemented in a timely fashion because of the leadership and support of the school's principal and director of special education. Although the teachers were initially skeptical, they were willing to use new information to understand Kyle better and to improve his academic performance. The effects of the systematic approach were apparent to Kyle, his teachers, and other students in the school.

During the crisis intervention process for Kyle, the regular education teachers and the principal got to know Kyle much better. Much to her surprise, the English teacher discovered that Kyle loved creative writing. Previously, the teacher had thought that Kyle was lazy and was not doing his homework at all. She learned that the reason he often failed to hand in an otherwise well-written story was that he was afraid it would come back covered in red ink signaling his errors in spelling and grammar. As a result, the teacher decided to focus her grading on Kyle's strengths instead of his weaknesses. For the first time Kyle was able to earn an A in creative writing by turning out several excellent stories and poems, though he still received D's in spelling. His other teachers developed similar insights.

Kyle kept his end of the time-out bargain by handing in most of his homework, attending all classes, and generally controlling his behavior—with only one or two slip-ups. Progress reports for the first 4 weeks of Kyle's new program carried the notation "showing improvement in work/attitude" for all courses. At the end of 9 weeks Kyle had "made considerable progress in all classes," and his grades "were improving."

One of the things that helped school staff understand Kyle's learning problems was the ability of the special education teacher consultant to work successfully with him to solve complex algebra problems. The teacher consultant understood that Kyle's distractibility was a major barrier to his completing his math assignments. She broke the task down and gave Kyle a step-by-step process to follow in solving problems. She then prompted Kyle by asking, "What is the first step?" "What is the second step?" and so on. When Kyle's math teacher observed Kyle completing an assignment with the teacher consultant, the teacher understood for the first time that Kyle's poor performance was not a function of lack of understanding or ability. In fact, the math teacher decided to apply some of these techniques with other students who were experiencing difficulty, to their benefit. Thus, the resolution of Kyle's crisis had a positive effect on other students in the class.

TEACHER INVOLVEMENT IN CRISIS PREVENTION AND INTERVENTION

The classroom teacher can play a strong role in preventing and managing crises. It will help prevent difficult situations from escalating into crises if teachers avoid the erroneous assumption that the student's lack of progress is the family's responsibility and substitute the view that lack of progress is a problem that can be solved through teamwork. They can actively seek additional information about the student's performance by asking questions such as What learning problems might account for the student's lack of progress? Under what conditions has this student been successful? and What are some new strategies I can try to solve some of these problems? Teachers can ask the student and parents to meet to discuss their concerns and ideas about the situation and to become part of a team seeking new information and remedies. Classroom teachers can ask for help from other professionals both within and outside the school system.

Teachers can help manage a crisis by being empathetic, creative, and flexible. They can listen actively, not respond to provocation, not blame, and not argue about past difficulties. It will help if they are willing to change some long-held beliefs and compromise in order to break stalemates and resume progress toward mutual goals.

After the immediate crisis is over, the teacher sits down with the student and parents to plan the educational program and activities that will help the student meet goals and objectives. The teacher's responsibility is to operationalize agreed-upon solutions. Ongoing communication among all parties is stressed. There is an emphasis on a new beginning.

Teachers can also learn crisis management skills. Consultants may not be available at the time they are needed. The qualities required of the teacher who acts as a crisis manager are fairness, objectivity, creativity, negotiation skills, and the capacity to manage his or her own behavior under difficult and stressful conditions. It is also important for the classroom teacher to recognize when additional help is needed, whether from another teacher, a social worker, a psychologist, a counselor, or an administrator.

SUMMARY AND CONCLUSIONS

Learning and attention problems present a difficult challenge, and sometimes their complexities result in a crisis situation for the student. A systematic problem-solving process is applied during crisis intervention. The person who intervenes adapts the process to the unique needs of each situation. Because of the highly charged nature of a crisis, it is often necessary to call upon somebody outside of the situation who is objective, can create trust, has the skills needed to resolve conflicts, and understands the complex nature of learning problems. Such individuals can be located either within or outside the school system.

During the intervention process, the crisis consultant adjusts the sequence and time frame to suit both the particular situation and the individual student. The consultant engages in a problem-solving process for dealing with the difficulties and preventing their recurrence. While doing so, he or she helps keep communication open between home and school.

The consultant must often deal with the emotional issues of the adults involved as well as the needs of the student. Each participant in the crisis situation may have some misconceptions and lack important information or skills. Participants tend to distrust one another's motives. To work together as a team, they must develop mutual trust and share common goals. In addition, they need to be assured that everyone cares and is seriously involved in addressing the crisis. Empathizing with all participants is an important part of the consultant's job. An awareness of the role of failure in escalating hostilities among families and schools, as well as of the healing that success can bring to all, is essential to planning an effective educational program.

5

Assessment

Wendy is a tall, pretty sixth grader. She is an active Girl Scout and a cheerleader for her brother's football team. Outside of school, Wendy is happy and has many friends. However, even though Wendy is almost 13 years old, she can't read. In-school testing has shown that she is of average intelligence and has learning disabilities. She has had the help of a resource room teacher. But nobody understands why Wendy can't read—least of all Wendy. Now Wendy is very unhappy in school. Her classmates often make fun of her. Her teachers are beginning to wonder if the problem has something to do with her parents' impending divorce.

Generally, teachers identify students with learning disabilities and ADD in grade school. For example, Wendy's learning disabilities were identified in second grade. However, the full extent of these students' problems often may not be revealed until middle school or high school—when, even with support, the student is not progressing. Wendy represents this type of student.

On the other hand, some very bright or gifted students have specific learning problems that escape detection by teachers until secondary school or beyond, often through extraordinary efforts on the part of the student and the parents. These students can achieve satisfactory grades with daily tutoring provided by parents and many hours spent on homework each night. The problems of some gifted students surface only during college. Then, when they enter college, they must confront their problems head-on. Their strengths (intelligence and diligence) can no longer compensate for their weaknesses.

Lacking even the most basic information about the nature and impact of their learning problems, such students are left with myths and superstitions about problems that they—and their teachers and parents—cannot explain. Unfortunately, these students often blame themselves for not succeeding, and their parents and teachers may blame them as well.

Wendy's problems baffle her, her teachers, and her parents. Teachers and parents seek assessment for students such as Wendy when these students are not performing as well as expected and when additional information is needed on which to base instructional decisions. Appropriate assessment can dispel the myths and superstitions and provide the hard data that students, parents, and professionals need to deal with learning problems. This chapter provides a brief overview of assessment for students with learning and attention difficulties. For more detail, the reader is referred to Salvia and Ysseldyke (1991), Sattler (1988), Taylor (1989), Wiggins (1993), and Wittrock (1983).

ASSESSMENT: PURPOSE AND REFERRAL

The goal of assessment is to gather information for making educational decisions about students. A comprehensive assessment serves several diagnostic and prescriptive purposes. It enables those concerned to make decisions about eligibility for special education and related services, improve educational program planning, improve the student's academic performance, and enhance student self-management through an awareness of strengths and weaknesses.

Assessment involves gathering information, observing students, administering tests, interpreting and reporting results, and recommending educational programming and instructional strategies. To be of maximum value to the student, the process must include not only a summary of test results and other diagnostic information but also an explanation of these findings and a set of recommendations. The recommendations become the basis for action.

Whatever its purpose, assessment is not merely a mechanical administration of tests or a statistical procedure for reporting scores. Assessment is a process, a search for information about underlying factors and relationships. It is an investigative and cooperative information-gathering process that will help the student understand and improve his or her school performance. In this regard, teachers play a critical and active role in the assessment process.

The referral for assessment is a formal request by a classroom teacher or parent to those outside of the classroom for information and assistance with a particular student. The starting point for the assessment process is referral.

Before referring the student, the teacher meets with the student and parent and identifies and describes problems or discrepancies in student performance. The teacher, student, and parents exchange information and insights. It is important to elicit student and parent involvement and cooperation from the beginning. Based on informal observations and interactions, the teacher identifies his or her concerns, provides examples of the problems as they relate to classroom learning or performance, discusses the instructional and/or management strategies that have been most and least useful, and suggests questions to address or areas to investigate. The teacher, parents, and student then jointly develop a list of questions they want the assessment to answer.

In Wendy's case neither the parents nor the teacher had any idea why Wendy was not learning to read. In addition, the teacher thought that she had done all she could to help Wendy.

COMPONENTS OF A COMPREHENSIVE ASSESSMENT

Assessment always includes the gathering of information from a variety of sources. Formal testing is only part of the process. Additional information is gathered through interviews, direct observations, error analysis of student work, curriculum-based assessment, diagnostic teaching, and student work samples (National Joint Committee on Learning Disabilities, 1987). Additional information can be collected from student self-reports, reports from other professionals, and previous assessment reports. Information is collected from both student and parents. The extent of the assessment process depends on its purpose, whether that be to document a learning disability, plan an appropriate educational program, or improve student academic or self-management skills.

Information from a variety of sources is necessary for several reasons. It provides a way to check the validity of results. It is required by special education law (IDEA) for determining eligibility for services. It completes the picture of the student by adding information not obtained from tests. Finally, it yields information on the student's performance in real-life settings, whereas testing shows how the student performs only in optimal or strictly controlled settings.

Depending on the student's history, referrals may be made for medical, neurological, psychological, or speech and language evaluations. For example, Wendy, who has a severe reading problem, will need both neuropsychological and language evaluations to show whether she has severe language disabilities and to what degree, if any, cognitive, emotional, or neurological problems are involved.

Information gathered concerns achievement, aptitude, social/emotional status, motor/sensory abilities, and medical, family, and developmental history. For a student with learning disabilities, information is needed concerning the following specific skills:

Expressive language—the ability to formulate age-appropriate spoken utterances

Receptive language—the ability to comprehend the spoken word

Basic reading—the fundamental ability to gain meaning from written text (includes reading decoding)

Reading comprehension—the ability to derive meaning from written text

Written expression—the ability to use written language to communicate ideas

Mathematics calculation—the concrete demonstration of calculations using mathematical symbols

Mathematics reasoning—the demonstration of understanding of mathematical concepts

In some cases, formal psychological assessments are necessary to provide information on the strengths and weaknesses of students with learning problems. These assessments can yield information on intellectual, perceptual, and language dysfunctions difficult to obtain in other ways.

The sources of information next described form the basis for a comprehensive evaluation.

Interviews

The goal of clinical interviews is to collect detailed information from relevant persons. This information serves to define and describe the problems and allows these problems to be examined from a variety of perspectives.

Interviews by psychologists, social workers, or teachers can set the tone for the entire assessment process. Often interviews are intense interpersonal encounters for the student and his or her parents. Messages are communicated in subtle ways, and respect and trust are important factors during the exchange of information between interviewer and student or parents. The interviewer's responsibility is to enlist the student's involvement and cooperation.

Family interviews can provide valuable information about the student's history, prior successes and problems, current interests and strengths, family dynamics, and stress that could affect the student's current performance. In addition, such interviews provide an opportunity to hear how the student acts at home or in community settings. However, it is important to focus on behavioral descriptions rather than labels, such as "single parent" or "adopted."

Work Samples

Work samples can provide a wealth of information about student performance and progress. Teachers should select and save typical work done in class and at home to illustrate student strengths and weaknesses. Work samples often reveal, in a way tests do not, attributes such as creativity and special interests.

Classroom work and homework are probably the most underused and underrated sources of information available in schools. Teachers can attach work samples to referrals to pinpoint or demonstrate the types of problems the student experiences.

Diagnostic Teaching

Diagnostic teaching can be helpful in investigating how a student learns. While conducting a 5- to 10-minute one-to-one "minilesson," the teacher focuses on the student as learner, closely observing the procedures used by the student to learn a concept or solve a problem. The teacher poses questions such as What is the method by which the student arrives at an answer? and When mistakes occur, do they occur because the student does not understand or follow directions, is unable to sequence or use reasoning or logic, or is unable to say or write the answer?

School Records

Schools are required by state law and school district policy to maintain certain records. In accordance with the Family Educational Rights and Privacy Act (Public Law 93–380), every school district must have a written policy governing the management and confidentiality of records and a procedure for parents and students to inspect, challenge, and correct records.

A cumulative record may contain personal identification data, attendance figures, report cards, achievement scores from district or statewide standardized tests, reports by teachers or consultants, and anecdotal notes. In addition, the record may contain psychological reports, medical records, summary or meeting notes from evaluation teams or committees convened to determine special education eligibility, IEPs, and correspondence between parents and school. Some files are kept in the school office for the teacher's easy access. More confidential information may be kept in a file in the central administrative offices. Teachers may use these records to identify trends and patterns. Such information can be invaluable when describing problems.

Observations

The purpose of conducting observations is to document the extent and frequency of a problem and the situations in which it occurs. Observations can provide baseline data that can be used to document progress. Observations can also provide information about student strengths. Behavioral observations can be conducted to assess on-task/off-task behavior, work habits, peer interactions, and teacher-student interactions (Mercer & Mercer, 1993). They are particularly informative when evaluating the effects of psychostimulant medication on ADD (observations collected prior to medication are compared with observations conducted after medication has been begun).

Observations of student performance can be informal, but they should be made on several occasions and in different settings. Systematic observations using commercially prepared forms are the most informative (Levine, 1986; Lindsley, 1992). It is good practice to have several different observers—such as a teacher, a special education teacher consultant, and a social worker—observing the student from different perspectives. Parents can be asked to observe the student at home during selected activities.

Student Self-Assessment

The teacher or psychologist can use various self-assessment activities to help elicit information from the student. This can include filling out checklists of characteristics and making lists of interests, strengths, and weaknesses. Levine (1986) has developed a good example of a self-administered student assessment for children 9 years and over. Bleuer (1987) has developed two checklists to help students analyze their report cards to determine the reasons they obtained good and poor grades.

Using such checklists, the psychologist or teacher can probe for more in-depth information. Kyle, the tenth grader whose situation is discussed in chapter 4, filled out a number of self-assessment checklists. The more mature student can discuss with an interviewer how his or her aptitudes and skills in various areas compare with those of peers.

This kind of student self-examination provides important information, helps the student gain self-understanding, and involves the student in the assessment process.

Psychometric Tests

A variety of individually administered psychometric tests are used in a comprehensive evaluation. Tests like the group-administered California Achievement Tests (California Test Bureau, 1985) provide norms for particular age groups and measures of test validity and reliability. (Validity means that a test accurately and fairly measures what it intends to measure. Reliability means that if students take a test on different days or if it is administered by different persons, the results will be approximately the same.)

Different types of tests identify current levels of academic achievement, achievement in specific content or skill areas, intellectual functioning, language proficiency, attention, impulsivity, and behavioral functioning. Comparing the results of each type of test helps define and quantify discrepancies within the individual student's profile. Comparisons are also possible between an individual student's profile and the profiles of other same-age students. Such results can then be compared with other information about student performance in order to make decisions about eligibility for services, program placement, and instructional strategies.

Teachers can administer individual achievement tests and diagnose academic problems; if so, the tests should be chosen not merely on the basis of ease of use but by how well tasks required by the test match the learning tasks in the classroom. Licensing is required to administer tests of intellectual functioning, as well as some language and projective tests. Good practice dictates that people administering tests have training in the appropriate use of tests and required procedures for administering tests, as well as clinical experience interpreting results.

Individual achievement tests

Individual achievement tests yield more specific information than group-administered tests and provide an opportunity for a trained professional to observe the student's behavior on a variety of tasks.

For example, the Kaufman Test of Educational Achievement (K-TEA; Kaufman & Kaufman, 1985) is designed to measure a student's achievement in grades 1 through 12 in mathematics calculations and applications, spelling, and reading decoding and comprehension. It is a reliable and valid test that is easy to administer and score. Tasks on this test resemble those generally required in the classroom. Similarly, the Woodcock-Johnson Psychoeducational Battery (Woodcock & Johnson, 1989) measures numerous areas of academic achievement and cognitive abilities.

The Wide Range Achievement Test (WRAT-3; Wilkinson, 1993) measures word recognition and pronunciation, written spelling, and arithmetic computation. It is quick and easy to administer. It is most useful for screening purposes and can suggest the need for further testing and some avenues to investigate. The arithmetic section is timed so that speed, as well as accuracy, is measured. Tasks on this test are similar to basic skills tasks necessary in the classroom. Reading on this test is limited to word recognition and does not include reading rate or comprehension. Therefore, this test should never be used by itself to rule out the existence of a reading problem.

Diagnostic tests of academic skills

Diagnostic tests of academic skills provide an in-depth picture—very specific information—about the nature and extent of a skill problem. Such tests help ascertain the student's strengths and weaknesses in an area, show where in a sequence of skills there are deficiencies or gaps, and form the basis for recommending strategies to improve performance. Tests are available for reading, mathematics, writing, and spelling.

Four tests of reading skills are the Stanford Diagnostic Reading Test (SDRT; Karlsen, Madden, & Gardner, 1977), the Woodcock Reading Mastery Tests (Woodcock, 1987), the Gray Oral Reading Test (GORT-3; Wiederholt & Bryant, 1992), and the Test of Reading Comprehension (TORC-3; Brown, Hammill, & Wiederholt, 1994). The SDRT can be administered to a group or an individual. It assesses a broad range of reading skills, including phonetic analysis, structural analysis, vocabulary, reading comprehension, scanning and skimming, and fast reading. The Woodcock Reading Mastery Tests assess five areas, including letter and word identification, word attack, word comprehension (analogies), and passage completion. The GORT-3 measures oral reading in terms of accuracy, speed, and comprehension of the material read. Although the test is limited to oral reading, it is useful for analyzing errors. The TORC-3 is a respected test of reading comprehension that includes sections on comprehension in specific subject areas, including mathematics and social studies. Scores for reading rate and comprehension can be attained with the Nelson Denny Reading Test (Brown, Bennett, & Hanna, 1993).

Tests of intellectual functioning

An individual test of intellectual functioning is a basic component of an assessment and is required to determine eligibility for special education services and, by implication, Section 504 accommodations. Although individual testing is required, it is not to be used as the sole basis for decisions about eligibility or programming.

The third edition of the Wechsler Intelligence Scale for Children (WISC-III; Wechsler, 1991) and the Wechsler Adult Intelligence Scale–Revised (WAIS-R; Wechsler, 1981) are the most commonly used intelligence tests. The WISC-III is designed to assess the intelligence of students from 6 through 16 years of age, whereas the WAIS-R is designed for persons 16 years of age and older.

These tests include a verbal section and a performance section, each of which is composed of subtests, some of which are timed. Scores are reported for each subtest, each section, and for the full scale. An IQ test is an important factor in investigating mental functioning but is never used alone to diagnose learning disabilities or ADD. Additionally, the full scale score may not be as accurate a measure of intellectual ability as several subtest scores that reflect higher order thinking (e.g., comprehension, similarities, block design).

A severe discrepancy between the scores of sections or subtests is often used as an indicator of learning disabilities, although such a discrepancy may also indicate other problems, such as emotional disturbance, stress, lack of experience, or traumatic brain injury. Grouping the scores on some of the subtests can often indicate freedom from distractibility and degree of perceptual organization. It is important to note that all students evidence some discrepancies among subtest scores. Increasingly, research indicates that greater variability exists within individuals than had previously been thought (Kaufman, 1979). Therefore, small within-test discrepancies do not necessarily indicate the presence of learning disabilities.

Language tests

Language problems may be a basic cause of problems in spelling, reading, and writing, as well as behavior problems. Therefore, tests of auditory processing and expressive language are commonly included in a comprehensive language assessment. More and more, research is indicating that language problems are the underlying cause of learning disabilities such as dyslexia. Despite the fact that students appear to hear and speak adequately, there may be signficant language problems.

Some commonly administered language tests include the Peabody Picture Vocabulary Test–Revised (PPVT-R; Dunn & Dunn, 1981), Test of Adolescent Language (TOAL-3; Hammill, Brown, Larsen, & Wiederholt, 1993), Test of Written Language (TOWL-2; Hammill & Larsen, 1988), Clinical Evaluation of Language Fundamentals–Revised (CELF-R; Semel, Wiig, & Secord, 1987), and Test for Auditory Comprehension of Language–Revised (TACL-R; Carrow-Woolfolk, 1985). These tests are commonly administered by special educators, speech and language pathologists, or psychologists.

Measures of Behavioral Functioning

The most common evaluation techniques for behavioral functioning are behavior rating scales, self-report measures, situational measures, and observation. These measures are used to screen for distractibility, hyperactivity, and impulsivity; in addition, they can yield information on other problems that may need further investigation, such as depression, anxiety, and conduct disorder.

Parents and teachers can use behavior rating scales such as the Conners' Parent Rating Scale (Conners, 1989a); the Conners' Teacher Rating Scale (Conners, 1989b); ADD-H: Comprehensive Teacher's Rating Scale (ACTeRS; Ullman et al., 1991); Attention Deficit Disorders Evaluation Scale (McCarney, 1989); Child Behavior Checklist–Youth Self-Report (Achenbach & Edelbrock, 1987). The reliability and validity of these behavior rating scales and checklists are somewhat questionable, but they do provide a place to begin.

Two tests of attention and impulsivity are the Test of Variables of Attention (TOVA; Greenberg & Waldman, 1993) and the Attentional Capacity Test (ACT; Weber, 1988). The TOVA is a computer-based test of impulsivity and attention involving visual stimuli; the ACT measures auditory attention.

THE ASSESSMENT TEAM

When the primary purpose of assessment is to make diagnoses and determine eligibility for special education services or Section 504 accommodations, tests must be administered by licensed professionals with appropriate technical training: school psychologists, clinical psychologists, neuropsychologists, and sometimes speech and language pathologists. The neuropsychologist can evaluate basic cognitive functioning such as attention and memory underlying more complex skills.

Many achievement and psychoeducational tests may be administered by regular or special education teachers and other educational or psychological consultants. Some special education teachers and consultants are trained to describe and interpret test results, respond to student and parent concerns regarding assessment, make referrals for further testing, and recommend educational programming and instructional techniques. Often, teachers and consultants conduct initial screening interviews, and clinical psychologists follow up with in-depth clinical intake interviews.

The assessment process provides a unique opportunity for a team approach to sharing information, engaging in problem solving, and recommending plans. The multidisciplinary evaluation team is composed of professionals from different disciplines who determine eligibility for special education services under IDEA. The team's first job is to determine what types of information are needed for a comprehensive assessment. Members evaluate student performance, share diagnostic information with one another, and develop reports to use in planning an educational program. This team can also be responsible for determining the student's eligibility for accommodations under Section 504.

THE ASSESSMENT PROCESS

Generally, the school psychologist is responsible for overseeing the assessment process, and the following discussion reflects this reality. However, a comprehensive assessment involves a collaboration among many individuals, in which the teacher's role is central. Teachers may not consider themselves an important part of the assessment process, believing instead that their responsibilities end once the referral has been made. Increasingly, however, teachers share in the responsibility for assessment. Because they are the ones who will ultimately translate assessment findings into classroom realities, they will need to be involved in all the phases of the assessment process next described.

Involving the Student and Family

The psychologist uses various methods to involve the student and family and facilitate a positive assessment experience. Specifically, he or she acknowledges feelings and allays concerns, discusses informed consent and ensures confidentiality, and shares problem solving and decision making.

Acknowledging feelings and allaying concerns

The prospect of assessment may create anxiety and apprehension. Often students report that merely thinking about a comprehensive evaluation triggers the feelings one has when thinking about having a tooth pulled. Diagnostic testing is viewed as an invasive procedure full of danger and uncertainty. Even if students believe that testing may be useful or necessary, they may prefer to avoid it.

Parents, too, often have negative feelings about assessment procedures. They are likely to feel that previous testing was an invasion of family privacy, that they had no say in the matter, and that they have been blamed for their child's problems. Parents may feel that the results did not accurately describe their child and/or accentuated the child's weaknesses. Even if they concede that the tests provided some useful information, parents often feel that the results were ignored and that the assessment was a waste of time. These feelings must be acknowledged before testing can proceed. The psychologist establishes a trusting relationship with the student and the parents and explains why this assessment will be different from previous ones.

The exchange between Wendy's mother and the psychologist coordinating the assessment process illustrates negative feelings about assessment and shows how such anxieties can be allayed. Wendy's mother was very angry at the school and refused to sign the year's IEP. She said, "It's the same old stuff they did last year and the year before. It didn't work. She still can't read. They don't know what they're doing. And now they're blaming me."

The psychologist explained:

I can understand why you are angry. Wendy is a bright student, but she hasn't been making much progress. We need more information about Wendy, a new perspective, and additional testing and evaluation to find out why we haven't been able to help her so far and to find out what new methods may help her learn to read.

In response to the mother's concerns that prior testing had been less than helpful, the psychologist said:

This time things are different: First, we will look for Wendy's strengths as well as her weaknesses. Second, we will have much more extensive testing to see if more is involved than learning disabilities. For instance, you say that Wendy sometimes doesn't seem to understand what you say. We need to find out why. Perhaps she has a language problem that we haven't been aware of. Third, you will be involved every step of the way—before, during, and after the testing. Fourth, if anyone seems to blame you for Wendy's problems, I will talk to him or her. What's most important is that we will use the information from the assessment to write out a specific educational program just for Wendy. And we will monitor this plan very carefully.

Obtaining informed consent and ensuring confidentiality

As with medical procedures, informed consent is necessary for evaluations conducted outside the classroom by a licensed psychologist or other professional. If the student is under 18, the student's parents must be fully informed of the purposes and extent of the proposed testing and give their written permission to proceed. If the student is over 18, his or her informed consent must be obtained directly.

Both the parents and the student should understand why a particular test or procedure is advised, what kind of information it will yield, and how the results may be used. Whenever possible, the interests of the student are integrated into the discussion. Parents and student are also assured that testing is voluntary, that they are entitled to ask questions or voice concerns, and that the results are confidential and reports may not be released to other parties without the parents' (or student's, if over age 18) written permission.

Sharing problem solving and decision making

Because information about their academic performance can help students manage their vulnerabilities and maximize their talents, they should be actively involved in the assessment process from the beginning. Before getting involved, students generally want to know how assessment can help them do better in school. The psychologist explains that the process will yield technical information about learning styles, strengths, and weaknesses and that the student is part of the information-gathering team.

Chances are that the student already knows some of the findings that the assessment will provide. Test results will usually confirm both strengths and weaknesses the student has described during interviews or indicated on self-assessment checklists. In addition, the assessment will help uncover other aspects of the student's performance that were previously hidden. The psychologist stresses the advantages of having this information in concrete form:

Until now you've dealt with your academic problems as best you could—working twice as hard as other students but getting only half the results, or none at all. The assessment should give you technical information and new ideas about how to work more effectively. Your teachers will also find the information useful in helping you learn.

The student and/or the parents list questions that are important for the assessment to answer. Following are some of the questions most commonly asked:

What are the specific problems called?

How do these problems affect schoolwork?

What can be done about them?

Why are there difficulties with a particular school subject?

Why do these problems interfere with concentration and/or memory? How can parents help the student?

Does having these problems mean that the student is not intelligent?

Wendy's mother had just three questions: "Why does Wendy have trouble following directions sometimes?" "Why does Wendy have such problems in school when she does so well outside of school?" and "Will Wendy ever learn to read?"

Collecting and Reporting Information

One of the psychologist's responsibilities is to ensure conditions for a fair and valid assessment. For best results students need to feel comfortable in the test environment and with the test administrator. The psychologist helps students view the testing as an opportunity to gain information about themselves and understand that the outcome will be most valid if they are actively involved in the testing process.

The psychologist explains the nature and purpose of any formal testing:

These tests will provide us with samples of your behavior at one point in time. If you took the same test on a different day, your score might be several points higher or lower.

We take this into consideration when we evaluate the test results. The results will be used with other information we've gathered to draw a more accurate picture of your areas of strength and vulnerability.

If appropriate, the psychologist then asks if the student has any questions and briefly explains any information that will help the student understand the tests to be administered—for example, that some sections are timed or that the student is not expected to complete all of the items.

In addition to conducting the actual assessment, the psychologist prepares a written diagnostic report that presents the reason for referral; background information on the student; behavioral observations; assessment results, including strengths and weaknesses; clinical impressions; and recommendations. The diagnostic report presents information on each area that has been assessed.

Analyzing and Interpreting Results

The psychologist analyzes test results and provides a written psychoeducational report. This report must in turn be interpreted by the special education teacher consultant and the classroom teacher, in light of school requirements and the student's current school performance. In order to use the information in the report to help the student learn, it is important to determine the answers to the following questions.

Was the assessment fair, or did factors interfere with the student's performance on the test?   In Wendy's case, the psychologist's report stated that "As there were no indications of significant anxiety or poor motivation, these results are believed to be an accurate measure of functioning."

Are the tests appropriate and valid for the problems to be investigated?   The tests used with Wendy had been extensively documented in terms of validity, reliability, and correlation with other measures of student aptitude and achievement. Norms for the tests were established on a large, representative sample of students of Wendy's same age and socioeconomic group.

What are the test results in terms of standard scores, scaled scores, stanines, grade level, or percentile?   Results of psychological tests and subtests are usually presented in these terms so that a student can be compared to others of the same age or grade level on specific measures. For example, on the WISC-III, most of Wendy's subtest scores were below 10, which is the average score. The percentiles were also given for the subtest scores. Wendy's percentiles ranged from 5 to 50, with the higher percentiles for the performance subtests. This type of scoring shows that Wendy's performance is a little below the performance of others taking the same test.

What are the student's strengths and weaknesses?   Wendy's report described a number of weaknesses and relative strengths. For example:

Auditory verbal learning is significantly impaired. . . .
She does not retain auditory information well upon delay.
. . . Her ability to recall visual information such as pictures and designs falls within the low-average range. She
also appears much more able to retain visual information,
accurately recalling what she had learned upon delay. . . .
Visuospatial and constructional skills and abilities generally
fall within the average range.

Are there large discrepancies between scores for the verbal and performance portions of the WISC-III, the WISC-III subtests, or aptitude and achievement tests?   The psychologist noted that in Wendy's case the verbal-performance IQ discrepancy and the discrepancy between level of intellect (ability) and reading and spelling skills (achievement) were statistically significant, meaning that these results did not occur by chance alone.

How do the assessment findings explain current academic performance, including grades, class tests, and work samples? Wendy's test results verify that she is generally cheerful and sociable but clearly frustrated by her learning disabilities and academic deficiencies. There are no indications of significant anxiety or poor motivation. The tests indicate that Wendy does have severe disabilities in reading (dyslexia) and in expressive writing. Although her speech is clear and fluent, she has word retrieval difficulties.

Her testing reflects serious weaknesses in verbal learning and verbal memory. However, Wendy has demonstrated that she is able to use context and visual cues to compensate for her verbal comprehension deficits. In addition, she has relatively strong mathematical and visuospatial skills.

From these test results, Wendy and her mother learn some of the reasons Wendy is unable to read and communicate effectively. Wendy's learning disabilities, combined with her language problems, explain why she has been unable to learn to read thus far. Her fluent speech largely masks her word retrieval difficulties and the severity of her verbal deficits.

What other factors could affect or account for the results (e.g., medical problems, emotional states)? In Wendy's case, the psychologist could not identify any medical or emotional problems.

What important areas were not evaluated (e.g., motivation, persistence, creativity)? What role do these play in the student's life? Although Wendy is discouraged by her failure to learn how to read, she is willing to try a new approach. In order to maintain her motivation, the psychologist suggests that Wendy's math strengths "offer an avenue for academic success" and that "nonacademic activities such as art may prove very reinforcing."

In preparing for program planning, teachers ask the following types of questions:

How are the student's vulnerabilities or weaknesses barriers to performance?

How can barriers be confronted or overcome?

What strengths help compensate for or circumvent vulnerabilities?

Are there situations in which weaknesses constitute insurmountable barriers to goal attainment?

Discussing the Report

The report can be used as a basis for discussion with parents and student about learning disabilities and attention problems. This discussion is an opportunity to reinterpret history, understand the present, and set new goals for the future. It typically covers topics such as the following:

Definition of the disability according to federal guidelines or psychological classification

Description of how the disability might operate in everyday situations

Description of the relationship between the disability and behaviors, thoughts, and feelings

Information on possible causes, if known

Reassurance that the problems are not the student's or parents' fault

Some options and possibilities, including legal and public agency services and support

Information about possible treatments, tests, or educational, psychological, and medical procedures

Permission to take all the time needed to fully understand the disability and situation

Encouragement to focus on strengths, special qualities, and abilities, as well as to realize that a learning disability is only one part of a person's identity

Often during the reporting session the student will express feelings of inadequacy. The psychologist may attempt to allay these concerns in the following way:

Many students feel that way. But according to these tests, you are intelligent. Most people with learning disabilities have at least average intelligence. You have some difficulties that interfere with your performance, so you haven't been able to perform consistently. I can see that you are a hard worker. The problem is that you haven't been able to focus all that hard work in a productive manner. And that's exactly what we hope to help you do when this assessment process is complete.

Even though the psychologist may have reported the results once to the parents, others involved in the assessment will likely be responsible for reinterpreting and making the information usable to the parents and student. To initiate discussion, that individual refers to the list of questions prepared earlier by the student and parents and attempts to answer these in terms of the assessment results. It is important to reexplain the nature and extent of the student's problems and strengths to the student and parents, pointing out any discrepancies that may account for the student's problems. It may be helpful to paraphrase the introduction or summary section of the report—even read sections of the report verbatim, pausing to explain and discuss the meaning of important sentences, phrases, or findings. Often it is enlightening to student and parents to explain strengths and weaknesses by examining the student's response to test items and relating it to classroom performance.

Because many students with learning disabilities have problems with language or auditory processing, it is helpful to illustrate the numerical results of tests with visual displays. In addition, illustrations may have a calming effect because they are less formal and more like the process the student has used in estimating his or her own levels of performance in various areas. While sketching the student's profile, the professional can comment on the assessment results and ask the student to compare them with his or her self-predicted scores and course grades.

Frequently, the student and parents enter a report conference in a highly anxious state. The professional puts them at ease as quickly as possible by summarizing the assessment results in a palatable way. For example, if student and parents have been able to predict areas of student strength and weakness with some accuracy, the professional confirms their predictions.

Of course, unpleasant surprises may have occurred in the meeting with the psychologist—for example, when the student scores much lower than expected in one or more areas. The professional needs sensitivity, good timing, and systematic procedures to restate and discuss difficult or disappointing information. He or she must proceed slowly in order to explain the test results fully, maintain trust, and limit distress. The student's strengths are reported and discussed first. The professional treats the disappointing surprises later, using a calm, analytical, and problem-solving approach:

The reason we are so surprised at the results is that your strengths have helped you compensate for your weaknesses so well that they have hidden your weaknesses. We didn't know about these weaknesses until now because you were able to do the work. Now, because you are faced with greater challenges, the weaknesses are coming to the surface. We will have to figure out ways to deal with them. You are the same person now as you were before we discovered these weaknesses. You haven't changed— we just know much more about you. And that's good because it can help us plan a good program for you.

In accepting the disappointment, denial, or anger that the student and parents may feel, the professional can provide empathy and positive direction. For example, although Wendy's mother is still coming to grips with the severity of her daughter's learning disabilities and language problems, she is actively working with Wendy's teachers on a new program. By recycling empathy and problem solving as needed, the professional can help Wendy's mother keep the severity of Wendy's disabilities in perspective.

To help Wendy understand her test results, the professional refers Wendy's mother to the book *Keeping a Head in School* (Levine, 1990). This book is written for students Wendy's age who have learning problems and includes many case studies that Wendy can relate to. By reading and discussing parts of this book with Wendy, her mother will be able to help Wendy understand her strengths and weaknesses and encourage her to find ways of addressing some of her problems. Many parents have reported that both they and their children learned a great deal from this book. For younger students the book *All Kinds of Minds* (Levine, 1993) is helpful.

Making Recommendations for Educational Planning and Instruction

The psychologist's diagnostic report includes a list of recommendations for educational planning and instruction to help the student succeed in school. Recommendations can concern the primary modality in which directions and information should be presented (e.g., auditory and/or visual); ways to focus student attention; use of repetition, reinforcement, and feedback; appropriate placement; supportive services needed; types of courses to avoid (e.g., in the case of a student with language difficulties, foreign languages); and further referrals (e.g., for counseling). The report may also include recommendations for parents.

However, recommendations are often incomplete or overly general. In addition, psychological and medical reports may be too long, too vague, too complex, or too obscurely written for teachers or parents to use. When the report is not readily usable, the special education teacher consultant and/or classroom teacher will need to meet with the psychologist in order to translate assessment results into the educational accommodations the student needs and to determine methods and strategies for supporting student achievement in the classroom.

Using all the information that has been gathered during the assessment, the teacher goes on to design specific classroom interventions. In Wendy's case, recommendations were written by the psychologist for the classroom teacher and for the speech and language teacher consultant and the learning disabilities consultant. Specific recommendations for addressing Wendy's learning problems include a systematic multisensory program that uses visual, auditory, and kinesthetic modalities to teach reading and writing. Because of the severity of Wendy's reading and writing problems, the teacher consultant will give Wendy one-on-one instruction for an hour a day in reading, writing, and expressive language/word retrieval.

Wendy will be placed in a regular education class for most of the day so she can maintain her age-appropriate social skills and her self-esteem. The regular education teacher will use a cooperative learning model, carefully plan and individualize Wendy's participation in small groups, and locate materials that will ensure success for Wendy while the other students are working on more difficult materials. Continual participation in extracurricular activities such as cheerleading and sports will bolster Wendy's self-esteem. At home Wendy will begin keeping a daily journal by dictating to her mother things of interest to her. The goal is for Wendy herself to begin writing in the journal as soon as possible.

To maintain Wendy's motivation during the slow process of learning how to read, the learning disabilities teacher consultant will videotape Wendy once a month reading aloud and discussing a reading passage; give her high-interest, low vocabulary books on subjects of her choice; and explain to her that learning to read is like learning any new sport or learning cheerleading techniques: It takes a lot of work and practice.

Conducting Periodic Reviews

For students like Wendy who receive special education services, a review is conducted each year as part of the IEP process in order to determine goals and objectives for the following year. A similar annual review would benefit all students with learning difficulties.

It is not always possible to predict how student vulnerabilities, as described in the diagnostic report, will affect the student's work in a new course. Teachers and other professionals need to review diagnostic reports periodically. When new difficulties surface, it is important to reexamine diagnostic findings in light of the present difficulties, review examples of the student's strengths and weaknesses, and try to understand why the difficulties have arisen.

Once the source of a difficulty is located, it can be explained to the student as follows: "This is your glitch in operation. You didn't cause it, you can't cure it, but our work together will shed light on how to cope with it." Prior assessment findings—or new diagnostic efforts—can help put the difficulty in perspective and suggest directions for change in the student's educational program.

SUMMARY AND CONCLUSIONS

Problems cannot be addressed effectively unless their underlying causes are completely understood. Comprehensive assessment provides valuable information that can be used to identify and explain the problem and to develop appropriate instructional programs.

Too often, assessment is synonymous with testing. However, testing is only one part of the assessment process, just as psychologists are only one part of the assessment team. The teacher has important information and skills to contribute to the assessment process, and the process is greatly enhanced when the teacher plays an active role before, during, and after assessment. The student and family are an integral part of the assessment team. At the very least, the active involvement of the student and parents in the assessment process increases the likelihood that assessment results will shed light on the student's difficulties and lead to greater academic success.

When multiple sources of information—such as observations, student self-assessment, and diagnostic teaching—are integrated with test results, students and their parents have a greater understanding of student performance. Such an assessment provides a strong basis for improving instructional strategies by identifying students' strengths and making them the center of an action plan. Accurate information allows for more accurate prediction of possible problems and pitfalls, thus allowing them to be planned for and overcome.

6

Program Planning

The clutch hit by Sam.

The to teams were coreys cubs and Rich's Suzuki. my team was coreys cubs. The score when I Came up was seven to six. There were two outs. There were two men on base. Key on first and Grant on third. Thecount was two balls and a strike. When I came up to bat I was nervous. after that count the pither threw the ball. I swong. I hit it. the first base couch slapped me five. and we scored two that inning. and my couch picked me up. I felt GREAT.

The goal of effective program planning for students like Sam, the author of the passage introducing this chapter, is to design a learning environment that maximizes the individual student's abilities and addresses the student's learning problems. In Sam's case, the teacher used Sam's interest in baseball to help him learn writing skills.

All students could benefit from individualized programs to help them become more successful learners. For the student with learning problems, an individualized program is critical. This discussion follows Sam through the program planning process to illustrate effective and ineffective practices for students with learning problems.

CASE EXAMPLE: A STUDENT IN NEED OF PROGRAM PLANNING

Sam is an animated, mischievous-looking 12-year-old. He tends to answer an interviewer in one-word sentences. Given a list of adjectives, Sam describes himself as athletic, likable, friendly, happy, and noisy. He says he is not lonely, quiet, or neat. The idea that he might be neat makes him laugh. He says that he likes to help people. His interests are baseball, baseball, and baseball. When asked if he would describe himself as intelligent, he refuses to answer and turns away, his eyes filling with tears. He says he often gets angry at his younger brother. Sam wants to be a writer for a newspaper when he grows up.

Sam has severe learning disabilities and severe ADD, thus making him eligible for special education programming and services. He is currently on medication for ADD. Intelligence testing has shown Sam to be in the low-average range, although he is probably brighter than that. Students with learning disabilities often have depressed scores on intelligence tests. He has severe deficits in expressive and receptive language, which further depress his IQ scores, as well as problems with written expression. However, Sam's reading decoding skills are excellent; he is a visual learner.

According to his mother, Sam is highly motivated and hardworking. This past year, despite having visual-motor skills below age level and poor spatial relations, Sam taught himself to catch a baseball. He set himself a goal of 100 catches. He achieved his goal after practicing almost every day for 3 months, and he now plays on a Little League team.

Sam's teachers and parents are frustrated by the combination of his disabilities. They feel that he is quite bright and that he could do well if they "could only rewire his brain." Sam is in a regular education class that is team taught by a regular education teacher and a teacher with certification in special education and an endorsement in learning disabilities. Team teaching seems ideal for a student like Sam. It allows him to remain in the regular education class while providing him with much of the specialized help that he needs.

Sam is just starting sixth grade, and he wants to learn. He had so much trouble last year that he felt he had not learned the fifth-grade material. In fact, at the end of the school year he told his mother and his teachers that he wanted to repeat fifth grade so that he could really learn the material and be prepared to enter middle school. He went on to sixth grade, however, because the teachers assured him and his mother that he could learn the material he did not know.

The Individual Education Program: A Model for Program Planning

An Individual Education Program (IEP), written each year by an Individual Education Program Committee (IEPC), is generated for each student eligible for special education services. The IEP specifies the following:

The student's current level of educational performance, annual goals, and short-term objectives

Special education and related services, such as speech and language therapy, transportation, or physical therapy

Amount of integration in regular education classes

Prevocational and vocational education

Transition planning for postsecondary options

The date for initiation of the program

Evaluation procedures for determining whether instructional objectives are being achieved

By law, the IEPC includes the parent or parents, at least one of the student's teachers, and an administrator or supervisor. Other participants (e.g., other teachers, a school psychologist, a school social worker, a counselor) are often invited to share information and participate in decision making.

The planning process under Section 504 of the Rehabilitation Act is similar to the special education planning process. Although this law does not specify which teacher(s) should be involved in program planning, best practice dictates that, at some point, teachers who will implement the plan be involved in the planning process. This may mean that the annual goals, objectives, and general accommodations are planned at the end of one school year, whereas the instructional objectives and strategies and specific accommodations are generated prior to the first day of class.

The IEP process provides an excellent educational program planning model that can be used for students who are not eligible for special education services as well as for those who are. The process can be expanded to include the selection of courses and teachers for the coming year and to project a 3- or 4-year high school course of study.

Even when individualized educational planning is required by law, program planning is unfortunately often a last-minute affair. For example, although Sam's sixth-grade teachers were chosen at the end of his fifth-grade year, serious program planning did not begin until the third week of school. This situation is not atypical: Program planning is usually done at the end of an academic year after teacher deployment and course offerings for the coming year have been finalized. Parents and students have at most a week to select courses for the following year—if all goes well. If the school has financial difficulties or is poorly organized, a student may find that some desired courses will not be offered, a preferred course is full, teachers have not yet been selected or hired, or the prerequisites for a particular course put it out of reach. Students may also find that counselors and teachers have little time to meet with them at the end of the school year because of the demands of giving final exams, determining course grades, and filling out end-of-year reports. At the beginning of the school year teachers may be equally busy. In addition, students and parents usually are not aware of all of the school's or district's course offerings. They need time to locate the information that will enable them to make informed choices. They need time to gather input from teachers and counselors. They need time to consider student goals, course requirements, and available options before making decisions.

Unfortunately, although they are done according to legal requirements, even formal IEPs tend to be prepared in a rush, with insufficient time allotted for thorough discussion by everyone concerned. Participants' roles and responsibilities, lines of communication, and lines of authority may also be unclear. Accommodations needed in the regular classroom are rarely spelled out, although this situation is improving.

In sum, there are five major barriers to effective program planning: lack of involvement of teachers who will be implementing the plan, insufficient time allotted for discussion and planning, missing or incomplete information necessary for decision making, unsystematic planning, and insufficient time allotted to get systems, staff, and accommodations in place. To help overcome these barriers to effective planning, we recommend beginning the process well in advance—during the winter term for the following academic year.

TAKING A SYSTEMATIC APPROACH

A systematic approach helps in planning effective educational programs for all students. Such an approach assures that there is an alignment between the assessment process, program goals and objectives, instructional strategies and accommodations, and resources. Most important, monitoring and evaluation procedures are listed, and the individuals responsible for evaluation are specified.

The program planning process described in the following pages is basically that found in the IEP process in special education.

Regardless of whether or not the process is officially mandated, the basic steps remain the same.

Program planning at the secondary level involves many people—teachers, counselors, parents, administrators, and others. Before detailing the steps in the process, it is therefore important first to delineate team members' roles and responsibilities in formulating and implementing the plan.

Participants in the Process

The classroom teacher

Traditionally, the classroom teacher is responsible for implementing educational programs and developing daily lesson plans and classroom rules. For individual students with learning problems, the teacher's role and responsibilities are expanded to include program planning. The teacher needs to be involved actively in the program planning process. Responsibilities may include the following:

Meeting with the parents and student to plan the program

Asking for help from the school administrator, special education teacher consultant, or other professionals regarding academic strategies and materials

Keeping up to date on new educational research and methodologies

Modifying teaching methods and making accommodations to address the student's disabilities

Trying alternative techniques until one is successful

Helping to design, facilitate, and ensure the effectiveness of homework assignment systems, note-taking systems, test-taking systems, and so forth

Designing checklists with the student

Designing individual reinforcement systems with the student, parents, and special education teacher consultant

Monitoring the program plan and modifying as necessary, based on feedback from all parties

Contacting the student and parents in a timely fashion regarding any problems

The special education teacher consultant

If the student is eligible for special education services, the special education teacher consultant will be part of the planning team. The role of this consultant is as follows:

Meeting with parents and student to plan the educational program

Providing in-depth information to regular education teachers regarding the student's abilities and disabilities

Providing a copy of the student's IEP to teachers and discussing it with them

Consulting with teachers regarding effective teaching strategies and/or special materials

Arranging for assistive technology

Helping to monitor the program plan and consulting regularly with teachers regarding student progress

Informing parents frequently of student progress

Helping to design homework assignment systems, note-taking systems, test-taking systems, and so forth

Helping to design individual reinforcement systems, in collaboration with the teacher, student, and parents

Providing direct instruction in academic support skills, such as cognitive and metacognitive strategies, test-taking skills, note-taking skills, and study skills

Relating school skills to work skills

Providing remedial instruction in subject content areas

Helping to monitor and modify the educational program

The student

It is the student who must put in the work to achieve the educational goals and objectives. However, unless the student is involved in setting educational goals and objectives, he or she will be relatively unmotivated to carry them out.

As the student matures, teachers and parents should encourage increasing involvement in program planning. It may take years, but this involvement is critical to the long-term growth and maturity of the student. By the time the student is in secondary school, he or she should be assuming the following responsibilities:

Developing self-awareness of strengths, weaknesses, and current level of educational performance

Helping to set educational goals and objectives

Selecting overall course of study and individual classes

Designing checklists with teachers and parents

Developing a personal reinforcement system

Determining additional help and support needed

Understanding and meeting routine responsibilities (e.g., completing class work and homework, following attendance policy, following school and classroom rules)

Monitoring his or her own educational program and asking for help, if needed

The parents

In order for parents to be fully involved, they need to understand the program planning process. This means that course descriptions should accurately describe what is taught in the class and avoid euphemisms for low-level classes; in addition, procedures for school and course selection should be clear and fair. Course selections should not be predetermined by the school; rather, parents should have the right to disagree and negotiate. The most effective educational programs are those about which the parents, school, and student agree.

The roles and responsibilities of the parents are as follows:

Being aware of the student's current level of educational performance, strengths, and weaknesses

Providing information to the student to enable him or her to make educational decisions

Modeling problem-solving and decision-making behavior

Allowing the student progressively more involvement in educational decision making and decision making in general

Encouraging the student to make career plans, plan for future education, and determine current educational needs

Providing career information, locating role models,
and facilitating early work experiences

Taking an active (and sometimes a leadership) role
in educational program planning

Acting as the student's advocate in difficult situations

Monitoring and evaluating the student's educational
programs

Keeping the student's educational records

Contacting the school with any educational concerns

Sharing information about medication and medical
concerns

Supporting the educational program by providing
a home atmosphere conducive to learning

Arranging for counseling or tutoring, if needed

Sharing information from private therapists as
appropriate

Reinforcing student strengths and interests

If parents lack the information and skills to fulfill these responsibilities, schools, parent-teacher organizations, and parent support groups often can provide parent training in these areas.

The school administrator

The school administrator—usually the principal, assistant principal, or class principal—has a leadership role in program planning. The administrator underscores the importance of planning by allocating program planning and consultation time with appropriate school personnel. It is also the administrator's responsibility to provide any necessary training and support for teachers and to encourage innovation and creativity in programming. The administrator attends planning meetings as needed, helps solve problems, and responds to concerns expressed by parents and students.

The vocational educator

Although special education law mandates vocational services for eligible students, there is a new emphasis on career and vocational education for all students. Everyone is expected to graduate with technical and employment skills. The attainment of these skills should be part of every educational plan.

The roles and responsibilities of the vocational educator are as follows:

Assessing skills and interests

Providing information to the student to enable him or her to make educational and vocational decisions

Encouraging the student to identify and explore career and educational options

Encouraging the student to make career plans, plan for future education, and determine current educational needs

Providing career information and locating role models

Teaching vocational skills and arranging for vocational experiences

The school psychologist

A school psychologist can greatly enhance program planning for a student eligible for special education services. He or she can interpret assessment information and help translate it into instructional activities. Unfortunately, school psychologists are kept extremely busy administering assessments and are rarely available for parent or teacher conferences. Even if unable to attend planning meetings, the school psychologist should be contacted to check or comment upon the appropriateness of the program plan as it relates to assessment findings.

The external consultant

Sometimes a student's learning problems are so complex that additional expertise is needed to plan an effective educational program. This is often the case when parents and school cannot agree on placement or program options. For example, Sam's mother had long been dissatisfied with Sam's educational program. She felt that the program was not appropriate and not based on Sam's individual needs. However, instead of requesting a formal hearing, Sam's mother asked the school to call in an outside consultant to help design an appropriate program for Sam. This step saved the school district hundreds of dollars and allowed Sam's program to begin almost immediately.

The external consultant is a professional educator paid by the school or parents. The responsibilities of the external consultant can include the following:

Meeting with parents, student, school administrator, and teaching staff to analyze concerns, issues, and constraints

Analyzing all reports and assessments to determine student needs and strengths and to evaluate educational methodology previously used

Interviewing the student and observing the student in class to increase knowledge of student strengths and needs

Observing the strengths and weaknesses of the learning environment

Helping to design an individualized program acceptable to parents and school

Suggesting educational methods, instructional strategies, instructional packages, textbooks, and/or software

The family advocate

A family advocate is someone chosen by parents who helps the family, usually on a voluntary basis, to obtain the educational program the parents consider appropriate for their child. Each state is required by the Developmental Disabilities Assistance and Bill of Rights Act (42 USC ss. 6042) to provide protection and advocacy services.

Many family advocates have children of their own with learning problems and most belong to parent organizations such as the Learning Disabilities Association (LDA) or Children with Attention Deficit Disorders (ChADD). Parent organizations often provide advocacy training.

Parents usually call an advocate when they and the school disagree on an educational program for the child. Most advocates will accompany parents to school meetings and conferences. Other responsibilities of the advocate include the following:

Meeting with the parents (and student) to discuss their problems and concerns

Helping parents clarify issues

Helping parents find out the strengths and needs of their child

Helping parents locate information

Suggesting ways to solve problems and address issues

Helping parents decide what educational programs
and services are important for their child

Helping parents prepare for an IEPC meeting

Accompanying parents to an educational planning meeting

Helping parents get their points across at school meetings
and conferences

Making sure parents are listened to respectfully, that they
understand everything that is said, and that the law is
being followed

With the parents' permission, negotiating with the school
to work out mutually acceptable educational arrangements
for all parties

Helping parents decide whether to agree or disagree
with the educational decisions of the IEPC

Informing parents of the steps to take if disagreements
are not resolved

The program planning team for Sam included the special education director, Sam's two classroom teachers (a regular education
teacher and a specialist in learning disabilities), Sam's mother, an
external consultant, a family advocate, and Sam himself.

Steps in a Program Planning Model

The program planning model next described incorporates and extends
the principles involved in the IEP process.

Beginning the process

An effective system usually has a facilitator who takes a leadership role. In educational program planning this can be a teacher,
a counselor, a special education teacher consultant, or a school administrator. This facilitator is sometimes called the *case coordinator* and
may or may not be the same person who leads the assessment team.

A program planning team includes, at the least, a teacher, the
parents, and the student. Ideally, the case coordinator convenes all

persons responsible for the student's program to discuss program planning. If all the people involved cannot meet together regularly, the case coordinator can discuss appropriate parts of the plan with each one, eliciting input. The involvement of all concerned in the planning process improves the likelihood that an appropriate plan will be devised and that it will be carried out effectively.

The case coordinator ensures that all participants are aware of the purposes of the planning process:

To gather information on the student's current level of educational performance, interests, strengths, and weaknesses

To determine educational goals and objectives

To select specific courses and teachers

To suggest instructional strategies and accommodations

To outline teacher management and student self-management strategies

To identify preventive measures, support services, and other school resources

To monitor, evaluate, and modify the educational program

Determining the student's current level of educational performance, strengths, and weaknesses

A comprehensive assessment of the student's current status should form the basis for program planning. Chapter 5 offered a detailed discussion of issues in assessment. As discussed there, information from several sources is required by law to determine the student's eligibility for special education services and for regular education accommodations. Such sources can include formal psychometric tests, achievement tests, self-assessment, data from school records, interviews, observations, and work samples. In general, information on the student's current level of educational performance comes from achievement tests and course grades, plus parent, teacher, and student reports. Figure 6.1 shows Sam's formal test scores and their interpretation, which, along with other information, form the basis for his program plan. In Sam's case, the WISC-III (Wechsler, 1991), the Kaufman Test of Educational Achievement (Kaufman & Kaufman,

Figure 6.1   Summary of Sam's Test Results

PSYCHOMETRIC TESTS

WISC–III
Verbal Scale	85

Note. Performance Scale was influenced by distractibility and perseveration and was not considered a valid test of Sam's ability.

Kaufman Test of Educational Achievement
Math applications	3.5 grade
Math computations	4.7 grade
Reading decoding	6.2 grade
Reading comprehension	4.8 grade

Unnamed Diagnostic Achievement Battery
Alphabet/word knowledge	6.4 grade
Reading comprehension (memory)	2.0 grade
Spelling	4.7 grade
Writing/composition	2.8 grade

Peabody Picture Vocabulary Test–Revised
7.3 years

OTHER TEST SCORES

Reading
Word recognition and word attack	6.0 grade
Oral reading (a combination of speed, accuracy, and comprehension)	1.9 grade
Silent reading comprehension	1.0 grade

Spelling
Spelling skills	4.0 grade

Informal Writing Sample
Poor

Auditory Skills
Auditory memory	5.0 grade
Sequencing	5.0 grade
Discrimination	17th percentile
Attention span	Range 4th through 7th year

INTERPRETATION OF TEST SCORES
Reading decoding	High average
Reading comprehension	Severe discrepancy
Receptive language	Severe discrepancy
Expressive language	Severe discrepancy
Written expression	Severe discrepancy
Math	Low average

1985), an unnamed achievement battery, and the Peabody Picture Vocabulary Test–Revised (Dunn & Dunn, 1981) were the formal measures used.

Translating psychological assessment data into educational programs and instructional strategies for a particular student may be difficult and time consuming. The case coordinator may need to ask the psychologist who conducted the tests to clarify the meaning of particular test or subtest scores in order to determine and prioritize goals and objectives.

As the test summary in Figure 6.1 shows, reading decoding skills are among Sam's strengths. His weaknesses are in expressive and receptive language, reading comprehension, and written expression. What the test scores do not show are his motivation to learn and his persistence in the face of challenges. Sam is highly motivated and goal directed. He has proved that by his approach to learning to catch a baseball and by his willingness to repeat fifth grade in order to be prepared for the sixth. Sam also has serious deficits. But he has already demonstrated how he can use his motivation (to play baseball) to overcome his weaknesses (visuomotor and spatial). The educational plan developed for Sam will need to be based on his interests, his strengths, and his strong motivation and persistence. The role of motivation is an important one in program planning and is discussed later in this chapter in more detail.

In addition, although Sam scores poorly on tests of reading comprehension, he loves to read and often spends his spare time reading books appropriate for his age level. Sam also loves to write. He produces brief stories on his computer almost daily, and he has written occasional sports articles for the school paper. This illustrates the point that test scores, even those derived from a valid assessment, tell only part of the story. Because Sam had so many deficits it was important to have a list specifying his strengths, as shown in Figure 6.2.

Determining program goals and objectives

Special education law requires that educational goals and objectives be determined annually for students eligible for special education services. Long term goals and related objectives are also advised for students with learning problems who are ineligible for special education services. Program goals and objectives are used by individual teachers to guide the instructional program.

Figure 6.2   Sam's Strengths

Motivation
Sam wants to learn. His motivation is strong. He has obviously had good home and school support. The educational materials and methods for Sam should be chosen for their motivational value to him. Individualized reading, writing, and math assignments should be chosen or designed for Sam based on competencies relevant to the sixth-grade curriculum as well as content that motivates Sam to succeed. (See Sam's interests, below.)

Persistence
Sam is a persistent learner, especially when there is something he wants to learn—like catching a baseball. He has also demonstrated persistence with the learning tasks in school. Sam will work hard if he can see his progress toward a goal, especially a goal he has chosen himself.

Goal Orientation
Because Sam is very goal oriented, he should be involved in setting his own short-term goals in specific areas. Progress and improvement toward specific goals should be charted or graphed for Sam on a weekly basis so that he can see how he is doing.

Visual Processing
The relative strength of Sam's visual processing means that all learning tasks should be presented to him in the visual mode as well as the auditory and/or kinesthetic (i.e., all directions should be written as well as oral).

Interest in Baseball
Tying some of Sam's learning tasks to his interest in baseball is very helpful to Sam—for example, using baseball-related topics such as biographies of baseball players for writing assignments; using hits, runs, and errors to monitor his learning; and using the home cities of teams to familiarize him with maps and map reading.

Interest in Writing
Sam's strong interest in writing means that with direct instruction he will be able to use writing as a means of expression, of remembering things of importance to him (i.e., writing notes to himself), and of boosting his reading comprehension and oral expression skills.

Interest in Computers
Because of Sam's interest in computers, the computer can be a powerful learning tool for him. The strong visual input from the computer helps Sam focus on a learning task. The keyboard and earphones (if available for a particular piece of software) bring in kinesthetic and auditory input, thus maximizing learning.

Goals can include mastery of subject matter skills (e.g., math, science), cognitive skills (e.g., study skills), social/behavioral skills (e.g., going to class, staying on task), and language skills (e.g., written expression, oral expression).

Objectives should be tied to measurable outcomes and should include performance criteria, evaluation procedures, and schedules for evaluation. Specificity increases as one progresses from program goals and objectives to instructional objectives. When designing instructional objectives it is important to include higher level skills such as critical thinking and problem solving.

Annual goals for Sam are written in the areas of reading comprehension, written expression, math, and staying on task. Clearly, Sam will welcome instruction to increase his reading and writing skills; these areas will receive top priority. The crucial auditory and expressive language skills will have high priority as well. Sample annual goals and preliminary objectives for Sam are listed in Figure 6.3.

Before goals and objectives are finalized, the planning team asks the following questions: Are these goals both challenging and attainable? Are these goals important? and Are these goals relevant?

Evaluation procedures for assessing the attainment of objectives can include tests, charts, observations, self-report, work samples, and parent reports.

Selecting courses and teachers

It is particularly important for the student with specific learning problems to be actively involved in planning the course of study and selecting individual courses. Courses should be chosen carefully on the basis of the following criteria.

Chance for success.   The student will be more successful in areas of strength and past success than in areas of weakness and past failure. The chosen course of study should be one in which the student and the parents have reason to believe the student will be successful.

Graduation requirements   The course of study must meet graduation requirements. Information on those requirements comes from course catalogs and policy handbooks. Advice on how to meet these requirements can also come from teachers, counselors, and school administrators.

Figure 6.3   Annual Goals and Preliminary Objectives for Sam

Reading Comprehension

Annual goal: Sam will improve his reading comprehension.

Objective 1   Sam will demonstrate his comprehension of reading material by writing responses, drawing pictures and maps, following a series of written directions, or doing a project in which the information is applied.

Objective 2   Sam will demonstrate his ability to use three comprehension strategies for understanding narrative and expository text (e.g., predicting, mapping, retelling using teacher prompts).

Auditory and Expressive Language

Annual goal: Sam will increase his ability to express himself in writing.

Objective 1   Given a series of questions by the teacher, Sam will write a story on the computer by answering them.

Objective 2   Each week Sam will be required to write a story one to two paragraphs long.

Objective 3   Given a topic, Sam will write his own questions and then answer them in a paragraph form.

Objective 4   Sam will reread and begin to identify areas to revise in his written work.

Math

Annual goal: Sam will complete fifth-grade math and begin sixth-grade math using a multisensory curriculum.

Objective 1   Sam will draw a picture of a story problem in order to solve the problem.

Objective 2   Sam will use the computer to learn and practice new math skills.

Staying on Task

Annual goal: Sam will increase his ability to stay on task.

Objective 1   Sam will return to task when cued or reminded by the teacher.

Objective 2   Sam will be allowed to go to the resource room to work when he thinks the classroom has become too noisy for him to concentrate.

Objective 3   Sam will learn to monitor his on-task and off-task behavior.

Creative ways of meeting graduation requirements should be considered for students with learning problems. For example, an independent study course with a supportive teacher or home schooling can fulfill a language arts requirement. Some vocational courses may be used to fulfill science, English, or mathematics requirements. Some high school students are able to take college courses to fulfill their requirements. Students eligible for special education services may also be able to fulfill an English requirement in a special education resource room. Advocates, other students, and parents frequently have information about alternatives for required courses.

Time and effort required.   The number of credits taken each semester should be determined on the basis of the amount of time and effort the student must spend on each course in order to succeed. Students with severe learning problems will have to invest more time and make a greater effort to complete the required work. For a student with learning disabilities or ADD, this might mean attending summer school or receiving outside tutoring. By taking a mix of courses, the student can borrow study time from the easier courses to devote to the more difficult ones.

Course sequence.   Particularly difficult required courses should be postponed until the student is more mature and better prepared to take them. Some students with certain patterns of strengths and weaknesses do better if they can take particular courses out of the usual sequence—for instance, geometry before algebra or physics before biology. Sometimes requirements can be waived. For example, a student with a severe language-based disability might be excused from taking a foreign language.

Relevance to the student.   Students with learning problems should select courses that they can relate to subjects they already know something about. For example, a student with learning disabilities might find it easier to learn information in a course on recent American history, which can be related to current affairs, than in a course on ancient civilizations. (Of course, a creative teacher might make the latter course very relevant.)

Teacher and program characteristics.   The teacher-student match is especially important to students with learning disabilities and/or ADD. A good match can make all the difference in the world to the student's chances for success. If a teacher and student are badly mismatched, the student should be allowed to select another teacher or another course to fulfill a requirement. For example, it would be a poor match to place Sam in a math class where the teacher uses only the grade level textbook or a history class where the teacher largely lectures.

The following teacher characteristics will make a good match likely for a student with learning problems:

Flexibility (e.g., in grading system, homework policy)

Positive expectations for the student's performance

Willingness to individualize methods and materials

Awareness of impact of learning disabilities and/or ADD on student performance

Positive attitude toward parent involvement

Because there are so many factors that must be taken into account in Sam's program, it is important to identify and list the strengths of his current program (see Figure 6.4).

Assessment methods used.   Alternative assessment methods, particularly student portfolios, can greatly benefit students with learning disabilities. Portfolios allow students to document achievement by using work samples and other evidence of performance such as photographs of projects, awards for community service, letters from employers, and the like. When using portfolios, students can easily observe and evaluate their own progress toward goals they have set for themselves. They are not competing with other students or working against the clock. For students who have difficulty taking tests, the program planning team should seek out courses in which student portfolios provide an alternative to formal testing. However, given the nature of ADD, teachers need to ensure that portfolios don't get lost.

Suggesting instructional strategies and accommodations

The program plan should include suggested instructional strategies to guide the teacher in his or her efforts to overcome or bypass student weaknesses and improve performance. A variety of resources

Figure 6.4   Strengths of Sam's Teachers and Program

Classroom Makeup
The 50–50 mix of regular education students and students with learning disabilities and other mild impairments helps Sam feel like a "regular" student and helps his self-esteem.

Emphasis on Cognitive Strategies
Research strategies, writing strategies, test-taking strategies, and so forth taught to students and posted around the room help Sam remember. Teaching such strategies and posting them provides Sam with the auditory and visual cues he needs.

Teacher Modeling
Having teachers model oral problem-solving strategies helps Sam develop his own problem-solving strategies.

Team Teaching
Team teaching with a regular education teacher and a special education teacher allows for modifications of the educational program and materials for Sam. Materials can be modified by the special education teacher during planning time or while the regular education teacher is leading large- or small-group instruction.

Availability of Individual Assistance
The availability of one or both teachers for individual assistance at all times can help Sam think through problems, stay on task, and organize his time.

Encouragement and Support
The positive climate of the classroom and the encouragement of his teachers motivate Sam to continue to learn.

The Computer Lab
Working in the computer lab is highly motivating for Sam. He is much less distracted in this setting. He focuses well and stays on task.

Accommodations
The availability of the laptop computer for writing assignments is also motivating for Sam. He wants to write. He no longer will have to concentrate on the handwriting process when he is trying to express himself in writing.

Additional Services
The support of the speech and language teacher consultant helps Sam with language expression and comprehension. Game formats such as treasure hunts and riddles are employed.

are available (e.g., McCarney, 1989; Rief, 1993). Figure 6.5 provides a detailed description of instructional strategies for Sam in many areas of performance and includes optional activities in each area to be based on teacher-student interest.

Identifying preventive measures and teacher activities

Whenever a student must take a course that will put pressure on an area of vulnerability or disability, an advance plan can prevent or minimize problems. Such plans should include the following:

Development of a reinforcement system

All reasonable accommodations in the regular classroom

Direct teaching of learning and self-management skills within content area courses

Arrangements for extra help from the teacher before, during, or after class

Arrangements for in-school peer tutoring or study groups

Timely feedback from the teacher on homework and tests

Timely and positive response by the teacher to problems as they arise

Help from the special education teacher consultant for students eligible for special education services

Careful program monitoring by student, parents, teachers, and the case coordinator

Arrangements for outside tutoring, if necessary

Establishment of a case management team that includes all the teachers working with the student, to prevent or solve problems

Arrangements for prelearning (e.g., reading the book and/or syllabus in advance of taking the course)

Use of assistive technology, such as computer-assisted instruction, spell-checkers, and calculators

Figure 6.5　Instructional Strategies and Accommodations for Sam

The following instructional strategies are proposed for Sam. Only some of them should be used. They can be modified and personalized by both teacher and parent. Additional materials can be located at the county school district learning resource center.

Reading Comprehension

Note: 20–30 minutes per day; one-on-one instruction by speech and language teacher consultant and/or special education teacher; out of classroom

Adapt the curriculum materials for word attack and comprehension for Sam.

Introduce the cloze method: Begin with a simple third-grade reading level story (perhaps about baseball). Work up to harder material. Play a treasure hunt game with Sam, using written clues for him to follow.

Help Sam build a simple model airplane or other project. Give him some choices. Help Sam follow the written directions. Work up to a science experiment. Have him follow the written directions.

Locate or write several riddles or short descriptive passages and help Sam figure out what they mean. Include humor.

Read to Sam aloud (fourth-grade current events newspaper material) as he follows slowly and carefully in the text. Discuss the passage with him.

Use a combined visual/auditory approach to introduce new reading material and increase comprehension. Audiotape his social studies textbook and have him read and listen simultaneously.

Introduce the SQ4R method for grade-level reading material.

Receptive and Expressive Language

Note. Both teachers in classroom; parents at home

Try not to ask Sam questions; tell him matter-of-factly what to do and how to do it.

Immerse him in language at home. Discuss current events, baseball, problem solving. Tell jokes. Read and discuss newspapers.

Model self-talk and self-instruction.

At home, when Sam is watching a baseball video, play "Who, What, When, Where, Why." Have Sam make a dial with a cardboard spinner. Have him write the *Wh* words on the dial.

Every few minutes, stop the video and spin the dial. Have Sam answer the question on the dial as it relates to the video. This will help increase active listening and comprehension.

Writing/Composition

Note. In large group; regular or special education teacher

Discuss with Sam some questions he might want to address before he does a writing assignment. Write out the questions for Sam to use as reference. This will help him organize his writing. Relate reading to writing, using SQ4R.

Give Sam his own writing process checklist to use as reference. Allow Sam to do all his written work on the laptop computer. The motivational power of the computer can be used to enhance Sam's writing skills.

Teach Sam how to use the computer to edit his work and check his spelling.

Make arrangements for Sam to take the laptop home to do his writing homework and any writing for the school newspaper.

Test Taking

Note. Special education teacher; one-on-one; in quiet place out of classroom

Allow tests to be untimed.

Cue Sam to stay on task.

Check for understanding of test directions.

Restate questions and probe for answers if necessary.

Give Sam his own test-taking strategies checklist for reference.

Allow Sam to demonstrate his understanding of the information in another way (e.g., hands-on, orally, in writing).

Math

Note. In small group; individualized, special education teacher

Modify math for Sam so that he does not become too frustrated. He is currently in the fifth-grade text but not keeping up.

Check the math software being used in the computer lab. Look for additional math software at the county school district resource center that might be appropriate. Utilize a situation-based and/or multisensory math program requiring Sam to draw a picture of the problem to be solved.

Figure 6.5 *(continued)*

Cognitive Strategies

Note. Checklists of strategies written (and laminated) for Sam by the special education teacher; strategies modeled by teachers in classroom and parents at home

Compile short lists of task-specific strategies for reading, writing, test taking, notebook keeping, and research for Sam to keep in his desk for reference.

Continue teaching these strategies to the whole class and posting them on the classroom wall.

Encourage Sam to read the strategies out loud to himself as he is working and check them off as he completes them.

Encourage Sam to use self-talk and self-instruction through the modeling of the adults around him.

Encourage Sam to write notes to himself as a way of organizing himself and remembering things he must do.

Staying on Task

Note. Both teachers, all adults

Monitor and redirect Sam constantly for off-task behavior. He is very distractible, especially in the classroom. Choose a seatmate for Sam who will model on-task behavior. Cue and reinforce Sam to remain on task, particularly in large-group situations.

As much as possible, place Sam in situations with a minimum of visual and auditory distractions. Some critical tasks like reading comprehension and test taking should not take place in the classroom because it is so distracting.

Select learning materials with heightened motivational appeal to offset the distractions of the classroom. Simultaneous visual and auditory (or multisensory) input may also increase on-task behavior.

Sam demonstrates the most focused, on-task behavior in the computer lab working with the math program. Use the motivating quality of the computer to help Sam stay on task. Carefully select additional software for Sam to use in any of the afore-mentioned skill areas.

Have parents develop checklists for home responsibilities and routines.

Have parents continue monitoring Sam's medication.

Handwriting

Note. Both teachers

> Give handwriting low priority at this time. Have Sam write as much as possible on laptop computer.

Charting Progress

> Start by using a progress chart just for reading comprehension. Involve Sam in setting goals for the week. Teach Sam on Monday through Thursday; assess progress on Friday. Involve Sam in assessment.

> To maximize motivation, continue the baseball theme on the progress chart by using balls, strikes, hits, home runs, innings, and so on. Ask Sam to help set it up.

For Sam, the computer is a perfect technological learning tool. The software chosen for Sam provides a multisensory approach to the learning of new material, allowing him to use his relatively strong visual skills to compensate for his auditory processing deficits. Sam finds the computer so motivating that he is able to screen out distractions and concentrate on learning.

Monitoring, evaluating, and modifying the educational program

Once a program plan is implemented, periodic checks on its effectiveness should occur. The case coordinator is responsible for ensuring that monitoring and evaluation are done systematically; however, each member of the planning team should help monitor and evaluate the program. Individual members can observe and chart the student's progress toward the educational goals and objectives.

Team members must communicate weekly, however informally, so that if problems arise they can be solved in a timely fashion. The team should meet as a group about 4 weeks after the initiation of the program to discuss any modifications that might be needed.

Most students enjoy monitoring their own progress. For example, Nathan, first introduced in chapter 3, monitored his progress on a brief checklist he and his teacher designed (see Figure 6.6). The checklist increased Nathan's awareness about his own behavior and achievement and helped him to feel good about himself. Eventually, he independently added items significant to him, such as "I completed my homework" and "I invited a friend home." He and the teacher designed a graph to track progress over time.

MOTIVATION AND REINFORCEMENT

As evident in Sam's case, test scores measure academic strengths and weaknesses, but they do not measure such things as interest, creativity, and motivation. The role of motivation and persistence in achievement cannot be overemphasized. Ability without the necessary drive and hard work will not turn someone into an opera singer, basketball player, or bank manager. However, strong motivation and persistence can propel a person with less natural ability into greater success than many people think possible. It is important to judge whether the student is sufficiently motivated to persist in the chosen course of study despite challenges and obstacles.

Motivation can be viewed as the degree to which a student independently approaches or avoids a task or a course. Motivation

---

Figure 6.6   Nathan's Daily Checklist for Self-Monitoring

Date _____

_____ I completed my math work in class.

_____ I spent _____ minutes reading.

_____ I expressed myself in writing.

_____ I met my spelling expectations.

My objective for the week is

_____

_____

_____

---

grows out of interest. A student who is interested in a school subject is more likely to want to do the required work and therefore more likely to pass tests. Motivation can also grow out of the expectation of success. A student who has already been successful or who expects to be successful in a course is more likely to work hard—to persist in the face of challenges—and thus actually to succeed (Deci, Vallerand, Pelletier, & Ryan, 1991; Schunk, 1991). Course selection should therefore be based on the student's interests and on previous success with a particular subject or teacher.

Some students who appear unmotivated in school often demonstrate motivation and persistence in nonacademic pursuits or out-of-school activities such as sports, art, music, or hobbies. A student who builds and maintains machinery at home, who plays musical instruments, or who plays on an all-city soccer team demonstrates the ability to work hard and succeed in an area of particular interest. Relating course work to nonacademic interests will help the student achieve success in school.

Teachers can increase student motivation by directly relating new information to what the student already knows. In addition, teachers should make sure students know why they are learning something and how they will be able to use the new skill or information in daily life.

The program plan needs to be appealing and reinforcing to the student to keep the student on track and contribute to the student's motivation. Courses that are of interest to the student are intrinsically reinforcing. They spark curiosity, creativity, and involvement. Courses that provide experiences of success are also intrinsically reinforcing. However, in a required course that a student finds particularly difficult, the teacher can implement a reinforcement system that uses extrinsic rewards to heighten motivation and encourage success. These concrete, tangible reinforcers can range from stickers and points for younger students to special activities and monetary rewards for older adolescents. Another valuable form of reinforcement is the intangible social reinforcement that comes from respected authority figures when they acknowledge and encourage student efforts, express respect for the student, or compare the student to an admired person who strives to overcome obstacles.

The following elements are necessary in an effective reinforcement system:

Student selection of short- and long-term
educational goals

Student commitment to work toward goals

Student selection of reinforcers

Charting of the student's progress

Involvement of both home and school in the system

Provision of appropriate instruction and support
to the student

Reward for incremental student progress
toward goals

BALANCING CONFLICTING PHILOSOPHIES, INSTRUCTIONAL NEEDS, AND SYSTEM DEMANDS

Sam's educational planning team must balance several conflicting instructional needs in developing his program. A large, noisy, stimulating regular education classroom can be devastating for a student like Sam. Because of his attention problems, he needs a quiet place in which to learn. On the other hand, Sam wants to be in a regular education class with his friends. It is important for his self-esteem and for his socialization that he feel like a "regular kid" and be a fully participating member of his class. This particular dilemma was solved by letting Sam choose where he wanted to do his work each day, depending on the particular circumstances. For example, if the noise level in class was bothering him, he could move to the resource room across the hall to do his work. Many students with attention problems are mature enough to make similar decisions.

Other educational planning teams face similar dilemmas stemming from conflicting philosophies, instructional needs, and system demands. Often they must choose between two less-than-optimal alternatives. Following are some current philosophies and system demands that may come into conflict.

Inclusion versus resource room.   Inclusion, the philosophy that all students, regardless of ability or disability, should be educated in regular education classes, often conflicts with the need of some students with learning disabilities or ADD for intensive one-on-one teaching by a professional trained in special education methodology. Too often, budgetary or political concerns preclude making these judgments on a case-by-case basis.

Many students don't like spending time in resource rooms or being pulled out of regular education classes for intensive one-on-one work. They feel that this stigmatizes them in the eyes of other students, and they often report being teased. The self-esteem and socialization needs of students with learning problems are often difficult to meet in separate special education classes or "pull-out" programs. Yet intensive one-on-one academic instruction may be what these students need at this point. Ideally, all students should be able to move in and out of resource rooms for intensive academic help if and when they need it.

Open versus traditional schools. Open schools, with their philosophy of ungraded education, can be an ideal setting for students with learning problems. However, these schools generally have large open areas instead of separate classrooms, a configuration that allows great flexibility in programming but unfortunately also creates much distraction for students with ADD. Often, even modest rearrangement of the student's physical environment can minimize distractions.

Cooperative learning versus instructor-led models. Cooperative learning can be an excellent way to involve students of varying abilities in working toward a common goal. However, for the student with auditory language problems or the student who prefers to work alone, cooperative learning situations can be confusing, distracting, or counterproductive. Cooperative learning tasks and groupings must be carefully planned by the teacher. Many students need to be taught how to work with others in a cooperative and productive way.

Magnet schools and schools of choice versus regular schools. Magnet schools and schools of choice, with their emphasis on an enriching education centered on a theme such as science or music, often make no plans to accommodate students with learning difficulties. These schools tend to attract more able students, often using placement test scores or grade-point averages as selection criteria. Students with learning problems may have difficulty passing tests and often have relatively low grade-point averages. Even though they may have As in their areas of strength, their weaknesses pull their averages down. Entrance criteria to these schools should be flexible so that these students are not automatically barred. Once they are admitted, accommodations must be made available for those who are eligible.

Gifted versus remedial programs.   Many students with learning disabilities and/or ADD are gifted in some areas. These students may have difficulty gaining admission to programs for the gifted due to poor grades. Their problems are twofold: First, their gifts are often unrecognized by the schools, who are concentrating on their deficits. Second, if their gifts are addressed by an enrichment program, they often cannot find help for their weaknesses. Appropriate educational placement for such students is very problematic and often means a choice between two evils—a program for gifted students without support for learning disabilities or a totally unchallenging remedial program that can exacerbate behavioral problems. Here, too, entrance requirements to gifted programs must be examined. Educational placement must include both remedial help and academic challenge.

SUMMARY AND CONCLUSIONS

A well-planned educational program can help a student with learning problems become a successful learner. Good planning must begin early and involve a team approach. There are active roles for the teacher, student, and parents. The program should be individualized for student strengths and weaknesses, motivation, and interests. Finally, the plan, when implemented, should be carefully monitored and modified as needed.

Individualized educational programs for all students with learning problems can be based on the IEP model in special education. Educational goals and objectives, effective teaching strategies, and accommodations should be specified. A systematic approach to program planning can yield great benefits for students with learning problems.

7

Self-Management

Every teacher's worst nightmare is a chaotic classroom in which the students are out of control. In this nightmare the students are in an uproar, either ignoring the teacher or refusing outright to do what he or she asks. There are constant interruptions, and nothing ever gets finished. Students throw things at one another, even though the teacher threatens dire punishment. No one is learning. Fear that this nightmare may become reality can cause teachers to place too much real-life emphasis on controlling the class and suspending individual students in order to prevent the escalation of negative behavior. In such a scenario the teacher is in charge—but at great cost to both the teacher and the students.

There is an old saying that epitomizes the ideal of self-management: "Give me a fish and I eat for a day. Teach me to fish and I eat for a lifetime." Extrapolated, this means that there are two ways to manage student behavior: First, the teacher or parent can attempt complete control, providing rules, regulations, structure, and discipline to manage student behavior. As long as the adult is there, presumably the student's behavior is under control. Second, the parent or teacher can teach the student self-management strategies to control his or her own behavior. In this way, whether or not the adult is present, the student's behavior is self-managed (Markel, 1981b).

The key to effective classroom management is student self-management. The purpose of this chapter, then, is to describe the critical importance of self-management in enhancing the learning and performance of all students, to stress the importance of teaching self-management strategies to students with learning and attention difficulties, and to emphasize the integration of self-management strategies into the regular education classroom. Self-management applies to all of the academic content areas; specific strategies to integrate self-management skills into various academic skill areas are discussed in subsequent chapters.

OVERVIEW

Students with learning difficulties often do not allocate their time or attention well, and they seem to cope poorly with frustration and disappointment. These students have poor self-management skills, which in turn can have a negative impact on academic performance and interpersonal relationships.

Regardless of their specific problems, students with attention or learning difficulties want to succeed in their courses and have positive interactions with peers and teachers. Even when they try to pay attention, control their behavior, or complete their assignments, they do not know how to achieve the results they want. Often they feel overwhelmed: They don't know where to start or what to do, and they don't understand what has gone wrong. They may have average or above-average intelligence, but they are unable to live up to their academic potential or their own good intentions. Some just give up. They "turn off and tune out," are classified as underachievers, and may eventually drop out. Others become disruptive and defiant and are inaccurately classified as troublemakers or seriously emotionally disturbed. These students are frequently suspended, and many also drop out. Many stay in school but are miserable and/or depressed.

One way students with learning and attention problems can achieve academic success is by mastering self-management skills. Self-management can provide students with the tools to act or behave in more attentive, focused, and productive ways (Meichenbaum, 1977; Schunk, 1990; Wood & Bandura, 1989; Zimmerman, 1989.) Often the inclusion of self-management training in students' IEP or Section 504 plans is the key to fostering performance breakthroughs for these students.

Research studies indicate that successful learners are aware of task demands and the appropriate strategies to use at a given time. They can monitor and regulate their own behaviors in classroom activities such as reading and are effective problem solvers (Borkowski, Day, Saenz, Dietmeyer, Estrada, & Groteluschen, 1992; Paris, Lipson, & Wixson, 1983; Paris & Newman, 1990; Schunk & Rice, 1987; Smith, Young, West, Morgan, & Rhode, 1988). These skills need to be taught to all students. Generally, the earlier students master self-management, the greater are the chances that a positive impact on academic performance will be realized.

Self-management is both a state of mind and a cluster of skills. Students take on responsibility for their own learning and academic success (Pintrich & Schrauben, 1992). Teachers help students learn how to assume and execute their academic responsibilities by teaching self-management skills. Self-management training incorporates a variety of strategies that simultaneously use and extend strengths, develop new skills, and manage difficulties. Students choose from an array of self-management strategies based on their personal styles and values. Specifically, components of self-management training include the following.

Self-control strategies.   These strategies enable students to limit interfering behaviors such as talkativeness, excessive motor activity, or responses to inappropriate stimuli so that they can better focus their attention and persevere at a task. These strategies are of particular importance to students with ADD.

Self-management of academic behaviors.   These skills increase students' efficiency and productivity in the classroom and at home. Students learn skills such as goal setting, time management, self-monitoring, and self-recognition of progress.

Self-regulation of cognitive processes.   Students learn how to think critically, self-correct, select appropriate cognitive strategies, and regulate reading or writing behaviors.

Coping skills.   Students give themselves positive messages, maximize their strengths, bypass their weaknesses, and maintain motivation. These skills are also of particular importance to students with ADD and learning disabilities.

Problem-solving strategies.   Through the medium of self-talk, these strategies help students to identify problems, self-interrogate, solve problems, maintain vigilance, confront challenges or overcome barriers, and adjust or modify strategies as necessary in order to improve continually.

Because students with learning difficulties do not develop or apply self-management or problem-solving strategies spontaneously, it is necessary to teach these strategies. In comparison to their same-age peers, students with attention and learning problems require the following:

Clearer explanations of the relationship between the student's actions, self-management techniques, and positive consequences

More personalized and concrete examples

More frequent reinforcement of progress and effort

More repetition of skills in different classes

Greater consistency throughout the school day

Greater coordination between school, home, and community or vocational settings

In addition, they need to practice self-management skills in different settings (Ellis, 1993; Schumaker & Deshler, 1992).

Training in self-management skills is most effective when it is integrated with and practiced in the content area classroom as all students develop reading, writing, and other academic skills. Training can be done by a content area teacher alone or team taught by a regular classroom teacher and a special education teacher in the regular classroom. Teaching self-management skills in the content area classroom ensures maintenance and generalization of these skills across learning situations and over time.

Self-management strategies become part of the instructional process and are used to help students set expectations and select goals, activate and maintain attention, maintain motivation during difficult tasks, manage time, select cognitive strategies, solve problems, and monitor progress. In teaching self-management strategies, the teacher tells the students what strategies are being taught, how using self-management strategies can help them learn, and when and where they can use the strategies. The teacher models each strategy using course material, provides guided practice, and provides feedback as students practice new skills.

These strategies help students manage their own resources and achieve greater academic success. The teacher helps students develop their own behavior checklists and reinforces successive approximations of self-managed behavior. Students learn to focus and sustain attention, arrange optimal conditions for their learning, manage their time, sequence their tasks, engage in cognitive coping, and recognize and reward themselves for their efforts.

Effects of the Learning Environment on Attention and Learning Problems

The learning environment can exacerbate or minimize the effects of students' academic problems, especially for those students with attention or learning difficulties. Such things as seating arrangements, the choice of instructional materials, and the classroom noise level, as well as classroom management procedures and the methods teachers use to present information, can either decrease or increase reading comprehension, recall of new material, attention, and other learning.

Teachers need to be aware of the role the learning environment plays in fostering self-management. Encouraging students to make choices, problem solve, and experiment enhances the development of self-management skills. Lack of clarity or predictability, poor instructional materials, or inadequate feedback all contribute to self-management difficulties. More specifically, unstructured time and transitions between activities are more difficult to manage than structured time. Clear classroom rules and routines help decrease distractibility and impulsivity.

Attention as a Self-Management Issue

Attention problems may seriously interfere with cognitive processing of information. Indeed, without attention there can be no real learning.

Many students with attention problems take psychostimulant medication to increase their attention span. Attention problems may warrant medication, but long-term results require teaching students how to manage their learning and behavior. With or without medication, students must learn how to focus and stay on task, control impulsivity, and avoid unnecessary distractions.

In chapter 3 we met Myles, an eighth grader with ADD and learning disabilities. Myles has varying degrees of distractibility, impulsivity, and hyperactivity, even with medication. We saw what can happen to a student and a school when the system stalls and has no appropriate educational plan for the student in place. Myles was unable to learn and consequently disrupted other students' learning. Myles' serious behavior and learning problems were the result of several years of educational neglect. What began as a mild disorder when he entered middle school became a huge problem through poor management and poor programming.

The resolution of this situation required the teaching of self-management strategies to Myles as part of his educational program. Myles' program plan exemplifies how self-management can be integrated into the daily schedule: After negotiations between the school district and Myles' mother were finished, a new Section 504 plan was designed for Myles by the teachers, school administrator, Myles' mother, and the outside consultant, with Myles' input. The new program was designed to minimize Myles' attention-related behavior problems. Myles' medication was reevaluated, and he was given a timed-release capsule to take at home in the morning before coming to school.

Myles was removed from several classes that were not a good match for his needs and placed in classes with high interest (law) and high structure (math), both of which contributed to his increased attention span. The teachers became aware of the effect a lack of structure had on Myles and made sure that Myles understood what was expected of him at all times. They provided him with checklists to help him structure his time and requested that he repeat directions. His teachers also helped him with organizational skills such as breaking large projects into discrete tasks; doing so helped him begin work immediately and avoid disturbing other students.

The following behaviors related to ADD were targeted by the 504 committee, with Myles as a full member, and placed on a checklist to be used by all his teachers. A consequence and reinforcement system was developed to support them.

Distractibility: Being on time to class (not dawdling or horsing around)

Impulsivity: Using appropriate and respectful language with staff (no cursing); following staff directions (without discussion)

Attention: Getting on task

Hyperactivity: Keeping hands and feet to himself (no patting or poking other students)

The following interventions were designed to help Myles manage his behavior:

Gathering of baseline data by the school counselor or social worker regarding the targeted behaviors

Instructing Myles in ways to monitor his own behavior

Developing a reinforcement system with Myles and his parents to provide short- and long-term reinforcement of appropriate behavior

Reinforcing the school behavior management program at home

Ignoring nondisruptive hyperactive behavior (e.g., jiggling)

Instructing Myles in ways to talk to himself to prevent impulsive behavior

Using checklists or teacher support to help Myles get on task and return to task

Charting target behaviors at frequent intervals to measure progress

Teaching Myles to record and recognize positive behaviors

Attending a meeting with Myles, his teachers, and his parents to evaluate progress at the end of 2 weeks

Myles' new program works well because it includes a specific plan for self-management and is responsive to his needs. His new program is very innovative: He takes three courses in middle school and two courses in high school. His program takes into account his weaknesses and his strengths. He loves his high school classes and works very hard at them.

There is now a written 504 plan for Myles with goals and objectives, targeted behaviors, teacher interventions, periodic reviews, and a self-management plan. Each of his teachers understands how to help Myles manage his behavior.

ROLE OF THE CLASSROOM TEACHER

Curriculum guides usually do not include self-management goals or strategies. Teaching self-management is indeed an added responsibility, but one in which the teacher has a vested interest. With self-management, students can learn more effectively and have greater control over their performance.

Students arrive in middle school with a wide range of self-management and academic skills. This is one of the reasons that middle school poses such a range of problems for teachers and students alike. In order to progress academically through middle school and beyond, students must be taught self-management skills as well as academic content.

At the middle school level, the goals of self-management training are to learn techniques such as self-selection of learning or behavioral objectives and self-monitoring of progress. Teachers provide a large percentage of the guidance and support students need (see Figure 7.1).

As students move from middle to high school, self-management enables them to shift into independent learning. The goals of self-management training for more mature students include the ability to tolerate ambiguity and lack of structure, the development of greater coping and problem-solving skills, and the recognition that progress or success depends on hard work rather than luck. With a focus on self-management, students can move from immature and impulsive

---

Figure 7.1   Classroom Decision-Making Model

Teacher Management	The teacher makes the decisions 75–100% of the time, allowing little input from the student.
	The teacher makes the decisions 50–75% of the time, allowing input from the student about 25% of the time.
	The student and teacher interact and engage in shared decision making, with neither involved more than 60% of the time.
	The student participates in decision making 50–75% of the time.
Student Self-Management	The student selects, directs, and evaluates activities 75–90% of the time.

---

thinking patterns to reflective and proactive patterns of learning and performing. In high school, students are required to self-select goals and tasks and monitor their actions in situations that provide less support and supervision. Strategies similar to those taught in middle school may be taught in high school, but at a higher developmental level.

In both middle school and high school settings, teachers provide direct instruction, modeling, and guided practice for each skill (e.g., time management) and within each subject area (e.g., science, history) during each academic year. Students with attention and learning problems will need additional modeling and practice time, as well as structure and support. The overall goal is to prepare students to work more independently as they mature.

In general, the teacher helps students target behaviors or skills that need improvement, generate goals, list activities, discuss problem solving, and track progress or performance. The teacher also prepares choices from which students can select behaviors, goals, and activities to target.

The teacher teaches and models self-managed learning while covering content. For example, in history the teacher can demonstrate how to use a systematic reading strategy to get the main ideas from a chapter of the text. It is helpful if the teacher coordinates the teaching of self-management strategies with other teachers at the same grade level. (Such curriculum coordination is already practiced in many middle schools.) The teacher can also help students apply self-management to homework assignments outside the classroom by providing information on self-management strategies to parents.

Throughout the process, the teacher encourages students to assume increased responsibility for decision making, as shown in Figure 7.1. The teacher discusses and demonstrates how skills are used in a variety of settings (e.g., during extracurricular activities or at home), then assigns practice both in and out of school. As students progress, they begin to see the subtleties that affect their behavior and achieve new insights about the interaction between themselves, the task, and the situation. Students gain greater accuracy in predicting the consequences of their actions and in noticing early warning signs of difficulties. For example, a student might say, "I did it again . . . I forgot about the test until the last minute. Doing that isn't helping me. I need to write all of the assignments in my notebook as the teacher writes them on the board."

INTEGRATING SELF-MANAGEMENT INTO THE CONTENT AREA

The teacher helps students improve academic skills, deal with attention problems, and develop organization and time-management skills through direct instruction, modeling, guided practice, coaching, and reinforcement. One or two skills are taught at a time. The skills are then integrated into academic activities throughout the semester (Alberto & Troutman, 1986). All skills are practiced in the classroom while students learn content material.

In a self-managed classroom, the teacher maximizes student learning and helps students overcome learning and behavior problems by taking the following steps.

Increasing Student Self-Awareness and Involvement

Awareness of the impact of their difficulties on their daily performance can motivate students to work on behaviors over which they have control and try to optimize their environment (Vernon, 1989; Zieffle & Romney, 1985).

To help increase student self-awareness, the teacher initiates class discussions regarding the need for self-management of academic behaviors and the kinds of problems students have completing learning tasks. The teacher listens to comments about how students see themselves (e.g., forgetful, always losing things, unable to concentrate, disappointed with their grades). The teacher also listens for clues about others' opinions. For example, students may make comments such as "My teacher thinks I'm nuts because I can't sit still and I don't follow directions," "My friends think I'm a jerk because I forget things," and "My dad yells at me because I don't listen."

The teacher explains that many people have these kinds of problems and that these problems are nothing to be ashamed of. He or she also points out that such problems must be addressed in order to improve performance and that doing so is no different from wearing glasses to correct poor eyesight. Finally, the teacher stresses that students can take more control over their school performance and grades than they imagine.

In order to get a commitment from students to learn self-management skills, it is important for students to understand how these skills can help them become more effective learners and, not incidentally, get better grades. Students are involved in selecting goals, determining criteria, self-monitoring, and setting up a reinforcement system. Without student agreement and involvement, there will be no self-management.

Helping Students Set and Reach Goals

The teacher includes one or more student self-management goals within the context of the class. In language arts, self-management goals for students can include asking the teacher for clarification of the writing assignment and allowing time in the study schedule for thinking about and planning the paper. In history, self-management goals can include preparing questions for the lecture, maintaining attention during the lecture, and reviewing and editing lecture notes. In math, self-management goals can include designing a nondistracting study environment for homework and checking work for completeness and accuracy.

The teacher and the students discuss the interaction between a student problem and the task or situation. Myles, for example, did very well in law class because of his great interest in the topic. Similarly, once Myles began his computer assignment he found the work so interesting that he had no trouble staying on task. His big problem in computer class was getting on task and not disrupting other students. The computer teacher explained to Myles how a checklist could help him get started. With Myles' input, she developed the checklist shown in Figure 7.2. Other checklists can be developed by more mature students, with teacher input, regarding particular behaviors they want to decrease or increase.

Students next list the positive behaviors they already have, which if used more frequently could enhance their academic performance. For example, a student who writes her assignment down twice a week could further enhance her performance if she recorded it four or five times a week. Students discuss the best ways to substitute effective behaviors for problem behaviors. For example, Myles' mother suggested that he use a chain to attach his pocket calculator to his belt along with his keys. Both could be kept in his pocket, where they would be accessible.

The students list problems they would like to gain control over and discuss the problems to determine how each can hinder progress. The students relate these problems to problems they have had in

---

Figure 7.2   Myles' Checklist for Computer Class

Teacher_____ Date _____

	Yes	No
1. Enter classroom quietly.	☐	☐
2. Read directions on chalkboard.	☐	☐
3. Pick up assignment sheet.	☐	☐
4. Sit in assigned seat, without talking.	☐	☐
5. Either begin assignment or listen to teacher directions/instructions.	☐	☐
6. Load file.	☐	☐
7. Work on assignment.	☐	☐

---

the past, to poor grades, and to difficulties they might have in social interaction. The teacher and students identify the possible benefits of increasing positive academic behaviors and/or of eliminating problem behaviors. During this process they also consider competing student goals and needs, such as the goal of increasing achievement in school versus the need for attention and approval from school friends. Both student goals must be given weight and a compromise worked out using "Grandma's rule": First you work, then you play.

The students then prioritize the problem or problems they want to work on first. Two to five problems are selected by the class, from which each student will later select one to work on at a time.

In the process of self-management, students may have to modify their goals and actions if unforseen circumstances make their goals unattainable. The teacher helps students modify their goals to reflect the reality of the situation and overcome their disappointment at not achieving goals. Many problems can be avoided or minimized if the teacher starts small, goes slowly, and allows time for practice and feedback.

Considering Individual Needs

When teaching self-management strategies, teachers can individualize by varying the instructional task, the reinforcement system, and/or the conditions of learning. Reinforcement systems should always include a greater emphasis on positive academic and social behaviors and pay less attention to negative behaviors (Sprick, Sprick, & Garrison, 1991).

Tasks can be broken down into smaller units and/or made more interesting, reinforcement can be made more meaningful, and time on task can be shortened. By individualizing, teachers can increase student self-management skills and students' sense of control over the learning process.

Although provisions are made for individualization in the content area classroom, students with more severe attention-related problems can receive more intensive training in self-control and coping skills in a nondistracting small-group environment.

SELF-MANAGEMENT STRATEGIES AND SKILLS

A variety of self-management skills and strategies have been demonstrated to be effective for students with and without attention and learning difficulties. Among these are the following.

Self-Observation

In self-observation, students increase their awareness of a behavior and systematically watch for its occurrence (e.g., Horowitz, 1986). This technique helps increase students' awareness of the relationship between their thoughts and behavior and their academic performance within the classroom. In addition, they become more sensitive to the conditions under which they perform best and worst.

For example, Myles saw the positive effects that resulted from using a checklist in his computer class. He completed more work, and the teacher seemed friendlier. He even thought similar checklists could help him in other classes.

Self-Selection of Academic and/or Behavioral Goals and Objectives

Students identify their own goals or target academic behaviors from a list of possibilities developed by the teacher (Morgan, 1987; Schunk, 1990). Students are encouraged to begin at a level that ensures success and move toward the highest level that is reasonably attainable. Teacher and students discuss various options and the consequences of various choices. For example, Myles selected the goal of beginning homework in class as the focus of his self-designed homework contract.

Self-Determination of Evaluation Criteria

After a discussion with the teacher about possible criteria to be used to evaluate their progress, students choose the criteria by which they will judge the adequacy of their behavior (Smith et al., 1988). Initially, quantifiable criteria are used so that students can more easily measure progress toward target behaviors. For example, students graph the number of problems completed or the percent of accuracy. This technique helps students to think about the critical features of a task or behavior and ways in which mastery can be defined.

Self-Contracting

After discussion with the teacher, students write out a plan for altering or maintaining their own behavior. This plan includes the objective or goal, criteria for evaluating progress, timetable, and recognition and reward for effort. The plan may include when, where, how, and how much assistance the teacher might provide. Research indicates that contracts written with and by students with learning or attention problems can increase appropriate academic behaviors (Homme, Csanyi, Gonzales, & Rechs, 1970; White-Blackburn, Semb, & Semb, 1977). Requiring the student to sign a contract written solely by the teacher or administrator will not have the same effect.

Self-Instruction

The effectiveness of self-instruction techniques has been demonstrated for over 25 years (Bem, 1967; Bornstein & Quevillon, 1976; Camp & Bash, 1985; Meichenbaum & Goodman, 1971; Palincsar & Brown, 1984; Palkes, Stewart, & Kahana, 1968). In self-instruction, students talk to themselves, providing directions for their own actions. Self-instruction can include self-directed commands, intention statements, guidelines or steps that should be followed, and error correction. For example, Myles had to tell himself continually to follow the teacher's directions without arguing and to get to class without stopping to fool around with other students.

Visualization

Visualization is an underutilized self-management strategy that can enhance classroom performance. Students are encouraged to visualize themselves as competent performers of some task that has presented a problem in the past. Unlike role-playing or simulation, in visualization students can design a total and personalized sensory experience that replicates their unique visual, auditory, touch, emotional, and physiologic sensations as related to particular courses and tasks (Suinn, 1990). During visualization, students can actually experience the way they look, think, and feel as they overcome some obstacle and/or effectively perform. For example, to help keep Myles on track in language arts class, the special education teacher consultant encouraged him to visualize himself in math class, where he performed exceptionally well.

Self-Regulation

Self-regulation is the conscious control of the learning process. It involves selecting appropriate strategies to use to achieve a particular academic goal and monitoring progress toward goals. In self-regulation, students talk to themselves, ask themselves questions, tell themselves to do something, and become more aware of their behavior when engaged in a task (Parker, 1990; Schunk & Zimmerman, 1994).

Self-Monitoring

In self-monitoring, students note the occurrence of some defined behavior using a journal, checklist, tally, or graph (Knapczyk & Livingston, 1972). Checklists and graphs provide information about student performance and increase self-awareness. In addition, checklists and graphs can serve as an intervention because, as students see evidence of their own performance, they tend to evaluate it and regulate it themselves in order to maintain or modify their performance.

This technique yields the best results when students are taught how to focus on discrete but relevant behaviors, how and when to record, and how to attain positive outcomes as a result of monitoring their own progress. For students like Myles, there is a rocky road to success. An almost immediate positive effect will likely be followed by regression, followed by periodic ups and downs. The goal is to maintain progress over time by analyzing the conditions surrounding the "peaks and valleys."

Self-monitoring can help meet adolescents' needs to control their own behavior. They are in charge of collecting information; often there is less resistance to this technique than to having the teacher monitor and correct behavior.

Self-Evaluation

When self-evaluating, students observe their own progress and compare it against their self-determined performance criteria (Bandura & Cervone, 1983; Shapiro, 1989). As they evaluate themselves, students maintain a focus on their progress. Students use information to self-correct and guide future performance. They ask, What did I learn about myself that can help me accomplish my goals?

For example, when Myles reviewed his tests with his science teacher, he realized that, even though he knew the information, he lost points when he did not take the time to read the questions carefully. Learning to read test questions carefully is an important objective for most students with attention problems. Myles earned more points on the next test. He could see that improvement occurred whenever he took the time to circle key words in the question.

Self-Recognition and Reward

Self-recognition and reward are powerful self-control tools when used alone or in combination with other procedures (O'Leary & Dubey, 1979; Rhode, Morgan, & Young, 1983). Teachers encourage students to recognize and reward themselves for on-task behaviors. Such behaviors may include sitting down and beginning work, completing assignments, and answering questions during class discussion. Checklists are a primary way for students to recognize progress toward such goals and to feel pride in their accomplishments.

Students determine the type and frequency of reinforcement and the particular circumstances in which rewards occur. Following this, students self-administer these rewards contingent on responses that meet the performance criteria. Self-administered rewards are highly individual and need to be selected by the students themselves. For example, Myles selected buying audio equipment (e.g., a microphone) and audiotapes, reflecting his interest in music.

Time Management

Time management is viewed as a combination of cognitive and self-management skills (Zimmerman, Greenberg, & Weinstein, 1994). All adolescents need training in how to manage their time effectively. They also need repeated opportunities to practice time management skills in a variety of situations.

The teacher increases student awareness of the benefits of effective time management: improved quality of work, greater productivity, time for other activities, and reduced stress. If students use effective time management, they can more easily get to class on time, complete homework assignments on time, and finish tests (Davey, 1985). Books on study skills for high school and college include sections on time management (e.g., Deem, 1993; Ferrett, 1994; Robinson, 1993).

When teaching time management skills, clocks, calendars, and daily planners become a staple of every classroom. For example, each day the teacher tells the entire class to take out their daily planners and record their assignments. Students learn and practice how to schedule tasks, prioritize according to importance, allocate sufficient time for each task, and check off tasks when completed. Students learn to divide long-term assignments into shorter tasks and apply other time management skills (see Figure 7.3).

By predicting potential trouble spots, teachers help students prevent time management problems (Adderholdt-Elliot, 1987b). Teacher scheduling and monitoring of homework assignments is a necessity for most students with learning and attention problems. It is especially important for teachers to establish a number of checkpoints for long-term projects and term papers (e.g., topic selection, outline, first draft, final due date) so that the student checks his or her progress before going further. In this way, the teacher can provide feedback and recognition for small steps and prevent unnecessary failure and frustration.

Finally, teachers help students learn to allocate their time according to their goals and priorities and in consideration of their unique strengths and vulnerabilities.

Stress Management

Teachers should expect to help students manage the stresses associated with learning new and difficult behaviors by including stress

Figure 7.3   Student Checklist for Time Management Skills

Estimating

_____ Estimate the time it takes to do some daily activities.

_____ Record the actual time it takes to do the daily activities.

_____ Practice to increase accuracy of estimations for daily activities.

_____ Estimate the time it takes to do homework assignments.

_____ Record the actual time it takes to do the homework assignments.

_____ Practice to increase accuracy of estimations for homework.

Breaking Down Assignments

_____ Break a big project into smaller, "doable" tasks and list.

_____ Complete the project.

_____ Add to the list important tasks that were overlooked.

_____ Write a list of tasks needed to complete another assignment.

_____ Arrange tasks in order.

_____ Complete the assignment.

_____ Add to the list important tasks that were overlooked.

Planning Daily Schedules

_____ List important daily tasks and activities.

_____ Estimate the time needed for each task or activity.

_____ Plan a daily schedule, listing activities and estimated times.

_____ Include short, frequent breaks.

_____ Include time for thinking, organizing, and problem solving.

_____ Include time for reviewing and revising.

_____ Try the schedule—check off tasks and activities completed.

_____ Record actual times for tasks and activities.

Adjusting Schedules

_____ List things that interfered with your following the schedule.

_____ List ways to overcome these scheduling problems.

_____ Rearrange the schedule to manage time more effectively.

_____ Try the schedule.

_____ Adjust as necessary.

management as a part of self-management training (Goldstein, 1988). Materials are available for use by students and their teachers (Adderholdt-Elliot, 1987a; Hipp, 1995; Roberts & Guttormson, 1990). Such stress management techniques can help students overcome disappointment and discouragement when lapses occur, plateaus are reached, or progress slows.

The amount of stress experienced in a particular situation can vary from student to student, and a particular student can react differently from situation to situation. The teacher offers general strategies to deal with normal stresses and strains related to learning.

Effective self-management skills (e.g., when students set realistic goals and use a checklist to show their progress) can help minimize stress. In presenting information about stress management, the teacher discusses the reciprocal interaction of stress with time pressures and daily health factors such as rest, exercise, and nutrition. The teacher also describes mental and physical ways to relieve stress once it occurs. Sometimes students can reduce stress by dropping nonessential courses and/or reducing work or family commitments. Other techniques to reduce tension include visualizing successful situations, meditation, relaxation exercise, fun and humor, and physical exercise (Girdano & Everly, 1979; Mason, 1980; Smith, 1985). Listening to comedy or music prior to studying can provide students with a quick and easy way to alleviate stress. Teachers can also introduce respectful fun and humor into the classroom as a stress reducer.

SUMMARY AND CONCLUSIONS

A systematic and integrated approach to teaching self-management can contribute to the short-term and long-term academic growth of all students, including those with attention and learning difficulties. Self-management training helps students to modify, regulate, and maintain positive academic behavior. Students learn the strategies and skills to manage their thoughts, feelings, and actions, and, in so doing, increase learning.

The benefits of teaching self-management are that students:

Overcome or circumvent barriers to attention and learning

Keep up with their assignments

Learn how to learn in a variety of subject areas

Feel as though they are in control of themselves

Feel proud of their effort and progress

Are better prepared to deal with difficult situations and unexpected problems (e.g., disappointment, peer pressure, extra work, illness, family problems)

Develop skills for independent learning that can be used throughout secondary school and in postsecondary or career settings

During self-management training, students progress from needing individualized assistance in the classroom to independent work in unstructured environments. Students can observe themselves progress from confusion and helplessness to clarity and control. Teachers do invest time and energy in teaching self-management skills, but the dividends are well worth their effort.

8

Reading

Students with learning and attention difficulties commonly read without either preparation or purpose. When asked how they begin reading, they say, "I just open the book, start reading on the first page, and keep going until I finish, fall asleep, or begin to daydream." In addition, they have specific problems, such as a lack of decoding skills, poor comprehension, slow reading rate, difficulty remembering or organizing information they have read, or distractibility.

Wendy, the sixth grader we met in chapter 5, is a student with severe reading problems. Wendy has poor decoding skills and is reading at least 4 years below grade level. Wendy has weaknesses in auditory learning and auditory memory, which, coupled with her problems in reading, have limited her acquisition of information. Sam, the middle-school student whose case is presented in chapter 6, has above-average reading decoding skills, but his comprehension is questionable. It is difficult to measure his comprehension because he has poor expressive language skills. Although he may not be able to answer a question directly, he often can demonstrate his understanding in other ways. Myles, whose situation is described in chapters 3 and 7, will be in high school next year. He has a different kind of reading problem. Although his reading comprehension per se is quite high, his problems with concentration seriously affect his reading. He reads much too quickly, often overlooking critical information, becomes distracted and loses his place, and doesn't take time to think about the implications of what he has read.

Reading problems are the most prevalent characteristic of school-age children with learning disabilities (Mercer & Mercer, 1993). In high school, reading problems can be more severe as the discrepancy between the student's reading level and course demands increases. A student with learning disabilities in tenth grade may read effectively only at a fifth-grade level. There is a delicate balance between trying to remediate the student's reading problems and providing accommodations to bypass reading so the student can take in new information.

Teachers at the secondary level often have in their classes sizeable numbers of students with reading skill deficiencies—both with and without learning disabilities and/or ADD. This chapter provides a general overview of reading and its development, describing ways the teacher can encourage such students to become more effective readers and an instructional process to help them master necessary reading strategies in the content areas.

OVERVIEW

The purpose of reading in the content area classroom is to acquire and use information. In this milieu, reading comprehension can be viewed as information processing. Reading is neither passive, nor is it mechanical. Rather, it is an active process that involves the student in a dialogue with the text in a search for meaning. It requires thinking before, during, and after the actual reading event (Borkowski et al., 1992; Schumaker & Deshler, 1992; Wong & Jones, 1982).

In extracting information from text, the effective reader employs a complex set of cognitive behaviors that includes decoding, previewing, questioning, organizing, and remembering. In addition, the effective reader learns to select appropriate strategies to use for different reading tasks (Brown, 1978, 1980).

In decoding, students learn to "break the code" by analyzing letters and sound units, synthesizing sound units into meaningful word units, and problem solving (i.e., matching a word's appearance and sound with the idea, event, or object the word represents). Comprehension requires the reader first to decode and understand the meaning of words, then to extract meaning from sentences, and finally to interpret the meaning of the message. Comprehension involves applying the thinking processes that lead to an understanding of what is read and using the information to problem solve. The self-regulation of all these behaviors is critical to effective reading and learning.

The content area teacher can play a strong role in influencing the acquisition of these reading and thinking behaviors and in increasing learning (Rosenshine & Meister, 1992).

Reading as a Developmental Process

Throughout their schooling, students progress through a sequence of developmental stages. The acquisition of reading skills is part of this developmental process and encompasses the skills of listening, speaking, reading, and writing. In the general population, there may be disparities in skill development that result in reading difficulties. Reading difficulties are more pronounced in students with learning disabilities (Levine, 1987) due to inconsistencies or deficits in any number of areas.

By the end of elementary school, students are required to locate and understand words, main ideas, and supporting facts and examples, as well as to follow sequences of events and draw conclusions. At the secondary level, students acquire more complex reading comprehension skills and learn to "master the message." At this stage, there is an increasing need to organize ideas and relationships and to incorporate multiple viewpoints. Specifically, students learn to comprehend the meanings of words in context, synthesize the meanings of strings of words to understand their message, and problem solve to find hidden or unstated meanings. In addition, they make predictions, draw inferences, and provide interpretations, as well as identify an author's purpose, tone, and opinion. Finally, they evaluate material and master in-depth content.

Although most courses at the secondary level require a great deal of reading and thinking, each subject area requires slightly different reading strategies. Effective readers are aware of the requirements imposed by reading materials in different content areas. Students will not succeed if they read all assignments in the same way.

Students must acquire general reading strategies and learn to apply appropriate techniques in different courses. In science, for example, students may need to analyze concepts, deal with long and complicated sentences, perceive relationships among concepts, integrate diagrams and illustrations with text material, and problem solve using definitions of unfamiliar and difficult terms. In history or social studies, students may need to synthesize information to make broad generalizations, find supporting details, and use different types of visuals such as maps and timelines. In English courses, the emphasis may be on critical analysis or interpretation.

In addition to mastering comprehension techniques, students must learn to read at different rates depending on the type of reading required (see Figure 8.1; McWhorter, 1980). For example, in analytical reading, especially of complex material, students read more slowly than they would merely to identify the main idea of a passage.

In advanced high school courses and in college, students are often required to conduct detailed analyses of what is read. They must integrate information from multiple—and often original and difficult—sources. They are required to summarize, paraphrase, integrate, apply, and evaluate information from print material and then to communicate their thoughts in writing. Increasingly, students are required to demonstrate mastery of such skills on college and graduate school admissions tests. For example, in the verbal section of the Scholastic Aptitude Test II (College Board, 1993), students are required to read, reason, analyze, apply, and synthesize in both single and double passages.

Teachers sometimes assume that students who can read at the elementary level will automatically be able to comprehend more difficult secondary texts. This assumption is simply false. Almost all students require training in reading strategies to comprehend and apply information to solve problems in the more challenging secondary school and college settings. Because of the critical importance

---

Figure 8.1   Purposes of Reading and Related Reading Rates

Purpose	Speed (Words per Minute)	Reading Materials
Detailed comprehension, analysis, critique	100–200	Argumentative writing, poetry
High comprehension and recall	150–250	Textbooks, reference materials
Moderate comprehension of main ideas, entertainment	250–350	Novels, newspapers, magazines
Overview of material, rapid location of specific facts	250–450 (flexible)	Textbooks, magazines, novels, nonfiction

---

of reading to the acquisition of information, every content area teacher has a responsibility to enhance student reading skills (Bos & Anders, 1992; Ellis, 1993).

Reading Problems

All reading problems ultimately affect comprehension and the learning of information. Poor decoding skills severely limit the amount of information that can be received from reading; a slow reading rate limits the amount of information that can be received in a finite amount of time; distractibility can affect both the amount and the accuracy of information gained. In addition, many students are unaware that they can organize their reading behaviors, selecting and applying strategies as appropriate. This lack of self-regulation can severely limit both the communication of information and the usability of the information gained.

Students with learning disabilities or ADD can have disabilities in any one or a combination of the problem areas just described or in visual processing, higher order cognitive processes, and auditory or expressive language. Visual processing difficulties directly affect the acquisition of information through reading by limiting decoding abilities; higher order cognitive problems can affect the sequencing or organization of information as well as memory. Language disabilities can severely affect the entire reading process.

It is not uncommon to find several students with one or more of these problems or disabilities in a regular classroom. Most classes have a three- to five-grade range of reading levels. This includes students reading both above and below grade level. The content area teacher can refer students suspected of severe reading or language disabilities for evaluation to a school psychologist, a special education teacher consultant, a speech and language specialist, or a reading consultant. These specialists can help the classroom teacher assess strengths and weaknesses and adapt reading materials to the needs of individual students.

Individual differences dictate that different approaches be employed when teaching students to read, especially those with learning difficulties (Pressley & Rankin, 1994). Wendy, Sam, and Nathan all attended elementary schools where reading was taught using the whole language approach, with its emphasis on reading for meaning rather than decoding. Sam learned how to read in this milieu; Wendy and Nathan did not. Both Wendy and Nathan went through third grade without learning how to read. Not until fourth grade, when his parents hired a tutor, did Nathan learn to "break the code" and start to read. Wendy remained at a first-grade reading level through fifth grade. Both of these students might have benefited from a thoughtful matching of reading methods with their individual strengths, weaknesses, and learning styles (Carbo et al., 1991; Dunn & Dunn, 1978).

Individualized approaches have helped deal with Nathan's and Wendy's decoding problems. Nathan's tutor used the Orton-Gillingham approach (Gillingham & Stillman, 1973). Wendy's special education teacher consultant used the Fernald (1943) approach. Both approaches utilize multisensory techniques, combining visual experience (seeing the letter or word), auditory experience (pronouncing the sound of the letter, syllable, or word), and kinesthetic experience (writing or tracing the letter or word), as well as learning the meaning of the word.

Both Wendy and Nathan have received remedial reading instruction outside the regular classroom. Sam has also received some reading instruction outside the regular classroom. However, in the regular classroom all three are learning how to use general reading strategies to become effective readers.

ROLE OF THE CLASSROOM TEACHER

Whether or not students have documented disabilities, they can benefit from systematic reading instruction in content area classes. All students need to develop their reading skills in every grade and in every subject. As academic challenges become more complex, teachers must provide direct instruction to develop advanced comprehension skills. Such instruction is best done in the regular classroom. However, some teachers of specific content courses may feel that they do not have the necessary time or training to teach reading, or they may not realize the need to do so (Menke & Davey, 1994). They may believe that reading improvement for students with learning problems should take place outside the content area classroom. Such teachers should know that reading strategies integrated with course content have been found to be more meaningful and transferable than strategies taught outside that context (Jones, Palincsar, Ogle, & Carr, 1987).

The teacher is in a position to organize the classroom environment, materials, and assignments to encourage systematic improvement of reading skills. Sometimes in collaboration with a special education teacher consultant or reading consultant, the teacher develops and suggests reading strategies appropriate to the subject, the text, and the students' skill levels. Reading skills are then integrated with other skills critical to mastering the subject matter: listening and note taking, test taking, writing, and completing homework. The teacher provides practice, feedback, encouragement, and opportunities for students to monitor their own progress.

Promoting Effective Reading Practices

In promoting effective reading practices, the teacher presents reading as a complex skill that can be learned, practiced, and improved—in secondary school and beyond. Students can control and regulate their reading activities through planning, monitoring, and adjusting their reading behavior. The teacher helps students develop a "tool kit" of general and specific reading strategies for use in particular courses and a self-regulatory system for deciding when to use each skill or strategy.

To help students become more active readers, the classroom teacher encourages them to do as follows:

Focus attention

Pose and seek answers to basic and higher level questions when reading

Relate new to previously learned information

Read with a purpose in mind

Periodically check whether they understand the material they are reading

Ask for help if they do not understand the material

Encouraging Positive Attitudes toward Reading

Many students with learning and attention problems report painful experiences and residual feelings of hurt, sadness, anger, and disappointment related to reading. Feelings of shame and avoidance are not uncommon in people of all ages who have reading problems. Educators should not underestimate the sacrifice asked of students with reading problems when they are repeatedly urged to read, try again, and hope for improvement. Many students with learning difficulties have experienced repeated failure and humiliation: Each new challenge may be accompanied by tension and fear of failure.

The teacher is a critical factor in increasing students' positive feelings toward reading, encouraging success, and reducing avoidance behaviors. By identifying small goals as "doable tasks," the teacher helps the student set a new course, welcome opportunities, and meet challenges. Such challenges can be exciting, although they require perseverance. Perseverance is important, even "heroic," behavior on the part of students with learning difficulties.

Specific ways to create a more positive climate include pairing reading with experiences that are humorous, enjoyable, and interesting or describing "bad habits" in a funny or exaggerated way. Students can also base their reading on their interests and daily needs, use appropriate computer software programs for reading and writing, and play reading-related games and exercises (e.g., crossword puzzles or language treasure hunts).

Individualizing

The classroom teacher individualizes instruction by matching methods and materials to individual learning styles, strengths, and interests. In doing so, the teacher explains the possible impact of students' personal attributes on their academic reading behaviors. For example:

> Each of us is unique, and our personal characteristics influence the way we read. The way you read is affected by your personal style, your thinking, your previous knowledge, and your past educational experiences. In addition to individual styles, readers have their own strengths and weaknesses. Some students find it easy to read at a relatively fast pace, whereas others read and reread the same material very slowly. Whatever your strengths and weaknesses are, you can benefit from reading strategies that are just right for you.

Individualizing means systematically describing both *what* to read and *how* to read it. Explicit and concrete explanations can help a student gain greater control over reading behavior. For example:

From your description, you are not a person who reads with concentration or comprehension for more than a few minutes at a time. We need to find the times when your capacity to concentrate is greatest, and we need to find the briefest but most important segments of the text to read.

Some students need improvement in subskill areas. Supplementary materials or exercises can be used within the content area classroom using small-group instruction. Many secondary textbooks provide extensive reading and learning aids that can be assigned as homework or for extra credit. Often reading consultants, curriculum specialists, or school librarians can locate useful supplementary materials in a variety of media formats.

Providing Accommodations

Usually, students with learning disabilities and/or ADD require accommodations in the regular classroom in order to learn effectively. If the textbook or any other required reading material is too difficult for the student, alternative methods for obtaining the information, to be implemented by the classroom teacher, should be described in the IEP or 504 plan. Following are some common reading accommodations:

Providing an audiotape of the textbook that the student can listen to while reading, thus giving the student the opportunity to take in information in both a visual and auditory way

Providing outlines of textbook chapters

Cuing students with ADD to stay on task during reading activities and tests

Adapting textbooks by highlighting main ideas, important points, and specific lines or passages to be read

Providing a substitute text with a lower reading level

Arranging for a special education teacher consultant to read texts and tests aloud outside of class to individual students with severe reading disabilities

Some students with learning problems require remediation because of the severity of their disabilities. Although remedial or supplemental instruction is best provided in the regular classroom, it can also be provided in tutorial or special education settings.

Estimating Appropriateness of Materials and Tasks

Many textbooks are poorly written and/or written at too high a reading level for most of the students in class. For example, the school district has just adopted a tenth-grade biology textbook that Kyle (whom we met in chapter 4) and many other students are finding very difficult. The text is 700 pages long and written at a beginning college level. Kyle's teacher might try to locate another text for him that covers the same material and is written at a lower reading level. In fact, the school district should try to find another text that is more appropriate for tenth-grade students, even though this particular text is considered to be state of the art.

A similar problem exists at Wendy and Sam's middle school. The seventh-grade teachers have just adopted an excellent multicultural geography text, but the text is written at a tenth-grade level and is much too difficult for Wendy and Sam. Almost half of the class is having difficulty with the text. However, there is no substitute text available. The challenge in this case is to adapt this valuable text and present the information in a way that students can understand. Wendy and Sam will need additional accommodations in order to access the information in the text.

Teachers will need to work together to assess the readability of texts and either reject or modify material that is too difficult. For help in determining the readability of a textbook or other material and in gauging its appropriateness for the class, teachers may use a readability estimate based on an examination of vocabulary and sentence complexity. A number of formulas can be used to determine readability and actual grade levels of textbooks (Bornmouth, 1968; Fry, 1977; Williams, 1972).

It is equally important that reading assignments be appropriate in length and complexity. The teacher may want to ascertain the time students need to complete their reading assignments at home. To obtain a rate/comprehension measure in this less structured setting, students can be asked to record the time required to read each page and/or to answer each question of the assignment. This information helps the teacher determine whether the assignments are appropriate in terms of length or difficulty.

TEACHING READING IN THE CONTENT AREA

Numerous reading and thinking strategies can be taught and demonstrated in the secondary classroom (Atkinson & Longman, 1988; Cook, 1991; Ellis, 1994). Materials to teach these learning strategies to high school and college students have been available for many years (e.g., Cohen, Knudsvig, Markel, Patten, Shtogren, & Wilhelm, 1973; Robinson, 1941; Smith, 1961; Walter & Siebert, 1992). More recently, researchers have shown these skills to be helpful for adolescents with learning disabilities (Schumaker & Deshler, 1992). The general goal of these approaches is for young people to use reading and thinking strategies to analyze and solve problems in both academic and nonacademic settings (Borkowski et al., 1992; De Jong & Robert-Jan Simons, 1992).

General Reading Strategies

Surveying

Surveying reading materials and posing questions about content are important first steps in the reading process. Teaching students with learning problems how to survey or preview reading materials can improve their comprehension skills (Wong & Jones, 1982). Before beginning to read, students survey the material to learn what will be covered in the reading and to get a sense of the scope and content of the information. When surveying, the reader looks at the major headings, the introduction, summary, and illustrations. Surveying provides a framework for identifying topics, organizing them, and relating them to past knowledge or experience. A survey helps establish the purpose of a reading task and readies the reader.

Questioning

When students generate or are provided with questions before beginning a reading assignment, they are better able to focus their attention and locate important information during reading (Rosenshine & Meister, 1992). In other words, they read to answer questions. Questions can also activate background knowledge and serve as a way of monitoring reading comprehension. A simple way of providing questions is to use the author's questions at the end of each chapter. The important thing is to get students to generate questions prior to reading in order to guide the acquisition of information and enhance comprehension.

In order to help students develop a range of questions, the teacher can use Bloom's (1956) taxonomy of educational objectives as a framework. Figure 8.2 presents a ladder of cognitive objectives and related tasks, based on Bloom's taxonomy. Lower level or knowledge questions ask students to list or define. Middle level questions require students to apply information. At the highest level, students are required to evaluate new information (Menke & Pressley, 1994). The use of higher order questions helps students use new information, gleaned from reading material, in innovative ways. This taxonomy can be useful in structuring objectives in any content area class or grade level, as well as for any learning style.

Paraphrasing

Paraphrasing takes place at intervals during reading. It requires the reader to stop at the end of a passage in order to translate a message or restate it in his or her own words. As students paraphrase or rephrase, they can elaborate, identify examples, or relate the message to their own experience. Paraphrasing at intervals helps readers become actively involved with the material.

Summarizing

Summarizing condenses or collapses information into a few sentences. It focuses students on the main points and helps them omit irrelevant or unimportant information. It is a closing activity, just as a survey is a start-up activity.

Organizing

Organizing information involves systematically classifying, sequencing, or categorizing information, then functionally relating the whole to its parts. When information is organized, the main points become more obvious, relationships are clarified, and information is easier to understand and remember.

Some techniques to enhance organization include charting, mapping, and outlining. The choice of organizational technique depends on the material and the requirements of the task. Students consider this question: In what order would you present the information to make the message clearer for a friend?

Nathan, Wendy, and Sam can all benefit from using these general reading strategies to increase their reading comprehension. Wendy will also need to learn a lot more about decoding before she can read fluently.

Using the SQ4R Method

The SQ3R method (Survey, Question, Read, Recite, Review) was first described over 50 years ago (Robinson, 1941); it was expanded in the early 1960s (Smith, 1961) to include writing and renamed SQ4R (Survey, Question, Read, Recite, [W]Rite, Review). A popular tool for all students, both with and without learning disabilities, SQ4R is a multisensory information-processing strategy to improve reading and learning skills. Lesson plans are available for using SQ4R in all content areas, including science and mathematics (Cook, 1991).

When using SQ4R, students engage in a series of cognitive activities to comprehend text material. An interactive process, SQ4R incorporates a variety of cognitive strategies: Students preview reading materials, ask questions, read text and illustrations, think aloud, discuss, write, and review material. Figure 8.3 shows a typical student checklist for applying SQ4R to textbooks. The following discussion examines the specific components of this approach as related to reading.

Survey

The survey provides an opportunity to preview and examine the reading assignment. More specifically, a survey helps the reader to do as follows:

See the text materials as a whole

Focus attention

Become aware of the scope of the topic and the sequence in which ideas are presented

Identify study aids

Anticipate challenges

Predict reading time required

Figure 8.2 A Ladder of Cognitive Objectives and Related Tasks

EVALUATION:
Making judgments
about the value of
ideas and material
for a given purpose,
using specific criteria

*Judge, assess,
critique, recommend,
select*

SYNTHESIS:
Putting parts
together to form
a new whole

*Plan, prepare, predict,
integrate, prescribe,
propose, create*

ANALYSIS:
Breaking down
material into its
component parts

*Analyze, detect,
explain, deduce,
formulate, separate,
outline*

APPLICATION: Using learned material in new situations

Apply, solve, demonstrate, use, conclude, complete

COMPREHENSION: Understanding the message or the meaning of material

Describe, discuss, estimate, classify, compare, contrast, distinguish, associate, compute

KNOWLEDGE: Remembering, recognizing, and recalling information or ideas

List, name, state, define, identify, trace, recite, repeat, write, draw

**Figure 8.3   Student Checklist for Applying SQ4R
to Reading Textbooks**

SURVEY each section to be read.

_____ Determine the organization of the chapter.

_____ Survey the first pages for basic information, such as the title, author, and table of contents.

_____ Identify any study aids, such as chapter objectives, introductions, illustrations, summaries, bibliographies, glossaries.

QUESTION the material.

_____ Say the chapter title aloud, converting the title of the chapter into a main idea question.

_____ Convert the heading or subheadings into questions.

_____ Add questions from the back of chapter.

_____ Be sure to include questions requiring interpretation, integration, and application of ideas.

_____ Begin to answer the questions, using prior knowledge.

READ to find the answers to your questions.

_____ Circle key words or phrases that answer your questions.

_____ Read figures and tables, then relate them to the questions.

_____ Think about what you are reading and reread passages that are unclear.

_____ Try to visualize or create pictures in your mind as you read.

RECITE the answers to your questions in your own words.

_____ Restate, paraphrase, summarize the information in your own words.

_____ Elaborate about the main ideas and relationships between ideas, using examples.

[W]RITE the answers to your questions.

_____ Write brief answers in your own words.

_____ Use charts, diagrams, and symbols to help answer the questions.

REVIEW.

_____ Read questions; recite/write answers; refer to text; and add, correct, or delete information.

_____ Ask the teacher to explain ideas that you did not fully understand.

_____ Repeat the review after a week.

Question

As noted previously, questions are tools for defining and structuring the reading task. They arouse curiosity and help determine the most suitable reading techniques. Posing and answering questions promotes efficient reading and motivates students (Wong & Jones, 1982).

In SQ4R, titles, headings, and illustrations from text are turned into questions, which the student then answers. Common lower level questions include the following:

What is the main idea?

What are important facts or examples?

What is the sequence or trend?

Who are the main characters or figures?

What are the critical time periods?

Where did the major events occur?

Students also pose and answer middle and higher order questions requiring them to apply, analyze, synthesize, or evaluate information. For example:

How can ideas be applied?

How can problems be solved?

What are the underlying assumptions?

How does _____ relate to _____?

Why did this occur?

What are the causes and effects?

Why was the impact significant?

What can be concluded?

What is the accuracy or usefulness of the information?

Do I agree or disagree with the author?

"How" and "why" questions are particularly good for encouraging critical thinking.

Read

Students read the assignment purposefully, to locate the answers to the questions. Most frequently, main ideas and major supporting facts are located in the introduction, at the beginning of sections, in illustrations, and in the summary. The student slows down to focus on and extract meaning from key words and phrases.

Teachers can advise students with reading problems to concentrate on main ideas and skip over detailed explanations, skim for an overall impression of content, and scan when a particular fact or answer is required.

Recite

Restating, paraphrasing, and summarizing information that answers questions is a critical aspect of the thinking and learning process. This step can include translating technical vocabulary or concepts into the reader's own words. Saying and hearing one's own version of the information helps focus attention, involve the reader, and promote understanding and remembering. In addition, it may serve as a self-check and provide the opportunity to elaborate.

[W]Rite

The answers to questions are recorded in the student's own words. Kernels of information are written using key words and phrases, abbreviations, symbols, or diagrams. Technical terms are defined. These brief notes serve to reinforce learning and retention of information. Later, these notes can help prepare the student for tests.

Review

Review of the text material, questions, and answers provides additional time for learning and retention, a check on accuracy and completeness, and an opportunity to organize and relate the information to larger issues. The review may involve repetition of any of the previous steps.

The SQ4R process is flexible and adaptable. It can be used with a variety of students in a variety of settings with a variety of materials. For instance, SQ4R is good for students who fidget because they can read for a few minutes and then stand up and move around. It also works well for students with decoding problems and can even make grade-level material accessible to students like Wendy and Nathan, whose reading levels are well below those of their classmates. With SQ4R, comprehension is increased, even though every word may not be read. Because it is a multisensory approach, SQ4R can be used at almost any grade level to increase reading comprehension.

The SQ4R process can also be used to improve student learning and performance in the areas of listening and note taking, preparing for and taking tests, and academic writing. Its application to these other areas will be described in chapters 9 through 11, respectively.

Self-Talk

Self-talk, or verbal mediation, is a learning strategy that enhances problem solving. Once learned, the strategy can be used and extended in a variety of situations (Berardi-Coletta, Dominowski, Buyer, & Rellinger, 1995; Cook, 1991; Davey, 1985; Meichenbaum, 1977; Short & Weissberg-Benchell, 1989).

Programs such as Think Aloud (Camp & Bash, 1985), a widely used verbal mediation approach, can be adapted to help students improve problem-solving abilities as they relate to reading. In general, this involves teaching students to self-instruct when faced with a task, generate questions and answers in order to access information, recite and restate information to remember it, and solve problems encountered during reading.

Before reading, general questions the student asks include What are my purposes? What do I already know about the topic? and What are my predictions? During reading, these questions are helpful: Am I understanding? What aspects are similar or different from my predictions? and How can I help myself do better? After reading, pertinent questions include What were the most important points of the material? and Should I reread any portions? Students direct their own reading process by asking themselves What will happen if I do this? and What should I do next? and by telling themselves to try different alternatives. Finally, they evaluate the effectiveness of their reading plan: That was a mistake, but this seems to be working.

Group Discussion

Recent research indicates that large- or small-group discussion or peer interaction can improve learning in general and reading comprehension skills in particular (Palincsar, Brown, & Martin, 1987; Palincsar & David, 1992). Group discussion helps students analyze information, relate new information to old, draw inferences, summarize, and use information acquired through reading to solve problems. This activity is especially appropriate for science and mathematics classrooms because students can learn and explain processes and sequences that may be difficult to grasp from printed text. Many students with learning disabilities need to discuss and express their ideas in small as opposed to large groups.

Visual Displays, Graphic Organizers, and Visualization Techniques

Visual displays and graphic organizers in textbooks not only supplement the printed message, they also emphasize the most important concepts and summarize information concisely. The most common visuals are pictures and illustrations, charts, and graphs and diagrams. Ideally, these graphics attract attention and telegraph meaning to readers. Unfortunately, students both with and without learning problems often ignore these visual aids.

Many students can understand and remember information and relationships better when they analyze a picture or graph than when they read (Atkinson & Longman, 1988; Hudson et al., 1993; Lenz, Bulgren, & Hudson, 1990; Naughton, 1993/1994). Some students who are otherwise unable to read the text can, with instruction, comprehend related graphics.

The SQ4R process can be applied to the visual displays found in textbooks to help students identify, organize, comprehend, and retain critical information. For example, a teacher could help a student survey the title of an illustration or graphic, its written explanation, and the actual graphic material. The student could turn the title into one or more questions, then answer the questions. Finally, he or she could relate the graphic to a main point in the text. This strategy empowers and motivates students as they realize that they can indeed learn from the book. For example, Nathan, whose situation was first discussed in chapter 3, is the type of student who can learn a great deal from the visuals found in textbooks. He is willing to spend the time examining and thinking about illustrations and other graphics; he can pick up details, see relationships, and understand complicated processes that he cannot understand from reading the textbook. Teaching

Nathan how to apply the SQ4R process to visual displays will great-ly enhance his comprehension and retention of course material.

Students can also generate their own visual displays or graphic organizers to help them understand facts, concepts, and relationships discussed in class or read in textbooks. Making any kind of graphic representation requires attention, organization, and understanding. It can also show what students know and do not know. Visual displays can be used during reading (to organize, summarize, and comprehend material) and/or after reading (as a review and retention enhancer). (Teachers can also provide advance organizers to students before reading.) Sam used the technique of translating story problems into pictures in order to solve them, with great success.

Sometimes students can improve their comprehension through the use of visual imagery (Clark, Deshler, Schumaker, Alley, & Warner, 1984; Rose, Cundick, & Higbee, 1983). For example, the teacher can suggest that students visualize a motion picture based on a novel they have read. By visualizing characters, events, sequences, and relationships, students are able to get beyond the literal level of the text into application and synthesis. Visualization makes reading much more interesting for them and increases their motivation. Visualization can be expanded to include points on an imaginary scale, as well as geometric figures or other symbols of people, events, and processes.

Cloze Exercises

For almost 40 years, the cloze procedure has been a valuable tech-nique for improving reading comprehension (Bloomer, 1962; Rankin, 1959). In a cloze exercise, every *n*th (e.g., every fifth or eighth) word is deleted, and the student is required to read and fill in the blanks using contextual clues in the passage.

The cloze technique is especially useful for students with diffi-culties in word retrieval, attention, problem solving, sequencing, and moving from part to whole. Sam's success with the cloze technique helped demonstrate his comprehension capabilities. He enjoyed the cloze exercises because they were like games. For the same reason, he also enjoyed solving riddles, another reading comprehension strategy.

Teachers can create their own cloze exercises, using text passages, for the purpose of review. They can also use these exercises to assess comprehension of the text or supplementary reading materials.

THE INSTRUCTIONAL PROCESS

Setting the Stage

Setting the stage for learning involves gaining students' attention and interest, broadening their perspective on reading, dispelling common myths, and creating a positive reading environment. It is important to engage students who are anxious about reading and assure them that they can be successful.

Students benefit when the teacher includes an overview of reading as it relates to academic performance. Depending on the course and the students' maturity, this overview may include a description of the reading process, a description of the variety of skills required to complete assignments, and an examination of the need for reading in adult life. For example:

> Reading requires a lot more thinking and skill as you progress through school. This means you must understand and learn information from text and then use the information to participate in class discussions, prepare for tests, write papers, and complete projects. If you have trouble reading or just don't like to read, there are some strategies that you can use to reduce the time and the amount you need to read. In addition, these strategies will help you increase the amount of information you learn and remember.

Before conducting class reading activities, the teacher arranges positive and nondistracting conditions for learning and employs techniques to help students focus their energy:

> Efficient reading is a complex academic task. Like athletes and musicians who perform complex tasks, readers can benefit from warm-up activities. Let's take a minute to relax. First, get comfortable in your chair. Take a few deep breaths, close your eyes, and get a mental picture of yourself at a time when you were performing well. After that, we'll be ready to focus on the assignment.

Collecting Information

To provide information necessary for instructional decision making, teachers are advised to conduct informal assessments of reading with class textbooks (Hughes & Smith, 1990). Informal assessments may involve some or all of the following:

Observing students as they read the text

Asking students about their reading skills or reactions to the text

Giving students a checklist to identify skills they currently use and those that need improvement

Administering informal assessments of vocabulary, reading rate, and comprehension, based on class texts

Examining existing student records for results of standardized reading tests

Given the constraints under which most teachers operate, the objective is to collect the most relevant information with the least expenditure of effort. The teacher saves time and energy by involving students in the process and by using class materials. Collecting data on vocabulary, reading rate, and comprehension can take as little as 30 minutes of class time—5 to 10 minutes to select materials, 5 minutes to administer a brief pretest or baseline assessment, 5 minutes for students to answer questions, 5 minutes for students to score the test, and 5 minutes to summarize and chart the results. Students can hand in their scores anonymously and be in charge of charting results to generate a class profile.

Baselines and pretests

The classroom teacher is wise to collect information on all students' entry-level reading skills early in the course. The goal of obtaining such information is to get a general idea of the group's entering proficiency with the text and/or their awareness of reading strategies (Miholic, 1994). Similarly, the teacher may administer a pretest on the subject matter. Both measures lead to data-based instructional decision making. The resulting data enable the teacher to (a) quantify the existing level of knowledge and reading proficiency; (b) adjust the level, rate, and type of classroom instruction to the needs of the class; (c) plan how to integrate reading into the course; and (d) monitor and evaluate learning outcomes.

Baselines and pretests benefit students directly by facilitating self-management. If students are to assume responsibility for their own reading and learning, they need information about their entering skill levels. With this knowledge they are in a better position to self-select goals, consider strategies, and manage time.

College admissions tests

For tenth- through twelfth-grade college-bound students, the verbal sections of practice college admissions tests and state proficiency exams can be used to assess reading skills. These tests can serve as relevant classroom performance measures of vocabulary and reading comprehension, especially higher order and college level reading skills. Practice college admissions tests such as the Scholastic Aptitude Test (SAT; College Board, 1993, 1995b) and the American College Test (ACT; American College Testing Program, 1993) are distributed free and available in all high schools. They are easy for students to use in a classroom setting or at home. For younger students, the Preliminary Scholastic Aptitude Test (PSAT; College Board, 1995a) is available. This test is shorter and not quite as difficult as the SAT or ACT. Statewide competency tests can be used in the same way. It is important to stress that teachers who use standardized tests in this manner are not "teaching to the test." Rather, they are alerting students to the demands that will be placed on them in the near future.

Analyzing Tasks

The teacher acquaints the class with multiple and increasingly difficult demands of reading by explaining that students have the responsibility to identify the purpose of reading assignments, examine related tasks, and select reading techniques and strategies accordingly. The teacher might say, for example:

> You need different clothes for different occasions. You
> don't wear hiking clothes or boots to the prom. In the
> same way, you need different tools for different jobs.
> You don't use the same tools to repair a truck as you do
> to build a house. The reading tools you use will depend
> on your purpose, the difficulty of the reading task, and
> your own strengths and weaknesses. An effective reader
> recognizes that reading for science and for history will
> require different tools. For example, science requires great
> attention to detail, such as formulas, technical terms,

diagrams, and data. History requires attention to facts, time sequences, and underlying relationships among people, places, and events.

In courses where inference and interpretation are appropriate, it is especially important for the teacher to model strategies to use when making inferences about or interpreting a passage. Students may be unaware that some of the most important aspects of reading involve not the words in the text but what is implied by or predicted from those words.

Setting Goals

The teacher determines class goals as related to the text on the basis of the assessment of students' entry reading levels. The teacher and students discuss the bench marks of expected progress as well as the desired results—for example, students will work the same amount of time but achieve better results, or they will work less and achieve an equal amount. Some students who greatly increase their skills can actually spend less time, learn more, and earn better grades.

The teacher also involves students in setting their own reading goals. To do so, the teacher provides a menu of reading improvement objectives. From this menu, each student selects an objective and then practices the relevant skill(s), using either recreational or academic reading materials. The goal is for each student to have a personalized reading improvement plan.

Teaching and Modeling Specific Strategies

Direct instruction in reading and learning strategies puts students in charge of their own learning (Ellis, Deshler, Schumaker, Lenz, & Clark, 1991). Students who learn such strategies not only improve their understanding and memory of text information but also feel empowered. Often students first feel a sense of control over the reading process when they begin to generate questions that the reading assignment will answer. Many students are elated when they discover that there is some system, some structure, that allows them to make accurate predictions about the content of a reading assignment.

The teacher chooses from among the specific reading strategies described earlier in this chapter and devotes classroom time to their direct instruction. With the teacher serving as a model and using class texts as an example, students observe and imitate a range of effective reading behaviors. The teacher provides feedback and support, with the expectation that students will eventually learn to conduct this process independently.

Providing Guided Practice, Feedback, and Reinforcement

Practice, feedback, and reinforcement are essential for students to master any specific reading strategy or technique. By integrating these mechanisms into classroom learning, the teacher helps students accomplish their reading goals.

Practice

Many students with reading disabilities do not practice reading often enough to improve. They need to make a commitment to improving their reading skills. Students may need to contract with others or with themselves to increase the amount of time or the number of pages read daily or within a week (Homme et al., 1970).

Practice is also necessary for students to master specific reading strategies. For example, once students are familiar with the SQ4R method, the process needs to be repeated. Some students with learning difficulties need extra demonstration and practice because they have trouble seeing the big picture or remembering sequences. Some students benefit most from going over several chapters in the same text; others gain more from applying the process to several different texts.

Feedback

Feedback lets students know exactly how they can improve their performance. The teacher provides timely and specific feedback on the student's use of reading and thinking strategies—for example, by identifying the omission of a step or redemonstrating a strategy. The teacher may review for students which skill to use, why, and when. The teacher can also describe discrepancies between the desired and the actual application of the strategy, as well as answer questions about why a strategy isn't working for a student and suggest alternative ways of applying it.

Depending on the situation and the student, it is sometimes wiser not to correct individual students but rather to incorporate the ideas into a future lesson. (Corrective feedback may have a negative effect on students with very fragile self-concepts.) Presented as part of the ongoing instructional effort, group feedback can take the form of "minilessons." These can be quite brief—perhaps no more than 10 or 15 minutes long. Topics can include ways to build reading efficiency, master technical vocabulary, and adjust reading rate according to the reader's purpose.

Reinforcement

As the old adage states, "Nothing succeeds like success." This is particularly applicable to the teaching of new skills, especially with students like Wendy, who have a high frequency of avoidance behaviors. It is up to the teacher to provide success experiences and frequent positive reinforcement. Such reinforcement may include, among other things, verbal praise related to work completed or effort expended; attention in the form of conversation about academic work, eye contact, smiles, pats on the back, or personal notes; allowing the student free choice of next activity; and recognition (e.g., positive notes home to parents).

Generally, students receive reinforcement only for learning content. However, it is also important to give reinforcement for progress toward the acquisition of reading and thinking skills. For example, students can be reinforced for using paraphrasing or summarizing techniques in class discussions as well as for posing and answering higher order questions and using information to solve problems.

Reinforcement should be individualized, based on students' entry level skills and goals. Newly acquired reading comprehension behaviors require frequent reinforcement to ensure their use and to enhance maintenance and generalization.

Monitoring Progress and Adjusting Activities

Periodic formal or informal assessment will help the teacher monitor student progress and determine whether it is necessary to change assignments or schedules, review strategies, or introduce additional techniques. Monitoring may reveal that some students require further evaluation, special services, and/or accommodations.

Many students with learning difficulties have underlying language problems that may become apparent only after some time has elapsed. Language problems can be very complicated and subtle, and the classroom teacher needs to be on the alert for any signs that one may exist. These include limited spoken vocabulary; difficulty expressing thoughts, feelings, and ideas; limited complexity of speech; and difficulty understanding multistep directions. Some students with auditory language problems have difficulty with "language on demand" (e.g., responding to a question) but have no difficulty with self-initiated language. Language problems can have a serious impact on learning, and the teacher may need to refer students suspected of having language problems for an intensive speech and language evaluation.

In monitoring performance, the teacher watches for avoidance or other problematic reading-related behaviors. Avoidance behaviors include not bringing the textbook to class, never opening the book, and rarely reading in or out of class. Other problematic behaviors include not using reading vocabulary in class or on tests and incorrectly reading directions on tests, homework, or papers. These behaviors must not be ignored. At a minimum, the teacher will need to create a more inviting or interesting environment so students will begin to attend to the material.

ENCOURAGING SELF-MANAGEMENT

It is important for students to track their own reading and learning behavior and to set goals for themselves (e.g., reading more books, answering more questions). Self-management contributes to motivation, which in turn enhances progress, which in turn reinforces positive behavior. Commitment to reading improvement can be solicited by having the entire class develop and implement verbal agreements or written contracts to complete supplementary readings or class vocabulary-building projects. A checklist of strategies like the example shown in Figure 8.4 can help students manage their own reading behavior.

Throughout the reading improvement process, students can establish nondistracting conditions, prioritize and schedule tasks, monitor the number of questions correctly completed, learn to cope with frustration (e.g., "This is hard, but I need to do it, and I can"), and reinforce and recognize their own efforts.

Figure 8.4   Student Checklist for Managing the Reading Process

Before Reading

_____ Review the reading assignment to identify
a purpose for reading.

_____ List one to three main idea questions.

_____ Make a plan and set goals (e.g., time allotted,
number of questions).

_____ Tell yourself the reading strategy you will use (e.g., SQ4R).

_____ Establish pleasant and nondistracting conditions
for effective reading.

_____ Gather materials (textbook, paper, pencils).

During Reading

_____ Activate attention.

_____ Search for clues to understanding (e.g., key words,
boldface type, illustrations).

_____ Monitor your comprehension; ask yourself,
"Do I understand this?"

_____ Reread when you do not understand.

_____ Organize information into visuals such as diagrams,
charts, or sketches.

_____ Relate new information to previously learned information.

_____ Take frequent breaks.

_____ Use self-talk to maintain attention and motivation.

After Reading

_____ Think about and summarize what you read.

_____ Create a picture or story in your mind.

_____ Identify information from other sources that confirms
or contradicts the information you have just read.

_____ Think about how you can use this information.

_____ Recognize your efforts.

_____ Reward yourself if you accomplished most of what
you set out to do.

_____ Set a realistic goal for the next time you read—for instance,
answering a certain number of questions.

For example, Wendy's personalized reading plan, implemented in both her social studies class and resource room, includes reading social studies materials at her level and using the information to participate in class discussion and design special projects. Wendy has always avoided reading, but this semester is different. Each week Wendy is encouraged to select a high-interest, low-vocabulary book for her special projects. She has also begun to keep a journal, with her mother's help. She dictates the important things she has learned that day, and her mother writes them down for Wendy to read and keep. These two strategies have made reading more enjoyable for Wendy.

To help Wendy monitor her own progress in reading, the special education teacher consultant has suggested that she videotape Wendy reading her textbook aloud at 3-week intervals throughout the semester. In addition to demonstrating Wendy's improvement, the videotaping appears to be highly motivating.

SUMMARY AND CONCLUSIONS

Reading is a complex task requiring active involvement of the student before, during, and after reading. Increasing reading comprehension in content area classrooms increases students' ability to learn and use new information. Effective readers employ various strategies, singly or in combination, to extract meaning from texts.

The content area teacher can provide effective instruction in reading skills and strategies for all students, including those with learning difficulties. Students can learn to select appropriate strategies based on their own needs and the requirements of the task. Teaching reading in the content area classroom requires a shift in the teacher's perspective but does not interfere with the teacher's goal of having students learn the content. Quite the contrary, integrating the teaching of reading strategies into the learning process can yield very positive results.

Finally, when dealing with students' reading problems, it is important for the teacher to focus on what *can* be done:

Do expect everyone to be a better reader.

Do incorporate direct instruction of reading strategies in content area classes.

Do appeal to students' interests and styles.

Do begin at students' current skill levels.

Do require thinking and discussion based on reading assignments.

Do help students learn to manage their own reading behaviors.

Do reinforce effort and progress.

9

Listening and Note Taking

Listening and note taking are activities neither seen nor graded by the teacher. They are, however, important skills. Because lecturing is a major teaching vehicle in the secondary setting, it is almost as important for students to learn to listen to and record verbal information as it is for them to read written information.

Many students with learning disabilities are passive learners who approach cognitive tasks such as listening and note taking without preparation or focus (Hallahan & Bryan, 1981; Wiens, 1983). Such students are often inefficient at organizing, remembering, and manipulating verbal information (Hall, 1980; Reid, 1988; Torgensen & Houck, 1980). Because of these problems and barriers, they often report feeling rushed, overwhelmed, and upset when entering a classroom. It may take them several minutes to settle down, arrange their materials, and feel ready to attend. By the time they are ready, the teacher may have completed the first part of the lecture. During the lecture, these students may misperceive, misunderstand, or fail to retain information. Some may be unable to remember complex explanations, numerical information, or technical vocabulary. After class they commonly lose or misplace their notes.

Cindy, a tenth grader, has problems with attention and organization. She has above-average intelligence and some auditory processing and memory deficits. She does not meet the eligibility requirements for learning disabilities under IDEA, and although she might be eligible for accommodations under Section 504, she does not want to be "labeled." Cindy acknowledges that she often "fades out" and daydreams during class. In math, she has trouble when the teacher faces the board while explaining the problem. Her difficulties become more evident when she is fatigued, when she is required to work rapidly, or when she is unfamiliar with the vocabulary. It is especially hard for her to pay attention during history lectures. Sometimes she views lectures as rest periods rather than active learning experiences. Sometimes she is bored. She takes few notes and remembers very little of the lecture. What notes she does take are practically useless when she prepares for tests. She knows that her grades suffer because of her poor note taking, but she doesn't know what to do about it. Cindy's history teacher can provide some general listening and note-taking strategies to the whole class that can help Cindy and others take more usable notes.

Kyle, introduced in chapter 4, is also in the tenth grade. He has been diagnosed with both learning disabilities and ADD. His auditory processing problems and writing difficulties directly affect his listening and note-taking capability. He literally cannot listen and take usable notes at the same time. He doesn't know what to do with himself during lectures and sometimes acts out and gets into trouble. Kyle is enrolled in the same history class as Cindy. Kyle will need some note-taking accommodations in the history classroom as well as general and individualized strategies for listening and note taking. The special education teacher consultant provides direct services to Kyle and consultative help to the history teacher.

OVERVIEW

Note taking is a complicated process that involves using two modalities simultaneously: receptive and expressive (i.e., listening and writing). Listening is not a passive process in which the student hopes to absorb a few facts, and note taking is not simply a mechanical act of recording whatever the teacher says.

Active Listening and Note Taking

Active listening is the conscious control of the listening act; like active reading, it involves the use of learning, thinking, and self-management strategies. It involves activities such as posing questions in advance and activating attention during the lecture.

Note taking provides a permanent record of the most important information presented in a lecture. The mechanical aspects of note taking involve fine motor skills and knowledge of vocabulary and spelling, as well as an ability to write easily and quickly using words that can be read by the student. However, note taking also involves the conversion of auditory information into a cohesive written message, under time constraints. This complex process involves the use of learning and thinking strategies before, during, and after the lecture.

Listening and Note-Taking Problems

Listening and note-taking problems occur for a variety of reasons. First, listening and note taking are unstructured, one-time-only events. Students have to get it right the first time. They cannot rewind the tape or flip back a page or two in the text to rehear or reread something missed. Second, students often do not know how to distinguish essential from nonessential information, how to decide what to write down and what to omit. They are unaccustomed to attending to the verbal and nonverbal signals that indicate what is important. Finally, most students do not know that they can improve their listening and note-taking skills.

Specific problems that contribute to listening and note-taking difficulties include deficits in auditory skills, short-term memory, concentration, fine motor skills, spelling, and organizational skills. Poor auditory skills, short-term memory, and concentration affect listening and severely limit the amount and the accuracy of information that can be obtained from lectures. Poor fine motor skills and spelling severely limit the amount of information that can be written during the lecture. Poor organizational skills affect note-taking efficiency and the usability of information. Students with learning disabilities or ADD can have difficulty in any one or a combination of these problem areas.

Students with learning difficulties or ADD may be particularly vulnerable to the effects of poorly organized or semiaudible lectures and particularly sensitive to distractions like noise, the movements of others, poor temperature control, inadequate lighting, and uncomfortable seating. In addition, they may have a lack of prerequisite skills in the subject matter; illegible, slow, and laborious handwriting; or insufficient basic sight or technical vocabulary. Impaired cognitive/language skills (e.g., slow information processing, poor problem solving, or difficulty with word retrieval and usage) also exacerbate problems. Students with high energy levels or hyperactivity may have difficulty sitting still during lectures and thus disrupt their own or other students' learning. Finally, emotional factors secondary to learning difficulties, such as fatigue or stress, play a part.

Sometimes intellectually gifted students may be able to listen actively and rely on their excellent memories instead of taking notes. Although some of these students can get by without taking usable notes in middle or high school, all students who plan to go to college will have to acquire note-taking skills.

Factors Influencing Listening and Note Taking

Some factors that influence listening and note taking are controlled by the listener (the student); others are controlled by the speaker (the teacher). The factors under the student's conscious control are how much and what to write. However, these are difficult determinations for many students. Some students attempt to record every word; they may understand the lecture content at the time of presentation but recall little afterward because they were so busy writing. Other students listen carefully but write only a few random words. They may be unable to recall later what the lecture was about because their sparse notes do not trigger any memory of the content. Still others with excellent memories but poor writing skills do not take notes at all because note taking actually interferes with their learning of the material.

Students need to learn how to listen for and record key facts, concepts, and relationships so that they can recall them when rereading their notes. In addition, they must avoid spending so much time taking notes that they fail to listen carefully to the lecture. The goal is efficiency in note taking, which means recording the maximum number of ideas using the fewest words or symbols.

ROLE OF THE CLASSROOM TEACHER

Classroom teachers can directly teach listening and note-taking strategies. They can also help students improve listening and note taking by modeling effective cognitive strategies—specifically, by relating new material to information already learned, emphasizing key words or vocabulary, and making new material relevant to the students' interests and previous knowledge. For example, if the teacher introduces a technical term, he or she uses it in context, provides visuals or examples, integrates it with previously covered material, and relates it to a reading assignment.

To help students learn to record lecture information, the teacher writes an outline, key words, or one or two main idea questions that the lecture will address on the chalkboard. This helps students pose anticipatory questions, attend to key words and phrases and note their meanings, put lecture notes into a meaningful order, and integrate the notes with other course material.

The teacher also helps students become more effective note takers by modifying lecture style and by individualizing and accommodating to meet students' needs in this area.

Modifying Lecture Style

Factors under the control of the lecturer include the rate of presentation, the density of information, and the lecture environment.

Rate of presentation

A significant discrepancy usually exists between the rate at which information is presented and the rate at which students can record it. Rapid presentation impedes recall of content. When information is presented too rapidly, students have difficulty writing complete and accurate information. They do not have enough time to process the material and often end up recording more superficial, easy-to-recognize facts. The teacher takes students' note-taking capacity into account when preparing lectures; students are encouraged to ask the teacher to slow down, pause, or repeat information when necessary.

Density of information

Density refers to the number of information units presented within a given time period. The greater the density, the more difficult it is to record or recall information. The average percentage of total lecture ideas recorded by students varies across studies from 11 to 70% (Hartley & Marshall, 1974; Kiewra, 1984). Generally, students record fewer than half of all lecture ideas. This means that teachers should decrease the density of their lectures by providing frequent examples and summaries, interspersing discussion, and telling stories and anecdotes. These digressions can also serve as informal rest periods and provide punctuation between main ideas and key concepts.

Lecture environment

The lecture environment greatly influences the ease and accuracy with which students can process and record auditory information. The teacher enhances students' note-taking capacity and improves their immediate and delayed recall of information by making sure that everyone can hear the lecture and see any visual displays, asking whether anyone needs special seating, and keeping the room comfortable and free from distractions.

In addition, the teacher promotes effective listening and note taking by including verbal signals in lectures. Some signal words—such as *first, next,* and so on—show sequence. Other words—*consequently, finally,* and the like—refer to conclusions. Signals such as *similarly* and *as opposed to* denote relationships. Phrases like *it is important to note, let me repeat,* and *I want to stress* indicate importance. Students are encouraged to pay attention to such signals and take down the information that follows.

Allowing time for discussion immediately following a lecture or some portion of a lecture can also significantly aid recall. Even a few minutes at the end of a lecture can provide a valuable opportunity for students to review their notes and ask questions.

Individualizing

Students vary in their learning styles. Some are auditory learners and learn best when information is presented orally; some are visual learners and learn best when they can read or observe. Some students are global learners and learn best when information is first presented as a global concept with details and examples following; some are analytical or inductive learners and learn best when a series of examples are presented first and build to a global concept or theory. Students also vary in the speed at which they process auditory information and in the speed at which they can write.

The auditory learner should have little or no problem learning from lectures, but for the visual learner, lectures present substantial difficulty. For the student who processes auditory information or writes slowly, the pace of the lecture is critical to effective note taking. For global and analytical/inductive learners the order in which information is presented is important.

The teacher designs lectures that appeal to individual student learning styles, needs, and strengths. For visual learners, the teacher writes an outline, key words, and new vocabulary on the chalkboard and provides additional visual input through overheads, pictures, or other graphics. For students who process information or write slowly, the teacher allows time for note taking by slowing down, pausing, or giving examples to illustrate main points. For students who have problems maintaining attention, the teacher poses questions to arouse curiosity and interest or break the lecture into shorter segments. And for the student with poor organization skills, the teacher summarizes periodically or provides visual organizers such as diagrams or charts.

Providing Accommodations

The classroom teacher is responsible for making reasonable accommodations to help students with learning disabilities and ADD in all educational areas, including listening and note taking. Following are some possible classroom accommodations for students with specific note-taking problems.

Difficulties with handwriting.   The student who has good keyboarding skills takes notes using a laptop computer; uses notes written by another student; or uses commercially prepared notes, if available, circling or highlighting important information. Alternatively, the teacher provides notes or an outline of the lecture.

Problems in auditory perception.   The student uses notes taken by another student or, if the student has good visual and reading skills, uses the chapter outline as a note-taking guide. Alternatively, the teacher provides notes.

Problems with attention.   The teacher seats the student nearby, away from noise and other distractions. In addition, the teacher seats the student next to a positive role model. The teacher cues the student to remain on task and reinforces on-task behavior.

Problems in rate of learning.   The student uses an audiotape of the lecture, audits the class before officially enrolling, or attends the same lecture twice (once at the regular hour and again at another time of day).

Because Kyle is eligible for special education services, a special education teacher consultant is available to help design an appropriate educational program for him. Because of the severity of his disabilities, the teacher consultant recommends that Kyle not be required to take notes at all during lectures at this time. The history teacher will arrange for another student to take notes for Kyle, and Kyle will focus on preparing for the lecture and listening actively during it. Kyle will be kept busy during the lecture with active listening and thus will not have time to misbehave. In addition, at the beginning of each lecture, the history teacher will write several key words on the chalkboard for Kyle to copy. Kyle will be encouraged to listen for and write down the definitions of the key words used during the lecture. This will be difficult at first, but with practice and continued support from the teacher consultant and the history teacher, Kyle should be able to achieve this goal before the end of the semester.

The teacher designs some options for Cindy that will be used by other students in the history class. To reduce daydreaming, the teacher suggests that students try to predict one to three questions to answer during each lecture based on the previous lecture or the chapter outline of the assigned textbook reading. These questions are to be written down and brought to the lecture. To increase focus, the teacher will introduce more questions into the lectures. To aid organization, the teacher will provide advance organizers such as maps, graphs, or timelines to help students record lecture material in an organized fashion. Last, the teacher will stop the lecture a few minutes early so that students can ask questions and review or reorganize some portion of their notes.

Though appropriate in many cases, accommodations for note taking do have some disadvantages. Specifically, designated note takers may be untrained or unreliable, and informal arrangements may break down, often at the worst times (e.g., right before exams). Listening to audiotapes is time consuming. In addition, audiotapes are often of poor quality and batteries run down and must be replaced.

To help avoid such difficulties, note-taking accommodations should be made systematically. In collaboration with the teacher, a staff member such as a school counselor or special education teacher consultant should be responsible for developing and monitoring the note-taking system. Note takers and their alternates must be selected in advance, and the system must be modified if it is not working. The student should also receive instruction in note taking and assume increasing responsibility as he or she becomes more competent.

TEACHING LISTENING AND NOTE TAKING IN THE CONTENT AREA

Researchers have discussed the benefits of teaching note taking for secondary and postsecondary students with learning disabilities, analyzed note-taking processes, and recommended ways to teach note taking (Beirne-Smith & Deck, 1989; Peck & Hannafin, 1983; Ruhl, Hughes, & Gajar, 1990; Saski, Swicegood, & Carter, 1983; Suritsky & Hughes, 1991). Curriculum developers have also described note-taking strategies that may be incorporated and integrated in the content areas (Cook, 1991).

Teaching effective listening and note taking in content area classes should begin in middle school and continue throughout the high school years. Specifically, teachers can help students learn strategies such as previewing the topic, establishing a note-taking format, and reviewing and editing notes. The SQ4R method can also be adapted for use in note taking.

Previewing and Questioning

Students must know the topic of the lecture in advance so they can prepare to take effective notes. To help students preview lecture content, the teacher suggests strategies such as the following:

Observe how closely lectures tend to follow the textbook and decide whether a chapter outline can serve as a lecture guide.

Review the information or issues discussed in previous lectures to provide a framework for absorbing new information.

Write down and become familiar with technical terms used in assignments.

List questions to answer during the lecture. Use a variety of resources, including reading assignments, handouts, class discussions, and board work.

Record the textbook page numbers of illustrations that may be referred to during the lecture.

Apply SQ4R to each reading assignment (see chapter 8).

The teacher encourages students to pose anticipatory questions and thus become involved in and responsible for their own learning. The questioning process raises curiosity, focuses attention, and defines a purpose—all conditions for effective listening.

Establishing a Note-Taking Format

A preformatted note page makes it easier to record notes in an orderly manner. Students can use a loose-leaf notebook with file pockets so that pages can be added or removed. A vertical line drawn 2 inches from the left-hand margin divides the page; questions, key words, or main ideas can be written in the left column before, during, or after the lecture. The right-hand side of the page is used during the lecture for recording notes that answer or relate to the questions or that describe main ideas. Figure 9.1 shows a sample page from Cindy's notes in history class.

The teacher helps students to design their own shorthand and select abbreviations and symbols, as well as to select the way in which they can most clearly differentiate main ideas from details and examples (e.g., use letters and numbers to outline, indent, skip lines). One or two words rather than whole sentences should be used wherever possible to denote key words or ideas. Students should be encouraged to share these organizational aids and discuss how to use symbols and abbreviations more consistently.

As an extension of the note-taking system, students can create their own visuals or graphics to describe, list, organize, and summarize information; artistic ability is less important than skill in visually presenting information. They can then bring in copies of diagrams, charts, or timelines to illustrate concepts or sequences of events.

Editing and Reviewing

Students need to learn the importance of reviewing and editing notes: Edited notes are much more readable and usable than raw

Figure 9.1   Sample Notes from Cindy's History Class

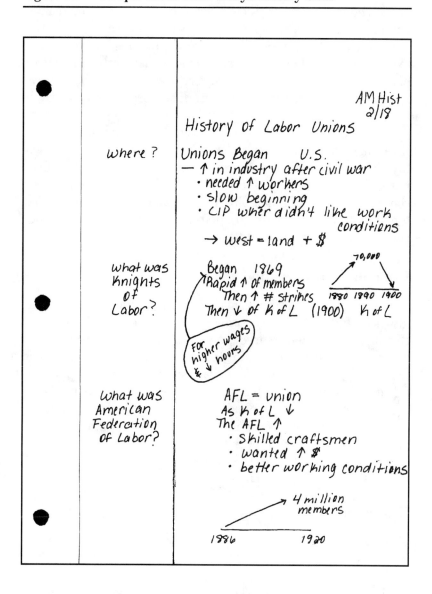

notes. The teacher helps students learn how to review, reorganize, and revise their notes by locating missing information, correcting inaccuracies, filling in details, and rewriting illegible words. The teacher may also show the class examples to demonstrate that good notes need not be very long or even very neat in order to be effective. Spelling and grammar are not a concern because notes are a private record.

Students are advised to review and edit their notes as soon as possible. They can remain seated a few minutes after the lecture to identify and correct sections that are incomplete or unclear. Immediate review is especially helpful for students with problems in memory, concentration, and penmanship. A brief review at the end of the lecture allows students to ask questions to complete their notes. They can further organize and edit their notes at home.

Using the SQ4R Method

The SQ4R method, discussed in chapter 8 in relation to reading, can also help students acquire information through lectures. When using this method, students survey, question, listen, write, recite, and review, as suggested in Figure 9.2. SQ4R enhances listening and note-taking skills and provides a framework for using new information in class discussions, on tests, and in writing assignments. Using the same skills in listening and note taking as are used in reading reinforces the learning of cognitive strategies and facilitates the integration of information from multiple sources.

THE INSTRUCTIONAL PROCESS

Setting the Stage

The teacher sets the stage by explaining that lectures and reading are both methods of gaining information and that effective note-taking skills can give a student a sense of control over lecture material. The teacher stresses that note taking is an important and complex skill that involves active listening, organization, memory, and writing. As in reading, certain strategies can greatly enhance listening and note-taking skills. The student learns to preview the lecture topic and prepare questions to guide active listening. The more prepared the student is, the easier it is to understand and remember the material.

Figure 9.2   Student Checklist for Applying SQ4R to Note Taking

SURVEY to identify main points.

_____ Identify the topic of the lecture in advance.

_____ Survey the assignment, previous lecture notes, and text material to be covered.

_____ Survey study aids such as chapter objectives, introductions, illustrations, questions, and summaries.

QUESTION to identify a purpose for listening.

_____ Ask questions based on main ideas of reading assignments or previous lectures.

_____ Write questions to address during the lecture or class discussion in the margin of a prepared note page.

_____ Write preliminary answers to the questions by using information from text material, table of contents, and/or previous lectures.

LISTEN to the lecture.

_____ Get ready to listen by facing the speaker, sitting squarely in your seat, and reminding yourself to be an active listener.

_____ Use your prepared note page or advance organizers as you listen for the answers to your questions.

_____ Try to visualize or create pictures in your mind as the lecture proceeds.

[W]RITE notes.

_____ Use key words, phrases, and abbreviations to answer questions or note new information.

_____ Write notes in your own words to improve recall of ideas and facts.

_____ Create charts, diagrams, and symbols to summarize and organize information.

RECITE the information.

_____ Repeat, paraphrase, and summarize the information in your own words.

_____ Elaborate about the main ideas and relationships between ideas, using examples.

REVIEW your notes.

_____ Reread and revise the notes to clarify and add information immediately after the lecture.

_____ Reread the notes to identify and mark the main ideas, supporting details, and examples.

_____ Refer to the text to check accuracy and completeness.

_____ Relate current to previous lectures.

_____ Highlight important information that might be used for test questions.

_____ Recite answers to questions without referring to notes.

After describing the purposes and benefits of active listening and note taking, the teacher points out that taking notes is a very individual matter:

> There is no one best way to take notes. The most important goal is for you to be able to use your notes for studying. As a class we will discuss a basic note-taking system, and then each of you will develop strategies that work best for you.

Collecting Information

Because effective note taking is so idiosyncratic, it is important for students to evaluate their own skills and develop their own strategies. Some students will need to write more information, some less; different techniques will work for different students.

Students can evaluate their own note-taking skills in two ways: The first is by reviewing their previous class notes, using a checklist like the one shown in Figure 9.3 to help them evaluate the effectiveness of their notes for learning and test preparation. The second is by evaluating their current skills by having the teacher present a one- or two-paragraph "minilecture" while students take notes (Cohen et al., 1973). The teacher then provides a list of the main ideas, facts, and examples included in the lecture. When students review their notes, they can determine the number of ideas recorded and the number of words written per minute. Students can also evaluate these notes according to the criteria on the evaluation checklist. Using the checklist, the teacher and class can then discuss note-taking strategies as related to the demands of the particular class.

Analyzing Tasks

The teacher shows the relationship of reading assignments to lectures and lecture notes to tests. The teacher says:

> Your task as note taker is to record the information covered in the lecture so it helps you identify and remember the most important topics, ideas, facts, and questions that the course addresses. Your notes are an important link between the information you read in your textbook and the information you are responsible for on tests and quizzes.

Figure 9.3   Student Checklist for Evaluating Lecture Notes

Are the notes

_____ Legible?

_____ Accurate?

_____ Complete?

_____ Organized?

Do notes include

_____ Spacing and format for additional information?

_____ Shortcuts (e.g., abbreviations, symbols)?

_____ Visuals (e.g., diagrams, sketches, charts)?

_____ Questions posed and answered?

_____ Summaries?

Setting Goals

The teacher assists students in setting goals based on the usefulness of their current notes. The students can use checklists such as Figures 9.2 and 9.3 to select personal goals.

An initial goal for Cindy was to use an advance organizer during the lecture to take notes. Kyle's initial goal was to listen for an explanation of key terms the teacher had written on the board.

Teaching and Modeling Specific Strategies

Teachers help students learn effective note-taking skills by employing direct instructional strategies that emphasize the procedural nature of note taking. As shown in Figure 9.4, the teacher provides the students with guidelines at three points: before the lecture, during the lecture, and after the lecture.

The teacher also helps students learn by modeling the entire note-taking process. A brief lecture is audiotaped and used as the basis for discussion. Before playing the audiotape, the teacher prepares the students by saying:

Listen as I describe my preparation for note taking.
Notice how I respond to verbal cues such as "the main

Figure 9.4   Student Checklist for Managing the Listening and Note-Taking Process

Before the Lecture: Plan and Prepare

____ Review previous lectures.

____ Read the assignment, using the SQ4R process.

____ Write questions that you expect to answer during the lecture in the margin or on sticky notes.

____ Gather necessary supplies or materials (paper, pencils, illustrations, etc.).

____ Establish note-taking format.

During the Lecture: Record

____ Arrive on time or a few minutes early.

____ Sit facing the teacher so that you can see and hear without straining.

____ Ask to sit where you will be the least distracted.

____ Tell yourself to listen for the answers to questions.

____ Write information in key words and short phrases.

____ Emphasize important points by printing, circling, or underlining them with a highlighter pen. Leave enough space to add notes.

____ Listen for signal words and phrases (e.g., "The main reasons . . .").

____ Use abbreviations, diagrams, and symbols.

____ Use your textbook chapter or table of contents as an aid.

After the Lecture: Edit, Organize, and Learn

Edit

____ Correct and/or rewrite inaccurate, incomplete, or illegible notes.

____ Define new terms.

____ Integrate information from lecture notes with information from texts.

Organize

____ Create charts and/or diagrams.

____ Write a summary of the main points.

Learn

____ Use SQ4R with lecture notes and ask and answer questions.

____ Create short answer and essay questions.

____ Take self-quizzes.

____ Check answers and review, if necessary.

____ Decide if you need teacher help.

reasons," "the primary aspect," or "three important trends." Watch as I convert these organizational statements into questions. Note how I try to consolidate the answers to these questions into short phrases and key words. I'm not just a transcriber; I am the boss. I can use abbreviations, diagrams, and symbols to explain, illustrate, and record information. Watch how I label portions of the lecture. If the lecturer says, "for example," then I write "EX" in large letters in the margin. Watch how I remind myself to edit or improve notes after class.

The teacher then shows how to take effective notes as the students listen to the audiotaped lecture.

The following tips will also help students better organize and record their notes:

Label portions of the lecture according to the teacher's remarks. If the teacher says, "first," then write "#1" in large print in the margin.

Use arrows to relate one idea to another.

Use numbers to place ideas in sequence.

Use large question marks where you will need to insert information after the lecture.

In the margins, write instructions or reminders for editing or improving notes after class.

If you lose track of the information, stop for a moment. Take a breather, skip a few lines, and go on to the next topic.

The teacher encourages students to use an evaluation checklist like the one shown in Figure 9.3 to improve their editing and review of lecture notes. Students can also work in groups to review and edit notes and take practice quizzes based on their notes.

Providing Guided Practice, Feedback, and Reinforcement

Most class members, especially those with learning difficulties, will need additional practice in active listening and note taking. Following class instruction in note taking, Cindy reported, "This stuff sounds good, but I can't do all that at once. I spend all my energy just listening. I can't seem to organize my notes." Cindy's history teacher assured her that other students have similar problems, explaining that it is useful to question and organize *before* the lecture, use organizational aids to ensure listening readiness and effectiveness, then practice newly learned skills. Kyle's special education teacher consultant provided him with more intensive practice with course lecture material in the resource room.

The teacher provides guided practice by giving students the opportunity to hone their note-taking skills during additional minilectures. He or she can also integrate opportunities to practice new skills into planned lectures by asking students to predict what questions will be covered in a lecture. During the lecture, students raise their hands when they hear the answer to a question they have predicted. After the lecture, they can practice such skills as reviewing and editing notes and filling in missing information.

Quiz and test scores can give students helpful feedback on how well their note-taking strategies are working. Students ask themselves whether their notes were detailed enough and included the right information, making adjustments if necessary. The teacher also helps students with this process by providing models of effective notes for particular lectures.

Finally, the teacher systematically reinforces these and other note-taking behaviors, as well as more subtle indications that students' skills are improving—for example, alertness, preparation, and the use of lecture information during class discussion. To provide reinforcement, the teacher integrates positive comments during lectures. The teacher also asks students how they are progressing with their note-taking efforts, empathizing with the difficulty of learning a new task. Perhaps the strongest form of reinforcement is the satisfaction students feel when their note-taking strategies enable them to answer test or quiz questions based on lecture material.

Monitoring Progress and Adjusting Activities

Observation and informal monitoring let the teacher know which note-taking activities to continue, change, add, or discontinue. One good way for the teacher to monitor class progress is to present questions based on the lecture on every quiz or test, as well as in every class discussion. The teacher observes the students' use of lecture information in their responses to these questions. Periodically, the teacher allows a few minutes of class time for student self-assessment.

ENCOURAGING SELF-MANAGEMENT

The teacher exerts much less control over listening and note taking than over other learning activities. The goal of teaching note taking is for each student to design a personalized system for recording auditory information in a form that is usable by that student. No one system is best (Saski et al., 1983); any strategy is better than none. Self-management forms the basis for effective listening and note-taking strategies.

In addition to designing a note-taking system, the student must be encouraged to plan conditions for effective listening and note taking. The teacher discusses with the class possible seating arrangements to improve listening and minimize distractions. Some teachers allow students to choose their own seats, at least temporarily.

Students with learning difficulties can be encouraged to arrive early so they can settle down and arrange their materials. They will also find it helpful to sit where they can maintain eye contact with the teacher. Watching the teacher's delivery and noting gestures and shifts in pace or volume that emphasize important points can improve their comprehension. In addition, sitting close to the teacher can reduce daydreaming, talking to classmates, and being distracted by open windows or doorways.

SUMMARY AND CONCLUSIONS

Listening and note taking are important skills that are often neglected by classroom teachers, who may assume that students will acquire these skills more or less naturally as they progress through school. Most students think that listening and note taking are mechanical processes rather than active thinking processes. They often underestimate the importance of these processes to the understanding of course material and to course grades.

Effective listening and note taking require planning before, during, and after a lecture. Students can improve their listening and note-taking skills if they prepare for lectures by asking questions in advance and answering them during the lecture. Extending SQ4R to the note-taking process can also enhance listening and note-taking skills.

Classroom teachers can help students improve their note-taking skills by teaching and modeling ways to prepare for, organize, record, edit, and review lecture notes. Special education teacher consultants can help classroom teachers individualize and provide additional guided practice for eligible students.

10

Preparing for and Taking Tests

Brandon is a bright ninth-grade student who is earning a C average. He continually reports problems with concentration and has difficulty attending to details. He has particular problems with tests. Brandon feels that he knows the material but cannot seem to do well on tests. Brandon's older sister has been diagnosed as having a learning disability and a subtle attention problem. When Brandon was given a diagnostic assessment, he did not meet the eligibility requirements for special education services, although his scores in some areas were low. The diagnostician noted problems with attention, distractibility, and impulsivity. Brandon's parents are currently pursuing Brandon's eligibility for regular education accommodations under Section 504.

Brandon worries about tests in general but says objective questions in his science courses are "the worst." He is afraid that he will do poorly on college entrance exams and that he will not be able to get into college due to his low grades. He worries because he knows that his courses and the tests in them are getting more difficult. Because he feels very insecure, he frequently changes correct answers into incorrect responses on multiple choice tests. The harder he tries, the lower his scores.

Kim, a senior at a highly competitive high school, experiences problems with essay tests. She found out about her learning disabilities during tenth grade. Like many students with learning disabilities, Kim has a history of failure. She is very concerned about her difficulties, sometimes blaming herself and feeling helpless. The diagnostic report indicates that Kim's scores on an intelligence test are slightly above average. She has difficulties in organization and in "seeing the big picture." Her reading rate is slow (in the 20th percentile), but her reading comprehension is at the 65th percentile. According to the report, "Reading speed and other information-processing speeds represent an area of significant difficulty for Kim. This is exacerbated under the pressures of time-limited testing."

Kim has difficulty preparing for and taking tests in her introductory psychology class. The reading assignments are long, and the essay tests are difficult. She reports feeling overwhelmed and makes statements such as "I don't know where to start studying. I never finish the reading or do well on essay examinations. I've begun having headaches the night before I have to take an essay exam."

It is important for students like Brandon and Kim to improve their test-taking skills for a number of reasons: First, tests are unavoidable. They are the primary measure of students' knowledge throughout their academic careers. Second, even though tests may not always be fair or valid measures of students' knowledge or skills, test results influence academic and career goals. Finally, tests are often the gateway to high school graduation or state-endorsed diplomas, to scholarships and financial support in postsecondary education, and to appointments and promotions in the workplace.

Test taking is an important but often neglected area of direct instruction. It is not invariably true that if students know the material, they will be able to demonstrate their knowledge on paper-and-pencil tests. Test taking requires the student to coordinate multiple skills under the pressure of time. This is a difficult process for all students and one that is especially difficult for students with learning and attention problems. Such students have particular problems preparing for and taking tests and, accordingly, get poor grades. They may know the course content and be able to apply it but have poor test-taking skills as a result of problems with reading comprehension, memory, time management, or test anxiety. They are often able to demonstrate their knowledge in other ways, but not within the constraints of the testing situation.

OVERVIEW

General Issues in Testing

A primary purpose of testing is to enhance student learning. By measuring student knowledge and skills, teachers can determine what and how to teach and adjust instruction accordingly. Tests can also challenge students to use, apply, or extend their knowledge and skills.

Secondary uses of testing include assigning grades to students or, in the case of standardized tests, comparing the performance of students, classes, and schools to state and national standards. It is in these contexts that testing often gets a bad name. In these instances, the outcome of testing is often unnecessary competition, failure, and exclusion.

Currently, testing and assessment are undergoing increased scrutiny in the fields of psychology and education (Archbald & Newman, 1988; Herman, 1992; Malnar, 1993). The validity of paper-and-pencil testing in assessing student knowledge and skills—especially higher order skills—is being questioned. There is general agreement that paper-and-pencil tests should not be the only method of assessing student learning but that assessment should also include alternatives such as portfolios, projects, products, and other measures of performance (American Psychological Association and Presidential Task Force on Psychology in Education, 1993). As discussed in chapter 5, alternative assessment methods are particularly helpful for students with learning difficulties. Alternative assessment allows such students to bypass their weaknesses and use their strengths to demonstrate knowledge and skills (Fuchs, 1994). It can also enhance their interest and motivation.

Paper-and-pencil tests are themselves undergoing closer scrutiny. Educators and psychologists suggest that these types of tests should focus on higher level skills rather than rote memory and that they should allow for creative expression and permit a range of plausible answers rather than prescribe specific "correct" responses.

The question of time constraints on tests is also being raised by educators and test designers. Many students have difficulty with timed tests. Although these students may know the material, they often need more time for thinking, for organizing or calculating, and for writing answers. The pressure to perform in a short time can cause such students to fail, even if they do know the material. Limiting the amount of time on a test may not result in a valid assessment of student skills, especially higher level skills. Although giving students unlimited time on tests may not be feasible, tests that can be completed and checked by most of the students in the class may be more effective.

Teachers will need to create tests that are helpful for making instructional decisions, measuring student knowledge and skills, and/or determining course grades. In addition, they must examine the commercially prepared tests that accompany their textbooks and ask whether these tests focus on higher level skills, allow for creativity and alternative answers, and serve the educational process.

Types of Tests and Test Questions

Standardized tests include statewide competency tests, standardized achievement tests, advanced placement tests, and college admissions tests. These tests, standardized on large samples of the school population in the United States, often include multiple-choice questions. These tests have always required some conceptual understanding, application, and analysis. Increasingly, they require that students possess high-level reading comprehension skills in the content area, the ability to manipulate information, and skills in problem solving. All of these skills are most effectively taught in the content area classroom.

Classroom tests are designed to show the extent of student learning, to identify strong and weak areas, and to document the degree of mastery. Classroom tests are usually designed by individual teachers and include combinations of objective, word problem, short answer, and essay questions. Unfortunately, in the interests of expediency, some teachers rely solely on commercially prepared textbooks and related tests. Such materials tend to neglect higher order learning and creativity.

Objective questions vary in form, including true/false, multiple choice, matching, and fill-in-the-blank. Frequently, such test items require only recognition or recall of correct answers to questions such as Who? What? Where? and When? Students with learning or attention problems can find objective questions problematic if their reading skills are weak or they are distractible. These students may have difficulty with multiple-choice questions because several choices often appear similar, but only one answer is considered correct.

Word problems are used largely in science and math tests. To answer a word problem, students first need to be able to read and understand the question. They must often apply technical vocabulary, rules, and formulas. To score well on tests using word problems, students are required to understand a concept, apply rules and concepts to solve problems, and check calculations. This type of question tends to pose problems because it requires sustained attention and a variety of reading, cognitive, and learning skills, thus making it more difficult to compensate for weaknesses.

Short-answer questions require the student to supply an answer or solution to a problem or to provide a written statement. Written statements typically include a main idea and/or fact or example in one or more sentences. This type of question is commonly found on tests in history and English.

Essay questions allow students a great deal of freedom in responding; they also require students to use higher level thinking (e.g., explain, trace, compare and contrast, analyze, summarize, evaluate). In middle school, students usually are required to write one or two paragraphs to answer an essay question. By high school or college, they may be required to compose one or two pages. In answering an essay question, students must write, organize, and revise their work so that the answer is legible, logical, and easy to understand.

In each course, teachers help students by examining and classifying the types of test questions (e.g., short answer, objective, essay, etc.). Teachers can then design test-taking strategies in light of the different cognitive and metacognitive skills required by each type of question.

Test questions can also be examined and classified according to Bloom's (1956) system of classifying objectives in the cognitive domain (see Figure 8.2). For example, true/false, matching, and multiple-choice questions require recognition and recall of facts, whereas short answer and essay questions more often require analysis, synthesis, application, and evaluation without many clues to trigger recall of information.

Test-Taking Problems

Many students, both with and without learning problems, have poor test preparation and test-taking skills. Some students who do poorly on tests simply don't understand the material covered and require more practice and explanation to learn it. Others may know the material but not know how to prepare for or demonstrate their knowledge on tests. Still other students who know the material may fail because they have poor reading or writing skills; as a result, they may have difficulty understanding test directions and questions, remembering and organizing information, and/or writing responses. Some students have good reading comprehension but a slow reading rate, which makes it difficult for them to complete tests in the time allotted. Many of these students have specific learning disabilities.

Students with ADD often have difficulty maintaining their attention during tests, and although they, too, may know the subject matter, they can lose points by simply omitting answers. Because of their impulsivity, these students may have problems with multiple-choice tests because they tend to select the first answer that seems right rather than evaluating each answer to find the best one.

Some students have test anxiety. When confronted with a test, their negative experiences with testing and resulting low self-confidence cause them to forget everything they learned. Given the history of failure often shared by students with learning difficulties, it is not surprising that they experience test anxiety. Frequently, such students do not discuss their anxiety but demonstrate it in a variety of other ways: avoidance (e.g., absence, tardiness, procrastination), direct action (e.g., crying, refusing, leaving), physical complaints (e.g., headaches, nausea), or lack of attention (e.g., staring, fidgeting). Ignoring such problems does not usually help them go away.

ROLE OF THE CLASSROOM TEACHER

Teaching students how to prepare for and take tests, as well as to analyze test results in terms of cognitive strategies, is an integral part of the instructional process. As the content area expert, it is the classroom teacher's responsibility to teach test preparation and test-taking skills as such skills relate to the specific area of instruction. Direct instruction can help all students, including students like Kim and Brandon, improve their test-taking skills (Markel, 1981a).

In addition to teaching specific strategies to meet the requirements of the various types of questions in each course, the classroom teacher helps students by providing a positive test-taking climate, individualizing, and providing accommodations for eligible students.

Creating a Positive Test-Taking Climate

Tests, by their very nature, are stressful, especially if they are viewed as measures of one's worth, critical for achieving a particular grade, or the gateway to a higher or more desirable level. Students with a history of doing poorly generally view tests as a method of collecting concrete evidence of their stupidity or failure. The teacher can remove some of the stress of test taking by providing a positive test-taking environment.

First of all, the teacher can help students develop a more positive feeling about tests by encouraging them to view tests as an opportunity to demonstrate what they know about a particular topic rather than as a competition for grades. For students to do well on tests, they need to feel they have a chance to succeed. The goal is to encourage students to consider tests an interesting challenge—a way of finding out more about themselves, increasing their knowledge of the subject matter, and demonstrating a personal best at any one period of time.

In order to modify negative attitudes toward testing, the teacher must remember that the real purpose of testing is to enhance student learning and must consider using alternate assessment techniques. They will also need to examine their own grading practices. Grading on a curve, which ensures that only a few students can get high marks, is not the most effective method of measuring individual student achievement, nor does it increase positive attitudes toward tests (Wood, 1992). An effective grading system reinforces correct answers instead of highlighting incorrect answers and gives partial credit for partial answers or for demonstrating good test-taking strategies.

Another way of making tests less aversive is to increase student motivation and interest. This can be done by using real-life situations in designing test questions and by making questions relevant to student interests. Humor can relieve stress and increase motivation during tests. In addition, the teacher can encourage students to contribute their own test questions and correct their own quizzes.

The teacher can make the testing environment itself more friendly by taking into account such things as lighting, distractions and noise, and room temperature. Students can also be encouraged to decrease stress by visualizing, relaxing, and stretching before and at intervals during a test.

Individualizing

The teacher considers individual needs in teaching test-taking skills, as well as in creating tests. Awareness of common test-taking problems, such as slow reading speed and difficulties with concentration, can help the teacher include specific strategies for overcoming these difficulties. A frequent comment of students is that they need more time to think.

The teacher designs test questions that take into account student interests and learning styles, making sure that every student has a few questions that are particularly relevant. Higher order questions and those that tap into creativity can allow students to individualize answers. Shortening test length so that all students have enough time to finish decreases stress and allows students greater opportunity to demonstrate what they know. Alternative assessment methods likewise tap into individual strengths and allow students to bypass weaknesses.

The teacher also individualizes the testing process by working with students to develop a personalized test-taking strategy for test preparation and for the actual test-taking event, as discussed later in this chapter.

Providing Accommodations

Under both IDEA and Section 504, it is the classroom teacher's responsibility to make reasonable accommodations for students with learning disabilities and/or ADD. These accommodations are usually delineated in the IEP or 504 plan. The teacher will need to read these plans, as well as the diagnostic reports included with the plans, in order to understand the needs of the student and the types of accommodations recommended. The special education teacher consultant can provide additional help for eligible students.

A variety of test-taking accommodations are considered reasonable and are currently in use in middle and high schools and at the postsecondary level (King & Jarrow, 1990). These include increasing the time allowed, providing a separate nondistracting environment, having a special education teacher consultant read the test to the student, allowing the student to answer orally, allowing the student to demonstrate competency in alternate ways (e.g., projects and portfolios), and allowing the student to use a word processor or calculator during the test.

TEACHING TEST PREPARATION AND TEST-TAKING STRATEGIES IN THE CONTENT AREA

As for reading (chapter 8) and listening and note taking (chapter 9), strategies for test taking can be taught and demonstrated in the classroom. Students who learn such strategies are more able to communicate and demonstrate the knowledge they possess. In general, students apply SQ4R and other cognitive strategies to the test-taking process, as well as using strategies to enhance memory and promote time management.

Using the SQ4R Method

The SQ4R method, discussed in detail in chapter 8 as it relates to reading, can be adapted to help students prepare for tests. When used for test preparation, SQ4R helps students integrate information from both reading and lectures. Briefly, students survey, question, read and reflect, recite, write, and review and edit. Figure 10.1 shows how these steps can be applied to the test-taking situation. Coupling the SQ4R method with test-taking strategies to use during the actual test can enhance student learning and improve test scores.

One of the more difficult steps for students in using SQ4R to prepare for tests is predicting test questions. Predicting test questions can help students learn how to differentiate between important and unimportant information, learn how tests are constructed and how to study for them, and feel a sense of control over the test-taking situation. When students are first faced with the task of predicting test questions, they often say, "That's impossible!" However, they do agree that it would be great to know the test questions in advance so they could zero in on what to study for the test.

The teacher points out that there are many clues students can use to predict test questions. Headings, subheadings, graphs, and charts are clues to important information in textbooks. Signal words point to important information in lectures. Questions at the end of textbook chapters can be clues to test questions, as can questions from previous tests. The amount of time a teacher spends on a topic in class can be used as evidence of its possible inclusion on tests.

Students begin by surveying all sources of information—textbooks, lecture notes, assignments, class discussion notes. They then predict both objective and essay questions, emphasizing high-level questions. (Students can also be encouraged to "play teacher" and create questions that they are particularly interested in.) After predicting questions, students try to answer them, seeking additional information as needed. When the test is over, the teacher and students discuss how well the students predicted the test questions. The teacher goes over the clues to important information and discusses how decisions are made about what questions to include on a test.

Figure 10.1   Student Checklist for Applying SQ4R When Preparing for and Taking Tests

SURVEY to identify topics to be covered on the test.

_____ Survey the test assignment, previous homework assignments, and previous lecture and/or text notes.

_____ Survey the text's study aids (e.g., table of contents, chapter objectives, introductions, summaries, glossary, illustrations).

_____ Make a list of the most important topics and key technical terms.

_____ Identify topics that are most and least familiar to you.

QUESTION to focus attention and arouse curiosity.

_____ Locate sample questions or problems that could be included on the test. These may be at the end of a text chapter or from lectures, class discussions, or review sessions.

_____ Create possible test questions by using lecture notes or headings from readings.

_____ Create different types of questions for each topic. Include How? Why? and What difference does it make?

READ AND REFLECT to understand the information related to your questions.

_____ Use your prepared questions to guide your reading and thinking.

_____ Attempt to answer the questions.

_____ Ask the teacher about possible topics and types of questions and locate portions of information to confirm or add to your answer.

_____ Reread portions of the text and lecture notes, circling or highlighting key concepts and facts that answer your questions.

_____ Sort out essential from nonessential facts, details, or examples.

_____ Visualize the information, explaining to yourself particular aspects of your mental picture that answer your questions.

RECITE the answers to your questions.

_____ Talk to yourself by restating or reexplaining answers to questions, relationships between topics, or steps to solve problems.

_____ Allow time to elaborate on the answers, including several facts and/or examples.

_____ Say the answers to the questions in your own words, without reference to your notes.

_____ Add details or examples.

[W]RITE answers to your questions.

_____ Write the answers in your own words.

_____ Use key words, phrases, symbols, abbreviations, or sketches.

_____ Organize the information and relate information from different sources or topics.

_____ Create a "miniquiz" and practice by taking an old test.

REVIEW AND EDIT your answers as soon as possible.

_____ Review your questions and answers.

_____ Check the accuracy and completeness of your answers.

_____ Reread, recite, redraw, or rewrite answers so the information is used in an organized and efficient way.

_____ List additional details and examples.

_____ Identify topics that need further explanation. Raise questions: How? Why? So what?

_____ Identify topics or sections to review or relearn.

Using Checklists

In addition to the checklist shown in Figure 10.1, based on SQ4R, other checklists can be devised to help students improve performance on objective tests (Figure 10.2) and essay tests (Figure 10.3), deal with test anxiety (Figure 10.4), and review test results (Figure 10.5). In class, the teacher introduces one section of a checklist at a time. After class, the teacher advises students with particular problems to spend additional time on one or more sections. The extent, frequency, and order of the instruction depends on the students' individual strengths and weaknesses and their perceived needs at the time.

Using Pretests

The results of pretests given before the actual test can give students concrete evidence of what they know or don't know before beginning to study. The teacher can design pretests for the class, or more mature students can design pretests for themselves from material at the end of textbook chapters or from the notes taken during reading and lectures.

Figure 10.2   Student Checklist for Taking Objective Tests

Review the list of steps. Star those that you intend to use. Check off each one as you complete it.

Before answering the questions

_____ Write your name on the test and/or answer sheet.

_____ Practice visualization and self-encouragement strategies ("I see myself feeling calm and relaxed as I take the test" or "I prepared well for this test and am ready to do my best").

_____ Circle key words in the test directions.

_____ Review the point system.

_____ Write or circle the number of points next to each question or test section.

_____ Preview the entire test to identify the different types of questions.

_____ Decide the order in which you will answer different test sections.

_____ Write down the time the test begins, the time the test ends, and the amount of time you will allot to each question or section.

_____ Decide whether or not to guess. (Guess if there is no penalty for guessing and if guessing does not take time away from answering questions you are sure about.)

While answering the questions

_____ Ask the teacher for help if you do not understand directions for a particular question.

_____ Answer the easy questions first.

_____ Skip the questions you don't know or are unsure about.

_____ Use a symbol (e.g., stars or question marks) to indicate the degree of difficulty of the questions you skip.

_____ After completing questions you know, go back and work on questions at the next level of difficulty.

_____ When answering questions you are unsure about, cross out those alternatives you know are wrong and make an educated guess from among the other answers.

_____ Be sure to answer those sections or questions that have the most points.

_____ Check periodically to see how much time you have left.

_____ Use self management skills to keep yourself on task.

_____ Don't rush. Stop to give yourself time to think.

_____ Check your work carefully. Do not change an answer unless you remember a fact that provides a reason for the change.

Figure 10.3   Student Checklist for Taking Essay Tests

Review the steps for taking objective tests (See Figure 10.2) and the list of steps here. Star those that you intend to use. Check off each one as you complete it.

Before answering an essay question

____ Read each essay question aloud.

____ Circle the key words in the question (e.g., *list, explain, trace, contrast*).

____ Restate the main question (and any subquestions) in your own words.

____ Ask yourself, What does this question ask me to do?

____ List key words to answer the question.

____ Sketch a diagram or timeline or write an outline of the essay.

____ Organize your key words on a chart, timeline, or diagram.

While answering an essay question

____ First provide minimal information to answer the main question and any subquestions.

____ Then add the following: supporting statements, examples, additional facts, inferences, conclusions.

____ Write an introduction and a conclusion or summary.

____ If appropriate, insert headings and subheadings as you would in lecture notes or a term paper.

____ When in doubt, qualify your answer (e.g., "The beginning of the 20th century" instead of a specific date).

____ If time permits, elaborate.

____ Write or print legibly.

____ Write an outline or list important points if time runs out.

After answering the question

____ Review the essay to check sequence and/or accuracy.

____ Include additional information if necessary.

____ Correct spelling or grammar.

____ Rewrite any words that are illegible.

Figure 10.4   Student Checklist for Managing Test-Related Stress and Anxiety

Review the list of steps. Star those that you intend to use. Check off each one as you complete it.

Before entering the room

_____ Arrive a few minutes early. Avoid feeling rushed.

_____ Check that accommodations you requested are available.

_____ Check that you have necessary materials or equipment.

_____ Avoid anxiety-provoking talk with others (e.g., "How much did you study?").

Before beginning the test

_____ Avoid anxiety-provoking self-talk (e.g., "I know I'll fail").

_____ Think positive thoughts (e.g., "I know how to keep myself on track").

_____ Establish a warm-up routine. Shift your focus from your tension to reading the directions aloud or writing helpful hints to yourself.

_____ Become aware of your feelings (e.g., "I'm feeling tense—this is a good time to stretch").

_____ Create positive images (e.g., "I can see myself working efficiently").

_____ Rehearse visually (e.g., "I can see myself walk in, arrange materials, take a deep breath, and begin to work").

_____ Breathe deeply and relax muscles.

During the test

_____ Think positive thoughts (e.g., "I'm using my test-taking strategies").

_____ Be prepared to confront problems (e.g., "If I come to questions that I can't answer, I'll skip them and do the ones I can").

_____ Create positive images (e.g., "I can see myself working steadily and staying calm").

_____ Use visual imagery (e.g., "I can see several possible solutions to this").

_____ Relax. Flex and stretch some muscles a few times during the test.

Figure 10.5 Student Checklist for Reviewing Test Results

Review the list of steps. Star those that you intend to use. Check off each one as you complete it.

Review

_____ First check that the test has been scored accurately.

_____ Identify any pattern of correct responses.

_____ Identify any pattern of incorrect responses.

_____ Indicate questions that you did and did not predict.

_____ Discuss the results with the teacher and get feedback.

_____ Identify test-taking skills that need improvement.

_____ List the content areas in which you were weak.

_____ List effective study techniques you employed.

Plan for the next test

_____ Discuss the test with classmates and schedule future study groups.

_____ Set goals for the next test.

_____ Project a study schedule and activities for the next test based on the results of this test.

Recognize accomplishments

_____ List the positive aspects of your test performance.

_____ Congratulate yourself for the positive aspects of your performance.

_____ Share your accomplishments or thoughts with another person.

_____ Reward yourself with rest, relaxation, and recreation.

A pretest enables students and/or the teacher to pinpoint areas that require only a quick review and those that require intense study. If the student discovers that he or she does not understand some basic concepts in a course, the student is then able to request supplemental instruction from the teacher or arrange for a tutor. Often, however, students are surprised at the amount of knowledge they already possess.

Enhancing Memory

It is often necessary for students to memorize information such as names, dates, formulas, and vocabulary. The teacher suggests strategies that involve using the information in some way in order to help students learn and retain new information. For example:

Writing and/or reciting new material, organizing it, and/or applying it

Connecting new information to something already known

Drawing pictures or diagrams or developing checklists

Visualizing a book, a page, or a diagram

Using rhyme and/or rhythm while reciting information

Using acronyms and other mnemonic devices (Cook, 1991; Deshler et al., 1984)

Students should be cautioned that it is difficult to memorize more than a little bit each day (e.g., more than three spelling words at a time).

Promoting Time Management

One of the most difficult aspects of test taking is time management. Students constantly complain that they run out of time during tests, feel rushed, and don't have time to think. Students also have difficulty planning study time effectively; they tend to leave studying for tests to the last moment and underestimate the amount of time needed to study for tests. Both of these difficulties with time management can have serious consequences for test results.

The classroom teacher introduces time management as a cognitive skill to use when preparing for and taking tests. A teacher-designed schedule for test preparation can free students from feeling rushed and allow adequate time for test preparation. Such activities are done at the beginning of the semester. The teacher provides various checklists to help students remember test-taking strategies or encourages them to design their own checklists and schedules of study activities in order to prepare for tests.

Time management strategies also enable students to allocate their time efficiently during the test so they can answer more questions. The teacher helps students develop a personalized strategy for taking tests based on individual strengths and weaknesses, the topics covered by the test, the types of questions asked, and the number of points per question. When using such a strategy, students do not answer the questions in the order presented; rather, they answer the questions in the order dictated by their personal strategy, most often with the easiest and most important questions being answered first.

The teacher begins by telling the students to survey the entire test before answering any question in order to understand what is required in each section and to determine how many points each section or question is worth. The student is told to write down the number of points next to each section. The student is further instructed to write down the time the test began and the time the test will end. To help students manage time during the test, the teacher writes the time on the chalkboard at 10- or 15-minute intervals during the test.

THE INSTRUCTIONAL PROCESS

Setting the Stage

The teacher sets the stage by explaining the general nature of tests and by providing a new perspective on test taking. The teacher says, for example:

> All tests require you to show what you know. Your job is to provide enough information in your answers to show that you understand and can apply the major concepts of the course. On objective tests you pick out the best answer, and on essay tests you write the answer. You need to prepare for both types of exams. In test preparation, you use many of the same planning, organizing, and thinking skills you use when you read assignments and take notes. The task is the same in that you ask and answer questions. The task

is different in that you must perform under time constraints and often in distracting and difficult conditions.

There are important differences between test questions in each subject area. For example, answering multiple-choice questions in biology is not the same as answering fill-in-the-blank questions for Spanish vocabulary, answering true/false questions about novels, completing story problems in math, or matching items using maps, names, and dates in history or geography.

The teacher tells students that the first tests taken during a semester can be considered learning experiences. Students are learning about their test-taking skills and about what the teacher considers important. This information helps students do better on the next tests. In each course, it takes a while for students to understand and practice the skills necessary to perform with speed and accuracy:

The more you practice test-taking skills, the more you will improve. If you don't do well on one test, you will have other opportunities to improve. Even college admissions tests provide several opportunities for you to practice and improve your test performance. For example, the PSAT is a preliminary test, a practice, given a year before the SAT.

All students can benefit from this type of explanation. Gaining a new perspective on test taking is a way to shift gears from being underprepared and overwhelmed to being task oriented and ready for action.

Because many students have a history of failure and feel helpless, the teacher identifies this common problem for the class by saying, "The focus of your attention needs to shift from what you can't do to what you can do and what you need to do to meet the requirements of the test." The teacher goes on to say that during the year each student can improve test performance by learning certain step-by-step strategies.

Collecting Information

The teacher reviews the results of prior tests to ascertain the types of questions or particular content areas in which students need more instruction or practice. The teacher collects information about test taking as a basis for setting instructional objectives and integrating the teaching of test preparation and test-taking strategies with course content.

Students usually can verbalize or use self-checklists to provide their views about tests in general and their study or test-taking skills in the particular content area (Weinstein, Schulte, & Palmer, 1987). Class or small-group discussion is another important way to obtain information, as well as to get students involved and motivated.

Analyzing Tasks

The teacher helps students with learning or attention problems improve their performance on classroom tests by analyzing ways in which test requirements relate to student performance. This means considering how the test format, topics covered, types of questions, time limits, and conditions surrounding test administration interact with individual students' learning strengths and weaknesses. Sometimes seemingly small adjustments, based on this kind of analysis, can yield a significant improvement in student performance.

Error analysis

Early in the semester the teacher involves the class in an error analysis using the students' previous classroom tests. The teacher identifies errors, cites examples, and distinguishes errors from each other. Analyzing the results of past tests increases students' chances of improving their grades on future tests. Specifically, the teacher does and says as follows.

Reviews correct answers:

The class demonstrated three areas of strength. These items show most students understand many of the basic concepts and remember facts. Now, look at the questions at the beginning of the test. Most of the answers are correct. These items demonstrate how well students can do at the beginning of a test when they are refreshed and not pressured for time.

Examines incorrect answers:

Now let's examine those items answered incorrectly. Although these are questions that most of you knew,

many of you circled the wrong answer. That may be due
to answering without thinking. You need to read through
all of the choices. Look at your tests. Are there any
questions you answered incorrectly, although you knew
the answers? Let's try to figure out why this happens.

Now look at the last question. Many of you got it wrong.
This information was in the last lecture. How many of you
reviewed your lecture notes when you prepared for the test?

Provides further analysis:

Look at the end of the test. Some students ran out of time.
Sometimes students omit or never reach questions they
know the answers to because they are spending so much
time on questions they are unsure of. The result is that,
although they know the information, they earn no points.

Sums up:

Let's count the number of points you would have earned
if you had enough time to finish the test. Efficient test
takers need time to check the accuracy of their answers.
What would have happened to your score if you had
taken a few minutes to review and check your answers?

Shows the benefits of test-taking skills:

In each of these circumstances, students lost points
unnecessarily. Some general test-taking strategies will help
you avoid losing points, and some special strategies based
on your unique profile will help you earn more points.

Analyzing types of test questions

The teacher helps students analyze the tasks presented by tests
by reviewing class tests, sample statewide tests, or sample college
admissions tests. Using these tests as examples, the teacher describes
types of test questions (e.g., short answer, objective, essay), the skill
requirements of each type of test question, and the structure of
answers. The teacher emphasizes the importance of understanding
and following test directions by circling the key words in the directions to each test section and asking students to paraphrase them.

Students can benefit especially from identifying the various aspects of complicated questions on objective tests. Often students are surprised at the number of decisions involved when they answer some objective questions. For example, depending on the subject, students may be required to respond to a combination of print stimuli: symbols, words, sentences, paragraphs, pictures, maps, diagrams, charts, tables, and so forth.

Students may need to respond in writing, and they may be required to use skills such as listening accurately, remembering directions, or following a sequence of steps. In addition to using visual, auditory, and memory skills, students need to sustain attention, screen out distractions, organize information, and problem solve. In addition, the student response rate for objective questions needs to be faster than for essay questions.

Objective tests.   The vocabulary used in objective tests can be a stumbling block for some students. It is often much more precise than the vocabulary used in essay questions. In objective tests, students must also be aware that there may be only subtle differences among the alternatives from which to select. They must make multiple discriminations in a short period of time. The teacher explains that objective tests may look simple but require a lot of thinking.

Essay tests.   The teacher describes the most common types of essay questions—in other words, those that require students to describe, trace, compare and contrast, or show cause and effect. In addition to describing main ideas and facts, students are expected to provide examples, draw inferences and conclusions, and, in some cases, express opinions.

The teacher can explain the demands of the essay exam by showing how a sample exam was completed. First, the teacher and the class analyze the essay question to decide what information is required. They divide the main question into several subquestions to be answered in the essay. The teacher points out the format that was used to answer the question: an introduction, answers to subquestions, and a summary or conclusion. The teacher explains that the length of the essay can vary from a few paragraphs to several pages; the longer the answer, the more details or examples can be included.

The teacher explains that this format can be used as a framework for answering all essay questions and encourages students to practice the following:

Using a checklist as a guide for preparing to take essay tests (see Figure 10.3)

Thinking and planning before beginning to write essays

Expanding the activity of writing key words (from note taking) to writing key sentences and phrases

Inserting additional supporting facts and examples

Providing structure to essays by writing introductions and summaries

The teacher again stresses the importance of reading, understanding, and following directions:

Too many students lose credit because they do not follow the question or test directions. No matter how well written your response may be, if it doesn't answer the particular question, it will be marked wrong. Your task is to read and follow each part of the question or test directions. For example, when the directions state, "Discuss similarities and differences between A and B," you need to include some information about each.

The teacher refers to the sample essay to illustrate this point:

Now look at the summary part of the answer. It describes the difference that is most significant and why. Did you notice the phrase in the question, "discuss similarities *and* differences"? In this summary, the most significant difference is discussed, but points are lost because no reference has been made to similarities.

Setting Goals

The teacher helps each student set goals based on individual strengths and weaknesses. For example, Brandon expressed his concern about his performance on a recent science test. The science teacher agreed to meet with Brandon after school to discuss the test results. The teacher reviewed Brandon's previous classroom tests and provided specific examples of how his strengths contributed to his score and how his weaknesses accounted for errors on the test:

> These answers demonstrate your sound reasoning. It is your skill and hard work, rather than luck, that account for this grade. You lose the most points for three types of errors: incomplete definitions of science vocabulary, selecting the first seemingly correct choice rather than selecting the best choice, and paying insufficient attention to details.

Therefore, two goals established for Brandon were to read aloud each alternative within the multiple-choice question before selecting the answer and to design mnemonics to aid his recall of all the elements included in the definitions of technical terms.

During a conference, the special education teacher consultant reviewed Kim's last essay test and circled the best parts of the answer and identified some critical errors. With respect to organization, the teacher said:

> Let's review each paragraph and identify the topic or main idea of the paragraph. In this paragraph, you stick to one topic. Let's highlight that as a model of a well-organized paragraph. Now let's look at the next paragraph. Circle the subject in each of the sentences in this next paragraph. Do you see how many topics are included? When you deal with so many topics in one paragraph, the reader experiences confusion. Using an outline or sketch helps you to organize your thoughts before you write them down.

A goal established for Kim was to design a checklist or map to help her include the following elements in her paragraphs: one main idea, an explanation, and one or two facts and/or examples.

Teaching and Modeling Specific Strategies

The teacher provides direct instruction in preparing for and taking tests, as discussed previously. Other specific test preparation and test-taking strategies are described in study guides for college admissions tests; these guides are widely available in bookstores, libraries, and the closets of older siblings. The strategies they detail are helpful to middle school and high school students in various content areas.

Teacher modeling provides the opportunity for students to learn test-taking strategies by imitation. Students need to see and hear a competent test taker as an active learner who is focused on and involved with the material. Students need to watch and listen as the teacher examines words and phrases, thinks aloud, creates a visual image, perhaps draws a diagram, and follows a step-by-step problem-solving procedure. Through the teacher's example, students begin to understand that they can use a systematic approach to improve their performance.

To lead students through a step-by-step strategy to answer objective questions, for example, the teacher might use a sample test:

> I will demonstrate a general strategy to answer complex multiple-choice questions by following a series of steps. Follow along as I work through this problem:
>
> 1. Place a pencil or index card under the line of print that you are reading.
>
> 2. Read each question aloud and rephrase the question in your own words.
>
> 3. Circle key words and phrases that qualify or quantify the information in the question stems or in the choices.
>
> 4. Answer the questions in your own words or estimate the answer, perhaps writing some key words.
>
> 5. Compare your answer with each of the choices and decide which is the best.

The teacher might say something like the following to model how to break down the task of responding on an essay exam in an easy but systematic manner:

> If I have three out of four essay questions to be answered in 60 minutes, and all the questions are worth the same number of points, then I have approximately 15 or 20 minutes to answer each question. Fifteen or 20 minutes per question is a short time. I will only be able to discuss two or three ideas per question, in addition to planning,

writing an introduction, writing a summary, and having time to check the answer.

Test-taking skills need to be upgraded as students move from middle school to high school because the tests themselves become more difficult, in the following ways:

The homework assignments and the textbooks on which tests are based are longer and more difficult.

The information presented by both lecture and text requires more time to understand, learn, and integrate with previous knowledge.

The answers to test questions require more thinking and often the integration of abstract and technical content (i.e., they rely more on application and problem solving than on recognition and recall).

Technical vocabulary often represents not single ideas but complex concepts.

Tests are longer, but the time allowed to complete them is often shorter.

Providing Guided Practice, Feedback, and Reinforcement

Guided practice

When students are asked what they do when they study for tests, they comment, "I reread the text," "I memorize the formulas," "I rewrite my notes." Some students create card files or make lists, but very few take a complete practice test under timed conditions, using the test-taking strategies learned in class. The teacher provides this "dress" rehearsal for the students. Guided practice and rehearsal are the only techniques that will ensure that students will be able to use the strategies they have learned once they are in the testing situation.

At first, students practice one test-taking technique at a time, using a practice test. Students practice each step, talking aloud, using the cues or signals they have established previously to make decisions or complete a task. The teacher provides corrective feedback and poses questions such as the following:

What is your reaction to taking a test in this way?

What part of the technique do you like best and least?

Would you like to try the technique again?

This step provides the opportunity again to individualize instruction according to students' particular needs and learning styles.

If needed, the tips for effective test taking are again explained and demonstrated to the class as a whole. For example, the teacher might model, once again, the technique of surveying the test and answering the easiest questions first. During practice, students discover how they can actually perform this task themselves.

The teacher explains ways in which taking practice tests can increase speed, accuracy, and endurance when students take objective tests. The teacher says, "Don't let the test itself be your practice experience. Practice and improve your skills before you have to give a final performance. Rehearsal is like playing exhibition or preseason games. It's a taste of the real thing."

The teacher also gives students the opportunity to review old tests and sample answers. This procedure is especially valuable before the first test, when students are largely unfamiliar with what the teacher considers of particular importance, in helping students decide the type and amount of information to be learned. Brandon practiced taking old tests and answering objective questions from the textbook. He investigated why individual choices on multiple-choice tests were either correct or incorrect. His skills at guessing improved as he discovered ways in which key words or phrases can distinguish one answer as the best one. Brandon now reads the questions and alternative answers much more carefully. As he practices, he increases the speed at which he completes the test and improves his scores. As a result, Brandon feels more optimistic and secure when faced with an objective test, and the test will more accurately reflect Brandon's knowledge of the subject.

Feedback

Both teacher and student need systematic feedback on the use and effectiveness of test-taking skills to adjust their future behavior. For the teacher, the purpose of collecting feedback is to adjust instructional activities, identify and circumvent barriers to student test-taking success, and provide corrective action.

For example, after midterm examinations, the teacher schedules a few minutes for students to discuss with one another their most and least effective test-taking strategies. To some students, it is most surprising to discover how much time their peers actually spend studying the material. In addition, the teacher can pose questions such as the following: How did you predict the exam questions? Did you use self-talk before or during the test? Were you able to better manage your time on this test? and How will you fine-tune your test-taking strategies for the next quiz?

Reinforcement

The content area teacher provides reinforcement for effective test preparation and test taking throughout the year for all students. In addition, designing their own goals and monitoring their own performance provides additional reinforcement for students like Kim.

Kim's test-taking goal was to answer at least one test question more completely, earning more points for the inclusion of more information. The classroom teacher was to circle each important point or fact in her answers. Following the plan was reinforcing because Kim could see her progress both on practice and actual tests. She was delighted because she knew the material and was ready to take the test. She made comments such as "I know this," "That's pretty neat," "I don't need to cram like before," "I'm not so nervous," and "I really feel better!" In addition, the teachers praised Kim's efforts and recognized her progress. Kim was proud to show her parents the tests because they highlighted her progress.

Monitoring Progress and Adjusting Activities

The teacher monitors progress in test taking by keeping track of quiz and test results, observing student behavior, and soliciting student comments. The teacher asks questions such as How do test results compare to knowledge demonstrated in other ways during class activities? The teacher analyzes errors, seeking to identify patterns and problems.

The teacher also observes student behavior during tests and quizzes in order to identify students who are confronting difficulties. Some common indicators of problems include the following:

High frequencies of crossing out, changing, or erasing answers

An inordinate number of questions about directions or test items

Seemingly nonproductive test-taking behaviors, such as daydreaming, sleeping, looking at the ceiling rather than the test, constantly turning pages back and forth, fidgeting, and dropping pencils and papers

Facial grimaces and body positions indicative of discomfort and tension

The teacher solicits student comments and provides opportunities for students to discuss progress and problems among themselves. The teacher directly asks for and listens to students' reasons or explanations for poor test performance. Only through such interchanges can the strategies utilized (or perhaps not utilized) be examined and corrected. New or more focused test-taking goals can be established by identifying problems from the students' perspective.

The teacher adjusts activities in order to allow students to relearn or review content material they missed, answer questions they might have, and continue to solve individual test-taking problems. Based on individual comments, the teacher identifies techniques to review and practice. Some of these may be related to other skills, such as reading, listening, note taking, or problem solving.

ENCOURAGING SELF-MANAGEMENT

Unlike many school-related activities, test taking is an independent activity in which students are solely responsible for the results. Students must therefore assume responsibility for preparing for the test (e.g., scheduling study tasks on a calendar) and managing their behavior during the test (e.g., focusing attention).

The teacher encourages students to develop self-management of test-taking behaviors in the following specific ways:

Providing class time for developing test-taking strategies

Providing class time to develop study schedules

Helping students develop personalized test-taking strategies

Helping students develop strategies to focus and maintain attention during tests

Helping students analyze their own test-taking behavior and set goals for improvement

Helping students recognize their efforts and progress, even when gains are modest

Providing time for students to review their tests to identify positive self-managed behavior

Helping students identify ways to enhance learning, memory, or performance based on test results

To achieve the goal of self-management, it is very important for students to evaluate test results and identify ways in which their thinking and behavior has influenced these outcomes. Too often, students throw away or lose their tests. They learn little from their mistakes and miss opportunities to set new goals or fine-tune their strategies.

Another critical component of self-management concerns test anxiety. The teacher discusses ways the student can manage stress and reviews guidelines for dealing with test anxiety before, during, and after a test. Students can use a checklist like the one shown in Figure 10.4 to help them review strategies for controlling stress and anxiety.

Because all students experience some degree of stress during tests, Brandon's science teacher decided to conduct a simple routine with the entire class before every test. Before the test, she encouraged students to use positive visualizations, then led them in simple stretching exercises for a few minutes. During the test, she periodically encouraged them to use their positive visualizations and take deep breaths.

Occasionally, test taking triggers anxiety reactions and avoidance behaviors that are best dealt with by professionals such as clinical psychologists, social workers, or rehabilitation counselors. It is the academic counselor's or teacher's responsibility to discuss these issues with student and parents and, when necessary, refer the student for diagnostic or counseling services.

In brief, self-management allows students to tap into their strengths to meet the demands of the test. Students learn to monitor, regulate, and evaluate their test performance and later to adjust and recognize their efforts.

SUMMARY AND CONCLUSIONS

Effective test-taking skills are necessary for all students. By the time students reach ninth grade, they should have a good understanding of the various types of questions used in classroom tests, statewide competency tests, and college entrance examinations. Test-taking skills are especially critical for students with learning disabilities and attention problems.

The teacher can apply a systematic approach to help students prepare for and perform well on paper-and-pencil tests. The goal is to ensure that student test scores are a valid measure of knowledge.

Teaching test-taking skills in the content area classroom increases student competence and confidence. Step-by-step procedures to review and prepare for tests lead to improved test performance. Competence is increased by identifying the causes of or barriers to effective performance and by providing techniques to overcome the barriers. Confidence is increased by monitoring progress, offering test-taking practice, and providing students with self-evaluative techniques. Ultimately, students are able to demonstrate to themselves that learning does occur, that they can perform, and that they can succeed under increasingly more challenging conditions.

11

Academic Writing

The paper was a mess! Scrawled along the margin were the teacher's comments that the paper was "disorganized, incomplete, and unclear." Covering each page were circles and arrows highlighting grammatical and spelling mistakes. Asondra, a high school senior with learning disabilities, was frantic: "I don't know what's wrong. I thought I had enough time. I rewrote it and rewrote it."

Nick is a tenth grader whose intelligence test scores are in the superior range. On standardized achievement tests his scores are scattered. For example, in vocabulary and comprehension he scores at the college level, whereas his written expression and spelling are at the fifth-grade level. His writing is incoherent. In fact, he usually does not hand in his written assignments; sometimes he forgets them, sometimes he loses them, sometimes he throws them away. Even though he is a leader in class discussion and does well on tests, his writing problems frustrate and humiliate him.

Michael is an average seventh grader who is not eligible for any special education services or accommodations. He does his homework most of the time, rarely participates in class discussions, and barely passes most of his tests. He writes very little—usually only a few short sentences—and rarely satisfies the requirements of any writing task. His writing is very mechanical and involves little thought. Writing is not a part of Michael's life. Even though there may be a newspaper to read, one can hardly find a pencil or writing paper in his house or the houses of his friends. Michael and his family feel they have little reason to write. Michael is an example of a student who might be ignored or dismissed as a low achiever.

Asondra, Nick, and Michael are students with writing problems. All three would be better able to demonstrate what they know if they were able to improve their writing skills. All three would benefit from systematic writing instruction in their content area classes.

OVERVIEW

Writing is a complex process incorporating fine motor, cognitive, and expressive language tasks. Levine (1990) refers to writing as a juggling act in which the student must remember and use many things at the same time—grammar, spelling, letter formation, vocabulary, ideas, instructions, and so forth. Writing is therefore not a mechanical act but a complex process requiring the student to consider and manage many different subskills (Englert, Raphael, Fear, & Anderson, 1988; Humes, 1983).

The primary purpose of writing is to communicate information and express ideas. Writing can also serve as an aid to short- or long-term memory (e.g., a shopping list or a permanent record of events, thoughts, and ideas). In addition, writing can promote the learning of new information because it requires the student to organize, paraphrase, summarize, form opinions about, and apply new information. Because of this relationship to learning, writing is an especially important academic task.

The writing task becomes increasingly more challenging as students move from elementary to middle to high school and on to college. In elementary school, students begin by writing single words and expanding them into sentences. As fine motor skills and vocabulary develop, students begin to write short passages comprised of three to four sentences. By fourth and fifth grade, students are writing short book reports as well as stories about a page in length. Sentence length increases. Written language approaches the fluency of verbal language (Levine, 1993).

In middle school, students move on to expository writing. They are required to express opinions and summarize information from several sources. More writing is required, and the emphasis is on planning and draft writing. Teachers are less tolerant of grammatical and spelling errors and have less time to provide individual help.

By high school, students are required to compare and contrast theories, use examples to illustrate concepts, and write research papers in their content area courses. At this level, students develop an individual writing style and begin to use different types of writing—creative, expository, and technical—for different purposes. Students are required to write longer and more conceptually challenging papers and to analyze and synthesize information rather than merely retell stories or list facts. Teachers require students to compare and contrast theories, use examples to illustrate concepts, and write research papers in their content area courses.

It is not only the writing task that becomes more challenging as students progress through the grades. The material to be read and discussed becomes more difficult, there is more of it, and it must be mastered more quickly. If students are not taught the skills to meet these challenges, they will become frustrated and fail.

Writing Problems

Students with learning or attention problems have many difficulties with written composition (Hammill, 1995). These writing problems can be traced to a variety of ability or skill deficits, as listed Figure 11.1. Although no student demonstrates problems in all areas, difficulties in more than one area are common. For students with learning disabilities, writing problems often continue during college (Gajar, 1989).

Many students have problems with writing simply because they have been unable to process and understand the information about which they are writing. Their poor writing reflects a lack of comprehension rather than a lack of composition skills. Too frequently, students just don't know what they are talking about, and their writing reflects this lack of understanding.

Even if they do comprehend the material, students with writing problems may have particular difficulty expressing their thoughts in writing, although their oral language may be average or better. The papers these students write are generally short, include limited vocabulary, and lack detail. These students have difficulty explaining complex ideas in written form.

Students with learning difficulties may have a variety of mechanical problems. Their command of grammar and spelling may be so inadequate that they lose their capacity to communicate effectively in writing. They write and rewrite individual words and sentences, never quite correcting their grammatical or spelling errors; often, in the process, they omit essential components such as an introduction or summary.

Some students may have laborious and illegible handwriting, or they may lack the visual tracking or fine motor skills required to write. Writing is slow, awkward, and frustrating for them. Even though these students understand the material, their papers are often short and unreadable, due to fatigue.

Figure 11.1 Common Writing Problems

Language

Limited skills in:

    Expressing or explaining ideas (verbally or in writing)

    Thinking of enough to say

    Using technical or mature vocabulary

    Retrieving words

Cognitive

Limited skills in:

    Understanding or remembering concepts

    Expanding or extending ideas

    Relating two or more ideas

    Understanding deeper meaning or significance

    Analyzing, synthesizing, problem solving, evaluating

    Building a logical argument

    Remembering

Self-Management

Limited skills in:

    Identifying the audience and/or purpose

    Planning, organizing, revising

    Selecting and using appropriate strategies and skills

    Knowing what to do to improve

Attention Difficulties

    High impulsivity

    Rapid, sporadic thinking/writing

    Missing details and words

    Distractibility

    Inconsistent work

    Burn-out, fatigue

Grammar/Spelling

Prevalence of:

    Run-on sentence or fragments

    Incorrect punctuation

    Incorrect verb tenses

    Subject-verb disagreement

    Incorrect spelling

Emotional/Motivational Difficulties
> Writer's block
> Frustration
> Low self-esteem
> Repeated failure
> Avoidance behaviors
> Passive learning style

Students with attention problems may spend an inordinate amount of time writing, although in reality they are often off task. They may write off the topic and appear disorganized. They may not spend enough time thinking about and planning their papers.

Students with learning problems often have self-management problems when it comes to writing. They miscalculate the amount of time required to learn, absorb, and integrate the new information about which they are required to write. In addition, they frequently misgauge the effort required to think and problem solve in relation to the requirements of the assignment and the organization of their writing.

Some students are overwhelmed by these problems and suffer emotional and motivational problems as a result. Procrastination or "writer's block" may develop. Overly critical teachers can exacerbate writer's block and inadvertently worsen rather than improve writing behavior. Asondra has become a procrastinator in response to her writing problems; Nick has stopped writing altogether. He suffers from perfectionism. When asked about his English paper, Nick says, "I didn't do it. I tried writing it a few times, but it just made me so mad. It just wasn't good enough!" Michael continues to write, but poorly. All three students know the material and want to do the work.

Finally, students both with and without learning difficulties sometimes have the "Hemingway Syndrome," a distorted vision of the writing process in which they picture a literary genius completing an enduring work in one fell swoop. What they often do not know is that Hemingway had an editor and wrote many drafts before his books were published and that even the creative process requires a systematic approach.

ROLE OF THE CLASSROOM TEACHER

Writing is generally taught in language arts and English classes; however, there is no guarantee that students will master the skills they need there or that these skills will transfer to specific content area classes. If the content area teacher requires students to complete writing assignments, instruction about the writing process is a legitimate responsibility of that teacher.

The goal of the classroom teacher is not to teach writing per se but to teach students how to write about the information and concepts important in the subject area. The teacher helps students master effective writing strategies (Harris & Graham, 1988), as discussed later in this chapter. More generally, the teacher promotes a positive writing climate, provides an audience for students' written communication, individualizes the writing process, and collaborates with other professionals to make appropriate accommodations for students with learning difficulties.

Promoting a Positive Writing Climate

The environment in which students write has a major impact on the work they produce and on the way they manage or regulate their thinking and writing behaviors. It is the teacher's responsibility to create a positive climate so all students are encouraged to write, especially those students who have learning and attention problems.

Pointing out the functional purpose of writing and giving students authentic writing assignments can increase student involvement and promote a positive climate for writing. For example, in history or government, students can write to congressional leaders to ask them to vote a certain way on an issue of national importance. In geography, students can devise a travel itinerary to another country. As with reading and other academic activities, interest in a topic increases student motivation to learn more about that topic and to share information about that topic with others.

The teacher stresses the importance of designing a supportive writing environment for oneself and asks about the conditions under which each student works best. It can be helpful if the teacher then lists the variety of styles and conditions represented in the class—for example, sitting for not more than 20 minutes at a time, having a quiet atmosphere (perhaps with some nondistracting background music), relaxing before or after writing, reviewing work with someone else, and talking about ideas.

Providing an Audience for Writing

The teacher serves as an audience for and critic of students' writing. Having an audience, even if only the teacher, can increase student interest and motivation. However, when writing is only for the teacher, students may tend to view writing in terms of grades or look on revision as punishment for inaccuracies. When students write for a wider audience—as they do when they participate in writing groups, computer networking, or the creation of class newsletters—they focus more on the communication of their ideas. Sharing the communication with a broad audience makes writing more interesting and fosters motivation to engage in all phases of the writing process, including the planning and revising steps (Calkins, 1986; Madraso, 1993).

Individualizing

The teacher explains that students will need to adapt strategies to suit their particular needs. In doing so, the teacher discusses different writing styles and patterns of strengths and weaknesses. For example:

> Some students are visual learners. If you learn best in this
> way, visualize, diagram, or illustrate your ideas before
> you write. Some students have problems with vocabulary
> and grammar, but their ideas are substantial. Focus on
> the ideas first, and leave the mechanics for last.

Some students tend to think faster than they write. Such students work best when they brainstorm first, quickly listing or audiotaping their ideas. They can then organize or diagram their ideas before they write. Some students prefer to begin with main ideas or the big picture, whereas others start with details. The teacher stresses that both details and main ideas are necessary and that, although a student may begin with one or the other, he or she will need to develop strategies to include both.

The goal is the same for all students: to improve skills in written expression within the given content area. To meet this goal while meeting the individual needs and interests of students, the teacher considers ways to modify assignments. These may include the following:

Giving students opportunities to select among topics

Being flexible in terms of due dates, make-ups, bonus opportunities, and number of written pages required

Incorporating outlines, drafts, and revisions as part of the assignment and grading process

Allowing students to elect to read their reports or stories to the class

Providing Accommodations

Students with learning disabilities and attention problems may lack many of the skills necessary to complete writing assignments. When classroom teachers work with such students, they follow the recommendations of the IEP or 504 plan. If necessary, they refer a student for remedial or support services in the language area.

Accommodations commonly helpful to students with learning and/or attention difficulties include using scribes and tape recorders to dictate ideas, oral or taped presentations, shortened assignments or alternative projects, and computer software. Word processing programs and other computer software (e.g., spell-checking, outlining, graphics) can be especially valuable in helping students improve mechanics, organization, and rate of production.

TEACHING WRITING IN THE CONTENT AREA

Instructional Strategies

A variety of strategies have been proposed to improve the writing process (e.g., Ellis, Deshler, Schumaker, & Alley, 1989; Hayes & Flower, 1986; Scardamalia & Bereiter, 1986). Such instruction focuses on the teaching of cognitive and metacognitive strategies. Investigating the mental processes used by skilled writers, many of these researchers have discussed how to apply their findings to students with learning disabilities (Graham, Harris, MacArthur, & Schwartz, 1991; Graham, MacArthur, Schwartz, & Page-Voth, 1992; Schwartz & MacArthur, 1990). Other authors stress teaching the process of writing along with the content of writing (Calkins, 1986; Cook, 1991). Calkins suggests offering writing workshops in the middle school curriculum. Still others stress the importance of group and collaborative writing at secondary and postsecondary levels (Belanoff & Elbow, 1986; Greenbaum & Schmerl, 1970).

Although they provide an excellent point of departure for students with and without learning or attention problems, these models may not always be appropriate for every student in every circumstance. Students do not have to start writing with word one, page one. They need options and alternatives and the flexibility to experiment. They need to combine, regulate, and balance systematic processes with spontaneous or creative efforts.

Using the SQ4R Method

Figure 11.2 helps students apply the SQ4R method to academic writing. In this application, students are encouraged to generate and write answers to questions that may be of interest to the audience. For example, Sam, described in chapter 6, wrote the story, "The Clutch Hit" based on a series of questions written by his teacher. The first step was to turn the title of his story into a question about one main idea, "What is a clutch hit?" Next, the teacher asked him questions such as What did you do? How did you feel? What was the score? At a later date, this short story became part of a larger paper about his love of baseball. (Similar step-by-step procedures are listed in Mercer & Mercer, 1993; Schumm & Radencich, 1992; and Schunk & Zimmerman, 1994.)

Teaching the writing process as a series of questions and answers helps students with writing difficulties break the writing task down into manageable steps and get "unstuck" when they are uncertain about how to proceed. The question-answer approach can help students like Asondra, who are overwhelmed by their writing problems, understand the requirements of the writing assignment. It also aids students like Michael in adding more information and detail to his papers. A side benefit of the discussion of the writing assignment and the generating of questions is increased learning of content.

Using Checklists

The checklist shown in Figure 11.3 takes the student through the writing process: The student begins by analyzing the assignment and

**Figure 11.2   Student Checklist for Applying SQ4R
to Academic Writing**

SURVEY the assignment.

_____ Determine the goal or intent of the assignment
and consider all of the requirements.

_____ Survey text(s) and class notes to identify basic information
that might be included.

_____ Survey or identify the study aids that might help organize the
topic—for example, table of contents, chapter introduction and
summary, graphs, and tables.

QUESTION to develop content.

_____ Say the assignment aloud, converting it into a main
idea question.

_____ Divide the main idea question into several briefer questions.

_____ Consider including higher order questions—for example,
What is the implication? What is the value?

READ AND REFLECT to answer your questions.

_____ Think about key words or phrases that answer your questions.
Visualize or get a mental picture of the topic or sequence
of events.

RECITE the answers to your questions.

_____ Answer your questions in your own words.

_____ Discuss your ideas with the teacher and/or other students.

*[W]RITE or sketch the answers to your questions on separate cards,
sticky notes, or pages.*

_____ Include drawings, diagrams, and symbols to visually depict
the answers to questions.

_____ Write a draft of the paper in your own words; include facts
and examples.

REVISE AND EDIT to ensure accuracy, completeness, and clarity.

_____ Reread the draft, checking for meaning and organization.

_____ Add, correct, delete, substitute, or move text.

Figure 11.3   Student Checklist for Managing the Writing Process

Plan

Analyze the assignment

_____ Read the assignment aloud and rephrase it in your own words.

_____ Convert each phrase or idea into a main idea question.

_____ Identify the general purpose of the assignment (e.g., explain, compare/contrast, trace, sequence, persuade, problem solve, generate controversy, discuss relationships).

_____ Identify length, due date, and preferred format for the assignment.

_____ Identify the texts and resources available for use.

_____ Obtain samples of papers that have received grades of A or B.

_____ Set priorities and begin scheduling.

Select the topic

_____ Consider your own interests, strengths, skills, and current knowledge.

_____ Brainstorm. Allow up to 5 minutes to list ideas related to the general topic.

_____ Include questions that require your analysis, criticism, and/or comparisons of different ideas.

_____ Disallow critical self-statements such as "My ideas are stupid."

_____ Collapse the ideas into no more than 10 questions.

_____ Sequence the questions in the order in which they will be addressed in the paper.

_____ Limit the topic. Plan a topic that is narrow enough to be completed in the assigned length and/or the available time.

_____ List additional questions and ideas for possible inclusion.

_____ Check with the teacher. Ask if the topic and the main idea questions you posed meet the requirements of the assignment. Ask for suggestions.

Organize

_____ Assemble materials, including textbooks, supplemental reading, lecture notes, and library materials.

_____ Apply the SQ4R process to reading and lecture notes to gather information on the topic.

_____ Schedule time to think about ideas and talk to others about the topic.

Figure 11.3 *(continued)*

_____ Talk to yourself about the topic. Think of different ways of presenting the information. Ask yourself about your audience and the message or information you want to communicate.

_____ Review tables of contents in textbooks to ascertain a method of organizing topics.

_____ Design charts, diagrams, or maps to answer proposed questions.

_____ Make a blueprint or plan to determine the order in which you will answer questions.

_____ To begin, write one of your questions at the top of a page and answer it.

Write

Prewrite

_____ Reduce stress or avoidance by engaging in relaxation or recreational activities before you engage in the writing process.

_____ Free-write to generate a flow of ideas or to answer questions.

_____ Write in short bursts. Set a kitchen timer and write for 2 to 5 minutes.

_____ Consider using an audiotape recorder or scribe to jump-start the writing process.

_____ Write an answer to each question. Use the key words as a basis for writing a main idea sentence.

_____ Write brief paragraphs that include a main idea, several supporting facts, and, if possible, examples.

Write

_____ Use the ABCs of writing:

        A = Always ask and answer questions.

        B = Be basic in organization and sentence structure.

        C = Clarity comes before creativity.

_____ Explain the purpose of the paper in an introductory paragraph.

_____ Complete the first draft by answering one question at a time or writing one paragraph at a time.

_____ Insert transitions between paragraphs and sections of the paper.

_____ Summarize the answers to the questions in the summary section. Consider including conclusions and recommendations.

_____ Take frequent breaks!

_____ Ask the teacher for feedback on the first draft.

Review

_____ Review the assignment. Check to see if the paper meets the requirements.

_____ Check that information is presented in a logical sequence.

_____ Compare the draft to the plan or outline and add, delete, or revise as necessary.

_____ Cut and paste to reorganize or resequence, if necessary.

_____ Clearly label introduction, sections, summary, or conclusions.

_____ Check that there are adequate descriptions of each major idea or critical issue.

_____ Check that there are adequate supporting information and examples.

_____ Check that technical vocabulary is included and used correctly.

_____ Obtain feedback from a classmate, parent, or teacher.

_____ Review and correct one problem at a time, including grammar, punctuation, and spelling.

_____ Ensure that the final version of the paper is neat, clean, and legible. Include a title page, page numbers, and references if assigned.

---

selecting the topic, using brainstorming to generate ideas or creating maps (Cook, 1991; Margulies, 1991). The next step, organizing, involves assembling materials and planning different ways to present the information. Prewriting and writing come next; during this step, the student answers the questions previously raised and generates a draft. A final review, including editing and feedback, completes the process.

When using checklists such as this one, it is important for students to understand that the amount of time needed for each step varies depending upon student strengths and interests. Because revision and editing take up considerable time and effort, the teacher will need to describe these processes at length. Students are encouraged to reread their drafts several times to check for accuracy, completeness, and clarity.

The checklists shown in Figure 11.2 and Figure 11.3 integrate the cognitive and self-management strategies necessary for effective writing; these checklists, adapted as necessary, can serve as a guideline for teaching. Students can use such checklists independently as they plan and write their papers, or they can collaborate to improve their writing. With the checklists as a basis, students can discuss their papers with other students, pair up to provide each other with feedback, create a writing support group, or write a paper as a group project.

THE INSTRUCTIONAL PROCESS

Setting the Stage

To set the stage, the teacher establishes a specific purpose for writing in the particular content area and describes writing as a way for students to communicate thoughts, express opinions, and, as appropriate, express themselves creatively. The teacher challenges students to explain and defend their ideas. To attain this goal, the teacher makes a commitment to help each student improve his or her writing skills.

The teacher provides a new perspective on the writing task, stressing the importance of being able to convey what has been learned. For example:

> Writing is a thinking and a communication task. With respect to schoolwork, the writer is the student, and the audience who receives and must understand the message is the teacher. The message must stand alone because the writer is not present to explain it. The writer has to think about questions that the reader or audience would have about the topic. Therefore, writing involves thinking and problem solving as well as the mechanical act of writing. Your paper must demonstrate to the audience—in this case, the teacher—that you understand the assignment and have learned the course material.

The teacher also provides the assurance that all students will improve their writing to some degree. It may be helpful for the teacher to stress the fact that even professional writers need to obtain feedback and revise their work.

Collecting Information

The teacher collects a writing sample on a content area topic and observes students' current writing skills. The teacher uses this information to adjust class assignments and individualize instruction (Ganschow, 1984).

Some baseline observations of extemporaneous writing are a necessity. The teacher may design a 20- to 30-minute writing exercise in which students read a portion of the class textbook and then write a summary—a sizeable paragraph or two—of what they have read. The teacher can collect the summaries, or students can be guided to evaluate their own work individually or in small groups.

The writing sample may be evaluated according to the following criteria:

Content: Did the student answer a main idea question and include one or two supporting facts or an example?

Language: Did the student communicate the message clearly and concisely?

Mechanics: Did the student write legibly with few mistakes in spelling, grammar, or punctuation?

Analyzing Tasks

To analyze writing assignments, students learn to identify the topics addressed in the assignment, the types of questions that need to be answered, and the amount or depth of information required to answer these questions. The teacher helps students analyze their assignments by specifically relating the writing assignment to various sources of information, such as lecture notes, texts, students' experience, current events, and laboratory experiments.

Checklists like the ones shown in Figures 11.2 and 11.3 can also help students structure the analysis step. If the teacher is successful in demonstrating exactly how a writer clarifies an assignment, then students will begin making comments such as "I never really knew how to start until now" or "I think I finally understand."

Setting Goals

Because few students spend adequate time thinking about writing, a major goal for an entire class can relate to planning. For example, students can learn how to brainstorm ideas that may be included in an essay and then practice selecting, reordering, and prioritizing them.

Students can use checklists such as Figures 11.2 and 11.3 to select individual goals on which to focus.

Asondra's goal was to learn how to use maps, diagrams, and outlines to plan writing projects. Michael's goal was to generate a series of questions to answer in his paper. Nick's goal was to follow a step-by-step procedure to manage his writing.

Teaching and Modeling Specific Strategies

In teaching writing strategies, the teacher provides examples and demonstrates ways of engaging in a systematic writing process (Welch & Link, 1992).

In addition, the teacher provides opportunities for students to review completed papers. Some students have never seen a completed paper, and reading others' papers is a first step toward the long-term goal of reviewing and revising their own work. Reviewing finished products emphasizes the organizational and structural aspects of writing.

The teacher also encourages students to evaluate textbooks and tables of contents to see how topics are organized and to use index cards, outlines, or diagrams to organize, record, and logically sequence information.

Throughout these processes, the teacher models the thinking processes and self-management strategies required of the writer. Specifically, the teacher clarifies how to progress from predicting questions to brainstorming and generating answers, to mapping, to outlining, to drafting, to editing and revising, to the final product.

Providing Guided Practice, Feedback, and Reinforcement

All students can benefit from practice in writing. Short writing assignments can be given on a weekly basis. The more students write, the less fearful they become and the better they write.

Depending on student needs, additional practice may be provided for an individual or a group. The teacher can do as follows:

Provide samples of questions that address increasingly complex cognitive requirements, moving from defining and classifying to synthesizing and evaluating (see Figure 8.2; Bloom, 1956).

Request students to think aloud to develop logical sentences or paragraphs.

Encourage students to express their ideas verbally prior to writing them.

Provide opportunities for students to write independently for brief periods of time, with teacher supervision and support.

Provide external prompts to increase length and add examples.

All feedback should help, not hinder, the writing process. The teacher identifies strengths as well as problems and errors. The teacher says, for example:

We learn from errors. We treat them as problems to be solved, not as examples of inadequacy. We will find and circle in green some positive examples of your writing. These will serve as guides and reminders for you when you are writing by yourself.

The teacher must remember to reinforce two critical and often overlooked parts of the writing process—thinking and planning beforehand and thinking and revising afterward. The teacher can do this by asking a general question (e.g., How are you doing?) and reinforcing any effective strategies the student is using. The teacher sets up individual dialogues with students in order to probe their thinking processes and reinforce successive approximations of productive writing behavior.

Monitoring Progress and Making Adjustments

Using the checkpoints, the teacher and class develop a chart to track the completion of specific writing tasks. The students place checks on the chart next to their names as they complete tasks. The teacher uses the chart to see how much time it takes to complete tasks and which tasks need more teacher attention. The teacher is available for individual consultation and coaching.

ENCOURAGING SELF-MANAGEMENT

Checklists of steps in the writing process like the one shown in Figure 11.3 can help students learn to manage their own writing behavior. In addition, the teacher suggests that students apply simple self-management techniques like the following:

Set goals: "It is only a four-page paper. I need to answer 10 questions."

Set schedules: "I need to work on the assignment an hour a day, but only in 15- to 20-minute periods."

Maintain a focus on one's own writing profile: "I always forget to put in conclusions."

Use strengths: "I seem to think best standing and walking around. Perhaps I will use a chalkboard."

Seize control of the writing process: "I am the writer who uses words as symbols, as tools to communicate information. Words are inanimate. I have the right, the responsibility, to change them. I control the paper—the paper does not control me."

Understand the necessity for revision: "When I have completed the first draft, I know I will need to reread and revise."

Monitor progress: "I answered two questions today."

Evaluate quality: "I used a checklist. I remembered to include a summary. I never can see my mistakes. I'd better ask my friend to look it over."

Reduce negative views: "I need to tell myself I can finish this project. I know I can do it."

Central to self-management in writing is the issue of motivation. Students frequently operate in a vacuum. They perceive writing assignments as tasks that have nothing to do with their individual interests, style, and strengths. Students often do not know the importance of selecting a topic that interests them. Most students are unaware they even have a choice in the matter. Writing on a topic of interest ensures that students will be motivated to work. Most teachers are generally happy to allow students to mold an assigned topic around a particular interest. The teacher gives students permission to discuss the matter by saying:

> Identify your own interests related to the assignment by asking questions such as:
>
> What are some things I would like to find out?
>
> What are some things I am not interested in?
>
> What are some things I know about already that I could expand upon for the paper?
>
> Do your own thing. Tell me some things you are particularly interested in that may or may not be directly related to the topic. Ask me for help in relating your interests to the topic. Ask me to help you limit the topic, if necessary.

SUMMARY AND CONCLUSIONS

Writing is an essential feature of advanced learning. It involves the learning and communication of new ideas and concepts. Along with teaching new ideas and concepts, the content area teacher has the responsibility to provide direct instruction in writing about them. Specifically, the content area teacher establishes a positive writing climate, serves as an audience, individualizes assignments, and helps design and implement accommodations.

The stepwise approach to writing in the content area described in this chapter helps students see writing as a process in which questions are asked, then answered. Checklists can help integrate cognitive and self-management strategies and enable the student to improve writing performance and become an independent writer. These checklists are especially important for students with learning and attention problems because they simplify and organize what is, for many such students, a mystifying process.

12

Homework

Mom: *Time to do your homework, Elena.*

Elena: *I hate homework. It's stupid!*

Mom: *You know you have to do your homework. Come on, get your books together.*

(Elena spends the next 10 minutes looking for notebooks, pencils, and books.)

Elena: *Mo-om, I left my social studies book in school, and I have a book report due tomorrow!*

Mom: *You've known about that book report for 3 weeks! You mean you haven't even started it?*

Elena: *I can't do everything! I forgot.*

Mom: (Beginning to yell) *And you forgot your social studies book, too?*

Elena: (Shrieking) *Leave me alone!*

(Elena runs to her room and slams the door.)

Elena and her mother have been having homework hassles for several months. Both are very upset. Elena is a sixth grader with learning disabilities, and her mother is afraid that Elena will fall behind if she doesn't do her homework. She loves her daughter, but she doesn't know what to do.

Variations of this scenario are played out in households across the country every night. Whether parents or children are the initiators, most of these exchanges end up in quarrels. These quarrels reflect the homework problems experienced by students with learning problems. Their assignments are often late, inaccurate, incomplete, lost, or forgotten. As a result, their grades and self-esteem suffer.

OVERVIEW

Homework assignments may appear deceptively simple and nonessential. However, brief but focused review and practice of new information and skills can be critical for learning new material (Rosenbery, 1989). Particularly in science, mathematics, and foreign languages, progress depends on the accumulation and integration of small blocks of information. Homework in these as well as other areas is critical for good progress.

Most teachers and parents assume that students will naturally develop good homework habits. However, homework involves working independently, generally without structure or guidance. Many students, even without learning problems, need to be taught how to do homework. Students who exhibit learning or attention difficulties in the structured school setting will certainly have problems when working independently at home (Frith, 1991).

It is only through reinforcement and practice that a skill is finally learned. The main goals of homework are to increase learning and student responsibility for learning, to help the student develop good work habits and independent study skills, and to extend or transfer knowledge and skills taught during the day (Wood, 1992).

Homework can also individualize learning. When working at home, the student can work at his or her own pace and focus on weak areas in order to gain competence. In addition, by working at home, students can complete work not finished in class.

Finally, homework helps students prepare for upcoming lessons. By reading a textbook chapter before the teacher's lesson on it, the student becomes familiar with the content and is therefore better able to listen actively and participate during class discussions.

Homework Problems

It is not surprising that homework is deemed a major problem in middle and high school. In these settings, homework accounts for as much as 50% of course grades and has a direct correlation with test scores (Mercer & Mercer, 1993).

Specific causes of homework problems include learning disabilities in reading or writing, auditory processing problems that make it difficult to understand oral directions, problems with attention and concentration, organizational and time management difficulties, academic deficits, and perfectionism and procrastination. Perfectionism and procrastination can lead to immobility, chronic failure, and demoralization, which in turn can prevent students from becoming involved in learning. In addition, many students feel overwhelmed by the lack of structure and supervision inherent in homework. Without a teacher's telling them what to do, many students simply do not know how to begin their work. Finally, most students who may appear lazy and irresponsible simply have not learned effective homework habits and skills.

Students with learning disabilities or attention problems often display the following kinds of difficulties:

Copying their assignments inaccurately or incompletely

Forgetting to bring their assignments home

Taking an extremely long time to write (and when finished having written work that is messy, poorly spelled, disorganized, and/or incomplete)

Being easily distracted and unable to concentrate for the time it takes them to complete their homework

Having no idea how long an assignment will take to complete and as a result turning in homework late or not at all

Impulsively jumping from activity to activity without completing any of them

Sometimes parents and teachers blame the student for homework problems: "If only the student worked harder, paid more attention, or were better organized." Some parents blame themselves for their children's homework problems: "If I were a better parent, this would not be happening." Teachers also blame parents for homework problems: "If only the parents were more involved in the child's education." Conversely, parents blame teachers: "The teacher gives my child too much homework"; "The homework the teacher assigns is just busywork. My child is bored and doesn't want to do it"; or "My child spends 3 to 4 hours a night on homework. That's too much." Homework problems are not necessarily the result of the student's lack of effort, poor parenting, or poor planning on the part of the teacher—although all three may contribute to difficulties.

Particularly during adolescence, homework can become the bat-tleground over which independence/dependence issues are engaged. The natural rebellion of the teenager clashes with the concern and control of the parents and school, and the student may refuse to do homework, preferring to spend more time with peers. This type of situation may require the help of a professional to resolve.

Stresses on the family can play a part in homework problems. Often both parents are working at full-time jobs outside the home. As a result, they may not be home to support and supervise home-work assignments, or they may simply be too tired to help when they come home. Some parents lack the basic skills to help their children with homework; others may not understand why the stu-dent has homework and therefore are not in a position to support homework in an informed and systematic manner.

Problems will occur if teachers fail to take into account the other demands on students and families besides school when planning homework assignments and when they are unclear about the purpose of homework assignments. Students quickly become uninterested in homework that they perceive to be merely busywork. Another fac-tor contributing to difficulties is the developmentally unsound prac-tice of giving large amounts of homework to students in elementary school.

Whatever the cause, many homework problems can be correct-ed or prevented when teachers teach and model the homework com-pletion process in their content area classes, involve students in setting goals, and inform parents about how to serve as a support system.

ROLE OF THE CLASSROOM TEACHER

Currently, although all students are expected to complete homework assignments, few teachers teach specific homework completion skills or encourage parents to become involved in a meaningful way. In addition to teaching and modeling specific homework strategies, the classroom teacher clearly delineates his or her own responsibil-ities, as well as the responsibilities of the parents and student; guides parents in supporting the student's homework efforts; individual-izes homework and the homework completion process; and makes necessary accommodations for students with learning disabilities and ADD.

Delineating Teacher, Parent, and Student Responsibilities

The teacher clearly defines his or her own role in the homework process, as well as the roles of the student and the parents. The teacher explains the division of responsibility to the student. For example:

> Our common goal is to increase student responsibility for learning. That means that we will all help you take charge of your homework and support you until you can do your homework comfortably and successfully by yourself. My goals are to teach you, to help you acquire knowledge and skills, and to demonstrate to you how to do your homework. Your parents' goal is to provide you with a good study environment at home. Your goal is to expand your own knowledge and skills.

The teacher bases homework on skills and content already learned in class. This means that parents will not be expected to teach the student new material. In addition, the teacher gives parents timely feedback on any homework difficulties. Teachers inform parents if the student has not handed in two or three assignments in a row so the problem can be corrected before it becomes a cause of student failure.

Specific student responsibilities include the following:

1. Developing a homework plan with help from parents: The plan may need to be modified if it is not working effectively.

2. Helping to decide when and where to do homework: When the student is given a voice in decision making, he or she becomes more invested in carrying out goals and objectives.

3. Following the homework plan without reminders from parents: Because the homework plan largely reflects the student's choices (i.e., when to play ball with the team, when to watch television, when to do homework), the student will be expected to follow the plan.

4. Completing homework to the best of his or her abilities in a timely fashion: The student understands that the homework should represent a best effort. It does not have to be 100% correct. However, it must be completed on time.

5. Checking homework for mistakes and legibility: The student is encouraged to check homework by reading it aloud. If the homework is illegible or something does not make sense, the student makes corrections before handing the homework in.

6. Handing in homework to the teacher in a timely fashion: Many students with learning problems do their homework but fail to hand it in to the teacher because they are ashamed of their poor writing or spelling or think their work is not good enough. This is part of an avoidance-of-failure syndrome, which must be overcome with encouragement from teacher and parents.

7. Asking for help when needed from parents or teacher: Many of us tend to think we are failures if we ask for help. In order for the student to become more comfortable with asking for help in school and at home, parents and teachers must not only tell the student that it is OK to ask for help but also model when and how to ask for help.

Parents' responsibilities include the following:

1. Helping the student develop a homework plan that includes days and times the student will do particular homework assignments.

2. Providing the student with a nondistracting, well-lit, comfortable place to do homework: The place is provided by the parents; the choice of place is determined by student and parents together.

3. Providing the student with basic materials (e.g., paper, sharpened pencils, a calendar): Providing basic materials allows the student to begin work immediately. Responsibility for basic materials can be transferred to the student when the student is ready.

4. Being available to help if the student asks: If the parents cannot help, they should tell the student to ask the teacher for help the next day.

5. Checking occasionally on student progress: If, when parents check, the student appears frustrated, distracted, or otherwise unhappy, they can ask the student if he or she needs help. However, parents must remember that a major purpose of homework is for the student to work independently.

6. Helping the student analyze homework problems: If the student is having difficulties, parents can help the student define the difficulties, then discuss, select, and try out solutions.

7. Expecting that homework will be done according to plan: Positive expectations greatly influence positive outcomes. Negative expectations work similarly.

8. Talking to the teacher about homework difficulties that cannot be solved at home in order to arrive at school-based solutions: Such solutions may include shortening or otherwise modifying homework assignments, tutoring the student in a content area, teaching the student organizational skills, and so on.

Involving Parents

When homework problems arise, parents and teacher discuss them and work with the student toward a solution. Some typical "red flags" include the following:

The student doesn't understand the assignments.

The student hasn't learned the skills covered in the homework.

The student is spending an inordinate amount of time on homework.

The student constantly complains about homework.

There are constant parent/child hassles about homework.

Homework is incomplete or inaccurate.

The student refuses to do the homework.

The student questions the validity and/or relevance of the assignment.

After a particularly aggravating homework session with Elena, Elena's mother called the teacher to tell her of their frustration and ask for her help. The teacher said:

> I understand completely what is going on. Many parents and students have problems like yours. Why don't you get out of the homework business right now and let me work out an arrangement with Elena to do her homework in school under my guidance for the next month? This will help her to upgrade some of her homework skills. In addition, I will send home some information for you on the homework process with some strategies that will help you support Elena when she begins to do her homework at home next month.

Often when homework problems exist the student has undetected or greater than anticipated learning and/or attention problems. The teacher and parents will need to take another look at the student's learning problems and diagnostic reports, then decide if program modifications would be helpful and/or if the student needs to learn new skills.

Most parents greatly appreciate information about helping their child complete and hand in homework assignments (Radencich & Schumm, 1988). The teacher can help parents provide support by giving them information about how they can assist the homework completion process. A checklist like the one shown in Figure 12.1 is useful in this regard.

Teachers in a particular school can also design parent workshops on homework. Parent-teacher associations can be the vehicle for distributing information to parents about homework several times a year. Such organizations can also sponsor a "homework hotline," peer tutoring, or a "study table" for students who forget their assignments or need extra help with homework.

Finally, in the interests of fairness, homework should not involve parents in a teaching role. Some parents who care deeply about their child's education cannot, for a variety of valid reasons, help their

Figure 12.1   Parent Checklist for Supporting Good Homework Habits

Provide a Good Learning Environment

_____ Encourage and reinforce the student for effort and progress.

_____ Minimize distractions (although complete quiet isn't necessary).

_____ Encourage the student to do homework as independently as possible.

_____ Allow the student to study with peers if good progress is made.

_____ Model good work habits for the student.

_____ Encourage the student to check his or her own work.

_____ Help the student learn from mistakes.

_____ Reward the student for completing homework.

Develop a Homework Plan with the Student

_____ Develop a weekly calendar of family events (e.g., outings, recreations, and responsibilities, including homework).

_____ Help the student decide on specific time(s) and place(s) for homework.

_____ Help the student develop realistic time management skills.

_____ Communicate your expectation that the student will follow the plan.

_____ Be consistent and stick with the plan.

_____ Allow for some flexibility for extraordinary circumstances.

_____ Encourage the student to set daily homework goals.

_____ Be positive—give praise even for small steps.

Don't

_____ Do homework for the student.

_____ Nag to ensure that homework gets done; allow natural consequences to occur.

_____ Check the student's work unless she or he asks for help.

_____ Try to teach the student.

_____ Tell the student how to do something. Either refer the student to checklists or ask questions such as "What do you think?" "Can you remember what the teacher said about this?" or "Does your assignment provide any information about this?"

child with homework. Homework should not be dependent on parent knowledge and skills; to avoid this situation, many teachers and schools arrange for students to do homework in school.

Individualizing

The homework process can be adapted according to each student's unique needs and the course requirements. For example, by allowing students to begin assignments in class, teachers can help students who have difficulty with planning and start-up. By giving the class assignments a month in advance, teachers can help students who have difficulty breaking down long-term assignments into shorter tasks and scheduling activities on a calendar.

When considering individual needs, the teacher takes into account the length and the difficulty of the homework assignment and the differing interests and learning styles of the students, then designs homework options accordingly. Students can be given a choice of equivalent assignments and methods of fulfilling the assignments and can be encouraged to build on their own interests and strengths in selecting topics for projects and reports.

For example, Elena has a great deal of trouble writing book reports, due to both organizational and expressive language difficulties. The teacher assigned a one-page paper describing the characters, plot, and setting of a book read in class. Elena struggled with the report for 2 hours. Upset, she told her teacher, "I just can't do it. I tried and tried." The teacher talked with Elena about what Elena found most interesting about the story; together, they worked out a plan for Elena to write a series of letters from one character in the book to another. In the letters, Elena showed her understanding of the book's setting, central conflict, and characters. She also revealed a sophisticated understanding of the letter writers' points of view, something that would not be possible in the more conventional book report assigned. With Elena's permission, the teacher read the letters to the class as an example of a creative way of conveying the information and suggested that, after consulting with her, other students could adapt future homework assignments to suit their particular interests.

A final issue in individualizing homework assignments concerns awareness of the homework assignments of other teachers and other responsibilities students may have outside of school. In order to determine what amount of homework is realistic for their students, teachers will need to monitor both of these situations.

Providing Accommodations

Students with learning disabilities and attention problems need homework accommodations in order to demonstrate their strengths and avoid undue penalties for their weaknesses. The following kinds of homework accommodations will go a long way toward preventing homework problems for students with learning difficulties:

> Writing all assignments for the student clearly, then giving the student the assignments for the entire week, month, or term

> Shortening assignments so the student has less writing or reading to do and can concentrate on learning the core of the material

> Grading on the content of the homework and not on appearance or spelling (except for spelling homework)

> Allowing the student to use an alternate modality (e.g., oral, demonstration, audiotape, etc.) to complete the assignment instead of writing

> Providing the student with an alternative textbook at his or her reading level or highlighting the main ideas in the grade-level textbook

> Designing a system to ensure that the assignment gets from school to home and the completed homework gets back from home to school

> If necessary, enlisting the aid of the special education teacher consultant to check that the student has the assignment, brings home the needed textbooks and notebooks, and completes the assignment in a timely fashion

TEACHING HOMEWORK SKILLS IN THE CONTENT AREA

The homework completion process can be taught in each content area class (Miller & Kelley, 1994; Olympia, Sheridan, Jenson, & Andrews,

1994). The classroom teacher targets homework completion skills as an important instructional objective (Mercer & Mercer, 1993; Wood, 1992).

The teacher clearly communicates the homework assignment to each student. For students with learning problems, assignments might have to be given both orally and in written form, clearly printed or typed. To check for understanding, the teacher might ask that students restate the directions in their own words.

After clearly communicating the assignment, the teacher helps students understand and manage the homework completion process for that particular assignment. The homework process is begun in class under the guidance of the teacher. The teacher guides students through the first steps and addresses any student questions.

A checklist like the one shown in Figure 12.2 is helpful. As illustrated, the homework process begins at school when the teacher makes the assignment and ends back at school when the student gives the completed homework to the teacher.

THE INSTRUCTIONAL PROCESS

Setting the Stage

Many students and their parents think of homework as busywork. Others see homework as interfering with what they perceive as more important or more interesting family business or fun. It is important for students and parents to understand why homework is given and what learning goals can be accomplished through homework. The teacher explains the purpose of homework to students and their parents. To students, the teacher describes the long-term benefits of learning to work independently:

> The ability to work on your own at home, without anyone
> telling you what to do or guiding you, is an important
> skill that you will continue using long after school is
> over—at home, at work, and in the community. For example,
> if you want to help someone win an election, or if you
> want to coach a Little League team, or if you want to plan
> a super vacation, you will need to figure out the tasks to
> be done, organize yourself and other people, and manage
> your time effectively, on your own.

**Figure 12.2   Student Checklist for Managing
                the Homework Completion Process**

At School
_____ Place each assignment in a notebook to be brought home.
_____ Read the homework assignment aloud and circle key words.
_____ Ask the teacher for help to break down the assignment into
      small steps.
_____ Ask the teacher for help understanding the assignment.
_____ List materials and resources needed to complete the homework
      assignment.
_____ Locate materials and resources.
_____ Bring home assignments, textbooks, and other necessary materials.
At Home
_____ Select a time and place to do homework.
_____ Read the assignment carefully, repeating each direction.
_____ List and schedule the tasks for that assignment, from last to first.
_____ Make a daily homework plan based on all assignments.
_____ Set the day's homework goals.
_____ Schedule reading, thinking, and writing activities for the number
      of minutes and at times of the day when you are most alert.
_____ Employ the reading and writing skills needed to complete the
      homework.
_____ Recognize your efforts by making positive statements.
_____ Keep on track by checking off tasks as they are completed.
_____ Decide when the homework is done by reviewing the assignment
      and any checklists you used.
_____ Check work for accuracy, completeness, legibility, and neatness.
_____ Place completed homework in the front of your notebook,
      ready to return to school.
_____ Praise yourself for your efforts and discuss your positive
      progress with a friend or family member.
Back at School
_____ Bring homework back to school and give it to your teacher(s).
_____ Bring textbooks, materials, and resources back to school.
_____ Revise and correct homework based on feedback from
      your teacher(s).
_____ Review and record whether you met your goal or stayed
      with your schedule.
_____ Save all completed homework in your notebook.
_____ Make a list and discuss with others your own "best homework tips."

You will use the skills you develop doing homework whenever you want to learn something new. You will find out that you have to practice a new skill several times before you really "know" it—like basketball or computer games or driving a car. That practice is the equivalent of homework.

The great thing about working on your own is that you can choose the best possible time to do the work and work at your own pace. You can spend more time on some things than others if you need to or want to, and if you finish quickly, you can go on to something else you want to do.

Homework is a very important part of learning and has a direct and positive effect on your test scores and grades. You, your parents, and I each have responsibility for making it a good learning experience.

Collecting Information

Information about homework completion can be collected using samples of student homework, checklists of homework completion, and student self-reports. Teachers already collect information using the first two methods. By including student input, teachers are able to get a more complete picture of homework problems. Information must be collected in a systematic fashion; clear criteria for judging the adequacy of homework must be employed. It will also be helpful to conduct an error analysis for homework assignments, as for tests (see chapter 10).

Analyzing Tasks

The teacher explains the complicated nature of homework and why it may be difficult to do. When completing homework, students are required to select and utilize various skills and strategies. Reading, writing, note taking, problem solving, self management, and organization and time management skills all come into play. The teacher breaks down the homework completion process into manageable units and explains the tasks listed on the homework completion checklist (Figure 12.2).

Setting Goals

Researchers have documented the importance of guiding students to set homework goals (Kahle & Kelley, 1994; Miller & Kelley, 1994). During instruction, the teacher focuses on homework process goals rather than on the content or accuracy of the homework. General process goals include bringing home the textbook and other resources needed to complete an assignment, starting homework in school, designing a distraction-free environment at home in which to do homework, and checking homework before handing it in.

Self-contracts may be used for students to provide more structure to the homework completion process. The individual tasks of self-contracting, such as the self-selection of goals and rewards, are described in chapter 7. Contracts and guidelines are available for use by students, teachers, and parents (Heacox, 1991; Schumm & Radencich, 1992).

Teachers encourage students to set daily homework goals and develop daily homework plans. A daily homework plan might include the following types of goals:

I will read _____ pages of _____.

I will answer _____ questions in chapter _____.

I will write _____ pages.

I will complete _____ problems in _____.

I will study _____ minutes for my test in _____.

I will complete _____ tasks for my long-term assignment in _____.

Daily homework contracts can begin with these types of goals and include such home-based rewards as watching a favorite television program or talking to a friend on the telephone. For completion of a weekly goal, use of the family car or a special outing may be an appropriate reward.

As a result of seeing the usefulness of the checklist designed by his computer teacher to help him get on task (see Figure 7.2), Myles became interested in using an expanded checklist, which included homework completion. He began to set some goals for himself and subsequently became increasingly more interested and involved in monitoring his own progress. Based on his successes, he became committed to the self-management process. He designed a self-management contract that included homework goals. Excerpts from this contract are provided in Figure 12.3.

Teaching and Modeling Specific Strategies

Effective homework completion involves specific reading and writing strategies combined with strong self-management skills. When doing homework, students must select and apply relevant learning strategies and employ effective organizational and problem-solving skills.

Specifically, the teacher shows how to apply the homework completion process to different types of homework assignments, deal with problems related to time management and motivation, and break assignments down into tasks or steps. Brief discussions of homework problems and solutions enable students to become more independent in the use of their skills in unstructured settings.

When assigning homework, the teacher models the learning and self-management strategies that can be used for homework completion, using a checklist like the one shown in Figure 12.2. Because many students report not knowing where to begin, the teacher pays particular attention to homework start-up. Students are instructed to begin right after they have listed all the tasks needed to complete the homework.

Providing Guided Practice, Feedback, and Reinforcement

To provide guided practice, the teacher models the homework completion process periodically during the course. When the teacher introduces the homework completion process at the beginning of a new term, the instruction is based on a general understanding of student learning difficulties. When instruction is repeated, the teacher bases the discussion on the individual student problems that have surfaced as the term has progressed. Over the course, strategies to complete different types of assignments and solve different types of problems are practiced.

Providing feedback on homework performance is another important teacher responsibility. In general, feedback should identify strengths to be maintained and explain clearly why these things are good; in addition, it should list weaknesses to be corrected and

Figure 12.3 Excerpts from Myles' Self-Management Contract

My long-term goal: College

My short-term goal: Pass all courses
                        Teachers will like me
                        Control my ADD

Objectives: Begin homework in class
                        Complete homework at home
                        Hand in homework to teacher on time

Obstacles: I sometimes don't understand what I'm
                        supposed to do
                        I often don't know how to begin
                        The work is boring
                        I'm always losing things; I can't find my
                        homework

Solutions: Ask teacher to explain directions
                        Ask teacher to help break down assignments
                        into steps

Resources: Use homework completion checklist
                        Use SQ4R checklist for reading
                        Parents (for rewards!)

How to evaluate: Homework completion checklist
                        Teacher says good things
                        Interim grades

Incentives/rewards: Charts and checklists
                        Feel good
                        Special rock concert

explain clearly how to improve these deficiencies. Feedback should also be timely; this means that the teacher gives back homework assignments in time for students to correct them and use them to study for tests.

It is important to remember that for some students, completing homework is a new behavior. To build good homework habits for such students requires frequent attention and reinforcement with gradual fading as the student becomes more successful and independent. Toward this end, the teacher provides opportunities for students to enjoy recognition and praise for work completed or attempted (i.e., effort). The teacher also reinforces students' use of cognitive strategies and self-management skills.

Some specific ways of rewarding improved homework behavior include the following:

Daily praise for any small effort or gain

Posting of completed homework checklists or papers

Specific comments on papers identifying work well done

Weekly recognition on bulletin boards

Positive notes to student and family

Showing the work to others around the school

Asking the student to explain what homework strategies have worked for him or her

The teacher encourages students to recognize their own efforts and to build in positive personal contingencies for working on the homework completion process. This contributes to students' feelings of self-control. Positive and fun-related group contingencies based on homework completion can foster the interest and involvement of otherwise uninvolved or noncompliant students.

Monitoring Progress and Adjusting Activities

Monitoring and evaluation of homework gives the teacher information about the effectiveness of the homework system and helps pinpoint any adjustments that are needed. The teacher continues to collect information on individual student progress. He or she focuses on answering the following types of questions:

Has homework been handed in?

Is it on time?

Is it complete?

Is it accurate?

Are there strengths that need to be emphasized
or extended?

Are there weaknesses that need to be addressed?

ENCOURAGING SELF-MANAGEMENT

Because the major goal of homework is to make the student more responsible for her or his own learning, the teacher and parents must gradually fade their support for homework completion. In order to accomplish this goal, the student needs a repertoire of self-management skills. Students engage in self-reinforcement first, because it is the easiest skill to learn and is also the most rewarding. Self-encouragement and coping statements can be used before the task to encourage start-up, during the task to maintain motivation, and after the task is completed, for reinforcement. Self-evaluation and self-monitoring are added later to help keep the student on task.

Cartoons or photographs illustrating the particular student engaged in a series of self-managed behaviors (e.g., using a calendar, working at a desk, triumphantly putting completed homework into a backpack) can help students who are visual learners. Such graphics can also be used as a checklist at home, providing an interesting and motivating support, especially for middle school students. In addition, signs (e.g., "Do Not Disturb") can be put on doors.

Integrating a variety of self-management skills ensures maintenance of learning strategies. Self-management skills can be used to keep the student on task and/or keep the student motivated. The techniques are modeled by the teacher, practiced by the student in class, and supported at home.

SUMMARY AND CONCLUSIONS

Homework increases student learning and student responsibility for learning. Because of this, homework has an important place in the curriculum. However, many students do not understand the importance of homework, have poor time management and organizational skills, and cannot work independently. Many students do not know how to apply reading and writing strategies to homework.

As with other complex behaviors, homework is a performance task that can be improved with a plan, coaching, and practice. Increased competence realized through better homework efforts is an effective way to build students' self-confidence and strengthen their academic capabilities. Teachers, parents, and students share in the responsibility for homework completion.

The teacher establishes a systematic process to help students improve the quality and quantity of homework. In addition to teaching and modeling homework strategies, the teacher individualizes instruction and provides any necessary homework accommodations. A critical role for classroom teachers is providing information to parents and encouraging them to provide support at home for homework completion.

13

Toward Performance Breakthroughs

Breakthroughs begin with the creativity and motivation of the individual teacher. The teacher provides vision, hope, commitment, and courage. Without vision, goals cannot be established and action plans cannot be developed. Without hope, possibilities cannot be realized and expectations cannot be raised. Without commitment, barriers and challenges cannot be overcome. Without courage, the first step toward breakthrough will never be taken.

Teachers set the stage for breakthroughs in their own classrooms and lead the effort for system change. They help students assume responsibility for their own learning. Like Michelangelo, the teacher combines art and science to discover the *David* in each student. The result of the breakthrough process is the development of a student who says, "I want to learn, and I can learn."

A student who attains a performance breakthrough is able to do his or her best when required. Throughout this book we have presented case studies of students with learning problems who attained performance breakthroughs. In all cases, regardless of the problem, the situation improved and the student started to make progress again. The students were members of diverse ethnic and socioeconomic groups. All were of at least average intelligence and in regular education classes in middle or high school. A few were exceptionally bright.

The following are some of the students and the critical factors behind their breakthroughs:

Nathan. A fifth grader whose transition to middle school was at question, Nathan had a generally good educational situation, and he was making reasonable progress. However, two important additions to his program resulted in a breakthrough. One was the team approach, which allowed the special education teacher consultant to recommend to the regular education teacher ways to individualize instruction for Nathan. The other was having Nathan monitor his own behavior, which served as a self-management tool and increased his motivation to complete work.

Myles.   Myles' situation was finally resolved. His breakthrough was due to a systems correction resulting in an educational plan that addressed both his strengths and weaknesses. Other important elements in Myles' breakthrough were his learning self-management skills and his ongoing counseling. Myles' complicated situation is an example of a problem that cannot be resolved quickly by one person or by one technique.

Kyle.   Kyle, a tenth grader with ADD and learning disabilities who was experiencing an academic crisis, achieved a breakthrough because of changing attitudes and expectations on the part of his classroom teachers. Once his teachers understood Kyle's abilities and disabilities, they were able to design an instructional program in which Kyle could demonstrate what he had learned.

Wendy.   A breakthrough for sixth-grade Wendy came as a result of a problem-solving approach to program planning. Using information from an in-depth assessment, Wendy, her parents, and her teachers were better able to understand her strengths and weaknesses—and, in the process, help her learn to read. Increasing Wendy's motivation to improve her reading skills was another important element in her breakthrough.

Sam.   Sam was experiencing difficulties at the beginning of his sixth-grade year as a result of severe learning disabilities and ADD. Harnessing Sam's strong motivation to succeed and building his educational program around his love of sports and his strong interest in writing helped move him toward his breakthrough.

Elena.   Elena's breakthrough occurred when her teacher tapped into her hidden creativity during a conference regarding a homework assignment. Many students with learning disabilities and/or ADD—like Elena, Kyle, and Sam—are extremely creative and can bloom when a teacher is willing to take the time to solve performance problems.

Performance breakthroughs for Brandon, Nick, Michael, Kim, Cindy, and Asondra came as a result of their learning new cognitive strategies in reading, writing, listening and note taking, and test taking. Sam, Nathan, Kyle, Wendy, and Myles also benefitted from learning new cognitive strategies. Systematic reinforcement of effort and progress by the classroom teacher also played a large part in their success.

The case examples described in this book illustrate the paradoxical nature of the breakthrough process. For example, the more teachers accept and validate students for who they are, the more apt students are to embrace change and increase their efforts. Self-monitoring and recording of specific behaviors can lead beyond the mere counting of those behaviors to student self-regulation. A focus on observable behavior can lead students to deal with deeper performance issues. Systematic problem solving can yield opportunities for creativity.

Many students are embarrassed by their learning problems or disabilities and try to hide them. They tend to feel that they are the only ones with such problems or taking medication. They are often teased by classmates when they receive extra help and therefore often do not want any help. They do not want to deal with their problems. They do not want to be "different." If they are to succeed in school, students with learning and attention problems need to understand their weaknesses and their strengths. They must ask questions to clarify things they do not understand. They must ask for help when they need it.

Teachers can help all students understand their unique patterns of strengths and weaknesses and how they learn best. Teachers can also strive to provide a learning environment in which all students can learn. In addition, teachers can phase out their own control over the learning process by involving students.

During the breakthrough process, a large percentage of the responsibility for student learning passes from the teacher to students. Students become increasingly aware of their strengths and weaknesses, more capable of setting their own academic goals, and more motivated to work toward those goals. Students become adept at self-monitoring and begin to feel more in control of their learning.

When teachers help students focus on strengths, students are more apt to embrace their talents than to ignore or trivialize them. When not driven continually to prove that they can achieve in areas of vulnerability, students learn to accept their weaknesses and put them into perspective. Breakthrough becomes a realistic goal when strengths and interests are combined with preparation, training, and practice.

Students who achieve performance breakthroughs experience positive life changes and become successful adults: They remain in school, graduate, keep and progress in their jobs, make academic or vocational plans aligned with their talents and skills, and develop positive social relationships.

It is important to stress, however, that breakthroughs for students with learning or attention difficulties do not necessarily lead to college. Educators will need to stress to both students and parents that the student has choices. First consideration should be given to options that combine students' strengths and interests and circumvent or deemphasize weaknesses. However, students should not be discouraged from choosing options that include some areas of weakness if they have the necessary motivation and understand the barriers they will encounter. In these cases students need to keep in mind alternative goals if success is beyond their reach. For example, college is probably not an appropriate choice for either Kyle or Wendy. For both, it will be difficult just to survive middle school and high school. In Kyle's case, the best alternative may be for him to join the family business. The work appeals to Kyle and matches his talents. Wendy wants to be an exercise coach. This is an excellent choice because her interests and natural physical attributes are aligned with this field.

FACTORS AFFECTING PERFORMANCE BREAKTHROUGHS

A number of factors affect performance breakthroughs, among them the broader context in which public education takes place, teacher attitudes toward students with learning problems, the conflicting demands that exist in the teaching profession, and parent involvement in educational programming.

The Context of Public Education

The vision of public education in the United States is one in which all children have a right to public education, and all students can learn. In keeping with this vision, educational programs as well as ancillary and supplemental aids and services are provided so that all students can benefit from free, accessible, and appropriate education. Students are expected to graduate from high school, find gainful employment, and contribute as adults to the welfare of the community. Too often, however, reality does not match this vision. Expectations for students with learning and attention problems, as for other students considered at risk, have been particularly low. Such low expectations and acceptance of inadequate or short-term solutions lead to negative long-term consequences for students and society. Rather than aiming for performance breakthroughs, many schools, teachers, parents, and students are content with mere survival.

Forces operating in the world, the nation, the community, and the school system affect the day-to-day educational problems we are attempting to solve. We need to consider where our students are going and how they will get there as we attempt to deal with their more immediate problems. We need to be aware of emerging trends in education, changing societal needs, and the probable shape of tomorrow's world. Such trends concern privatization of education, immigration, racial and ethnic conflict, violence, drug abuse, teen pregnancy, political and religious movements, and economic conditions.

Specific forces within education also have a profound impact on the learning of individual students. Changing definitions of learning disabilities and attention deficit disorders make it difficult for teachers to decide if the student has a problem or not, if the teacher is legally required to make accommodations for the student, and what techniques would be helpful. Teacher union contracts, designed to protect classroom teachers from unfair working conditions, can affect the number of students with disabilities who can be placed in each regular education class.

The philosophy of a particular school with regard to inclusion can affect where a student with ADD or learning disabilities is educated for all or part of the day: Schools with an inclusion philosophy educate all their students with disabilities in regular education classrooms, sending teacher consultants into the regular class to help the student. Other schools provide these services outside the regular classroom.

On the one hand, breakthroughs for students with learning problems do not necessarily require the allocation of extra resources—

money, staff time, or materials. Resources currently within the education system can be mobilized to help these students achieve. On the other hand, school budget constraints are certainly part of the picture, as are the needs of other students in the school.

Teacher Attitudes

Against the backdrop of legislation and social, economic, and educational trends are attitudes toward students with learning problems. Unfortunately, attitudinal barriers can interfere with the delivery of appropriate educational services.

Having seen many efforts to reform education come and go, some teachers may be skeptical of new trends. They may doubt that their students have learning disabilities or ADD, even if these problems have been identified by IEPCs or Section 504 committees. They may fear that making accommodations for students with learning disabilities or ADD lowers academic standards or gives such students an unfair advantage. Teachers need to know that educational research has demonstrated that these students learn as much or more in regular education classes as they do in special education classes (Carlberg & Kavale, 1980; Reynolds, Wang, & Walberg, 1987; Will, 1986) and that both Section 504 and IDEA stipulate that students with learning disabilities belong in the regular education classroom as much as possible. Making accommodations for students with learning disabilities or ADD is as fair as allowing nearsighted students to wear their eyeglasses in class.

Some teachers may feel that modifying teaching strategies to accommodate students with learning disabilities and ADD will require them to expend more time and effort than their already overburdened schedules will permit. Although it may be necessary to expend additional time and effort at first, there will be a savings in the long run because learning problems will be limited and remediated instead of exacerbated. Many of these modifications will help everyone in the class, not just students with learning problems. In addition, teachers are protected by Section 504, which states that efforts to adapt the regular classroom for students with disabilities must be "reasonable" and not cause "undue hardship" to teachers and/or the school.

Special education teacher consultants can help classroom teachers see the value of and integrate appropriate accommodations. In one case, a student who was having difficulty with math worked through a math problem with the assistance of a teacher consultant while the math teacher watched. The teacher consultant told the student to put the problem into his own words. The student complied. Then the teacher consultant asked the student, "What should you do first?" The student answered, "Decide what 'a' represents and then what 'b' represents, then write out the equation." The student proceeded to do this slowly, talking aloud as he did so. The teacher consultant encouraged him to keep checking on the question to be sure that he was writing the equation correctly. When he was ready to solve the equation, the teacher consultant again asked him what he should do first. He told her, then began to work. The teacher consultant occasionally asked him additional questions to keep him on task and to probe for understanding. The math teacher was astonished at this display. He was now convinced that the student knew a lot more about algebra than he had thought. He also understood for the first time what the teacher consultant was actually doing: She was not giving the student the answers. She was keeping the student on task and providing an organizational framework for him within which he could solve the problem. This math teacher became an advocate for other students with learning problems in the school by convincing other teachers of the importance of accommodations.

Finally, students with learning disabilities and ADD often work very hard in school and at home, with little to show for it. Teachers need to understand that these students are not lazy, crazy, or dumb. By definition, students with learning disabilities are at least of average intelligence—and they can be gifted and creative. The right strategies can help these students experience performance breakthroughs.

Conflicting Demands

The schools and classrooms in which we operate are complex and dynamic. Similarly, the behaviors of students with learning and attention difficulties present complicated problems. Working toward solutions requires that educators balance the following types of competing values, demands, priorities, and consequences within their classrooms.

Structure versus flexibility. Students with learning and attention problems need to have school activities structured so that they always know what to do next. On the other hand, teachers must be innovative and flexible in instructional matters in order to solve performance problems.

Control versus independence. Students need to feel that they are largely in charge of their lives. Within a supporting framework designed by teachers and parents, students need to function as independently as possible.

Short-term versus long-term goals. The teacher relates a skill to be learned in the here and now with a positive long-term image of the student. For example: "You are the type of person who can be a leader when you get to the work force. The skill you need to work on now, budgeting time, is a skill needed by an executive."

Group versus individual focus. The teacher conveys the idea that the student is unique and requires individual attention, yet is also a part of the group and needs to cooperate and collaborate.

Strengths versus weaknesses. Focusing on weaknesses in order to remediate them while simultaneously focusing on strengths in order to maximize them and use them to overcome weaknesses has long been the teacher's juggling act. In addition, the teacher works with specific strengths and weaknesses while dealing with the whole person.

In some situations with some students, there are more questions than answers and no perfect, fair, or lasting solutions. Although educators should strive to find solutions, it is important to recognize the following truths:

Some problems don't have perfect solutions. There are times one must choose the best among bad alternatives—at least on a temporary basis.

Some situations are so complicated that it takes a long time to solve them.

Some solutions are a compromise between the educator's best judgment and the parents' and student's preferences.

In some situations there is no right and no wrong—just different opinions and values.

Parent Involvement

Parent involvement may be difficult to achieve, especially in a secondary school environment, where every student has five or more teachers and every teacher has 100 students. In addition, most parents are working and have little time to meet with teachers. However, the role of parents is critical: Any one of a range of parent involvement activities can support the student's educational program, from encouraging students to work hard in school, to helping students with homework, to helping plan an educational program.

GETTING STARTED WITH THE INTEGRATIVE MODEL

The breakthroughs for the students described in this book came about because of the additive effect of the components of the integrative model, discussed at length in chapter 2:

A systems approach

Teamwork

Student involvement

Motivation and student interest

Individualization

A problem-solving approach

Positive expectations

A focus on thinking strategies

A focus on self-management skills

Communication and collaboration with parents

Many of these students had several of these components in place from the beginning. Almost all of them had caring and concerned teachers, willing to go the extra mile in order to discover appropriate instructional strategies to help them learn.

Teachers can foster breakthroughs by implementing the integrative model in content area classrooms. They begin by using aspects of the model they feel most comfortable with and those that can be most easily adapted within their classes. Some teachers begin by using one component in one class once a week while others may be ready to adapt more broad-based changes in their classrooms. In some schools, teachers faced with many students with learning and attention problems may collaborate and integrate aspects of the model in several content areas.

For example, a teacher with little experience working with students who have learning or attention problems may select one or two students in the class who have problems taking lecture notes. Although their problems may be more severe than those of other students, perhaps 50% of the class could also profit from systematic instruction in note taking. The teacher could design one lecture that includes a cognitive strategy and a self-management skill, design a preset format for taking notes, or write three to four main ideas on the chalkboard before the lecture (see chapter 12). Another teacher, perhaps one who has been contemplating improving general reading skills, might provide practice using SQ4R with the text two or three times a week (see chapter 8). In some schools, eighth-grade teachers may teach test preparation and test-taking skills in each of the content areas (see chapter 10). In another school, each eighth-grade teacher may teach a different skill as it applies to his or her own content area.

Once a goal and a plan are set, the teacher considers how he or she can involve and motivate the student. The teacher asks, How can I provide visible, concrete evidence (feedback) to myself and the student about positive outcomes? How can the student become aware of what works and what does not? and How can this feedback be used to help set more challenging goals and extend this work with others in the classroom?

Personal preference, attitudes, previous successes and failures, system conditions and consequences, and training all play a part in the extent to which teachers decide to adapt or experiment with the integrative model. At the simplest level, the goal is to try to help one student and then extend the success to others.

The more teachers apply and add components of the integrative model, the more sensitive they become to the subtleties associated with learning and attention problems. The more intense and specific the investigation, the more obvious the cues pointing to appropriate strategies that enhance performance. As teachers solve problems, they can apply discoveries, insights, and solutions to other students in the class. At the end of the year, they can consider restructuring their class for the following year, based on the year's results.

Classroom teachers need information and resources in order to help individual students overcome learning problems. They need training and support as they strive for breakthroughs. Although individual teachers can achieve breakthroughs for individual students through creativity and hard work, breakthroughs are more easily achieved through a team effort. A team can provide the expertise to help the teacher make appropriate instructional decisions for a particular student. In those systems where training or resources are unavailable or teaming is not currently in use, the classroom teacher can lead the effort for change.

SUMMARY AND CONCLUSIONS

Designing an educational program that fosters breakthroughs for students with learning difficulties means using an integrative model. The individual classroom teacher can do much to help students achieve academic goals by applying the model.

Why envision breakthroughs for students with learning and attention difficulties, especially when progress is lacking and crises are frequent? All students have untapped potential and strengths—and many more than we imagine have hidden gifts and talents. Each teacher has the power to help create a future Thomas Alva Edison, Winston Churchill, W.B. Yeats, Albert Einstein, or Leonardo da Vinci. All of these individuals had learning problems. Not every student with a learning difficulty in school is a genius, but each student deserves to be the best he or she can be.

References

Achenbach, T. M., & Edelbrock, C. (1987). *Manual for the Child Behavior Checklist—Youth Self-Report.* Burlington: University of Vermont, Department of Psychiatry.

Adderholdt-Elliot, M. (1987a). *Perfectionism: What's bad about being good.* Minneapolis: Free Spirit.

Adderholdt-Elliot, M. (1987b). *Tips for procrastinators.* Minneapolis: Free Spirit.

Alberto, P. A., & Troutman, A. C. (1986). *Applied behavior analysis for teachers.* Columbus, OH: Merrill.

American College Testing Program. (1993). *ACT Assessment Test (ACT).* Iowa City: Author.

American Psychiatric Association. (1995). *Diagnostic and statistical manual of mental disorders* (4th ed.). Washington, DC: Author.

American Psychological Association and Presidential Task Force on Psychology in Education. (1993). *Learner-centered psychological principles: Guidelines for school redesign and reform.* Washington, DC: American Psychological Association.

Anderson, W., Chitwood, S., & Hayden, D. (1990). *Negotiating the special education maze: A guide for parents and teachers.* Rockville, MD: Woodbine.

Archbald, D., & Newman, F. M. (1988). *Beyond standardized testing: Assessing authentic academic achievement in the secondary school.* Reston, VA: National Association of Secondary School Principals.

Atkinson, R. H., & Longman, D. G. (1988). *Reading enhancement and development.* St. Paul: West.

Ayers, G. (1994). *Statistical profile of special education in the United States* (Supplement No. 26). Alexandria, VA: Council for Exceptional Children.

Ayllon, T., & Azrin, N. H. (1968). *The token economy.* New York: Appleton.

Baer, D. M., Wolf, M. M., & Risley, T. R. (1968). Some current dimensions of applied behavior analysis. *Journal of Applied Behavior Analysis, 1,* 91–97.

Bandura, A. (1977). *Social learning theory.* Englewood Cliffs, NJ: Prentice-Hall.

Bandura, A. (1986). *Social foundations of thought and action.* Englewood Cliffs, NJ: Prentice-Hall.

Bandura, A., & Cervone, D. (1983). Self-evaluation and self-efficacy mechanisms governing the motivational effects of goal systems. *Journal of Personality and Social Psychology, 45,* 1017–1028.

Baren, M. (1994a). ADHD: Do we finally have it right? *Contemporary Pediatrics, 11*(1), 96–124.

Baren, M. (1994b). ADHD: Management and therapy. *Contemporary Pediatrics, 11*(3), 29–30, 33–40.

Barkley, R. (1990). *Attention Deficit Hyperactivity Disorder: A handbook for diagnosis and treatment.* New York: Guilford.

Becker, W.C., Engelman, S., & Thomas, D.R. (1971). *Teaching: A course in applied psychology.* Chicago: Science Research Associates.

Beirne-Smith, M., & Deck, M.D. (1989). A survey of postsecondary programs for students with learning disabilities. *Journal of Learning Disabilities, 22,* 456–457.

Belanoff, P., & Elbow, P. (1986). Using portfolios to increase collaboration and community in a writing program. *Writing Program Administration, 9*(3), 27–40.

Bem, S.L. (1967). Verbal self-control: The establishment of effective self-instruction. *Journal of Experimental Psychology, 74,* 485–491.

Benjamin, L., & Waltz, G.R. (1989). *Reference for the 90's: Counseling trends for tomorrow.* Ann Arbor: ERIC Clearinghouse on Counseling and Personnel Services.

Berardi-Coletta, B., Dominowski, R.L., Buyer, L.S., & Rellinger, E.R. (1995). Metacognition and problem solving: A process-oriented approach. *Journal of Experimental Psychology, 21,* 205–223.

Bijou, S.W., & Sturges, P.T. (1959). Positive reinforcers for experimental studies with children: Consumables and manipulatives. *Child Development, 3,* 151–170.

Blalock, J. (1981). Persistent problems and concerns of young adults with learning disabilities. In W. Cruickshank & A. Silver (Eds.), *Bridges of tomorrow: The best of ACLD* (Vol 2., pp. 35–55). Syracuse, NY: Syracuse University Press.

Bleuer, J. (1987). *Counseling underachievers.* Ann Arbor: ERIC Clearinghouse on Counseling and Personnel Services.

Bloom, B.S. (Ed.). (1956). Taxonomy of educational objectives. *The classification of educational goals: Handbook 1. Cognitive domain.* New York: David McKay.

Bloomer, R.H. (1962). The cloze procedure as a remedial reading exercise. *Journal of Developmental Reading, 5,* 173–181.

Borkowski, J.G., Day, J.D., Saenz, D., Dietmeyer, D., Estrada, T.M., & Groteluschen, A. (1992). Expanding the boundaries of cognitive interventions. In B.Y.L. Wong (Ed.), *Contemporary intervention research in learning disabilities: An international perspective* (pp. 1–21). New York: Springer-Verlag.

Bornmouth, J. (1968, April). The cloze readability procedure. *Elementary English, 45,* 429–436.

Bornstein, P.H., & Quevillon, R.P. (1976). The effects of a self-instructional package on over-active boys. *Journal of Applied Behavior Analysis, 9,* 179–188.

Bos, C.S., & Anders, P.L. (1992). A theory-driven interactive instructional model for text comprehension and content learning. In B.Y.L. Wong (Ed.), *Contemporary intervention research in learning disabilities: An international perspective* (pp. 81–95). New York: Springer-Verlag.

Brown, A.L. (1978). Knowing when, where, and how to remember: A problem of metacognition. In R. Glaser (Ed.), *Advances in instructional psychology* (Vol. 1, pp. 77–167). Hillsdale, NJ: Erlbaum.

Brown, A.L. (1980). Metacognitive development and reading. In R.J. Spiro, B.C. Bruce, & W. Brewer (Eds.), *Theoretical issues in reading comprehension* (pp. 453–481). Hillsdale, NJ: Erlbaum.

Brown, J.I., Bennett, J.M., & Hanna, G.S. (1993). *Nelson-Denny Reading Test, Forms G & H.* Chicago: Riverside.

Brown, V.L., Hammill, D.D., & Wiederholt, J.L. (1994). *Test of Reading Comprehension (TORC-3).* Chicago: Riverside.

California Test Bureau. (1985). *California Achievement Tests.* Monterey, CA: McGraw-Hill.

Calkins, L.M. (1986). *The art of teaching writing.* Portsmouth, NH: Heinemann.

Camp, B.W., & Bash, M.A.S. (1985). *Think Aloud: Increasing social and cognitive skills—A problem-solving program for children (Grades 1–2).* Champaign, IL: Research Press.

Carbo, M., Dunn, R., & Dunn, K. (1991). *Teaching students to read through their individual learning styles.* Boston: Allyn & Bacon.

Carlberg, C., & Kavale, K. (1980). The efficacy of special versus regular education placement for exceptional children: A meta-analysis. *Journal of Special Education, 14,* 295–309.

Carrow-Woolfolk, E. (1985). *Test for Auditory Comprehension of Language–Revised (TALC-R).* Chicago: Riverside.

Clark, F. L., Deshler, D. D., Schumaker, J. B., Alley, G. R., & Warner, M. M. (1984). Visual imagery and self-questioning: Strategies to improve comprehension of written material. *Journal of Learning Disabilities, 17,* 145–149.

Cohen, R., Knudsvig, G., Markel, G., Patten, D., Shtogren, J., & Wilhelm, R. M. (1973). *Quest: Academic skills program.* Orlando, FL: Harcourt Brace Jovanovich.

College Board. (1993). *Scholastic Achievement Test II: Subject Tests.* New York: Author.

College Board. (1995a). *Preliminary Scholastic Assessment Test.* New York: Author.

College Board. (1995b). *Scholastic Assessment Test I: Reasoning Test.* New York: Author.

Conners, C. K. (1989a). *Conners' Parent Rating Scale.* North Tonawanda, NY: Multi-Health Systems.

Conners, C. K. (1989b). *Conners' Teacher Rating Scale.* North Tonawanda, NY: Multi-Health Systems.

Cook, D. M. (1991). *Strategic learning in the content areas.* Madison: Wisconsin Department of Public Instruction.

Davey, B. (1985). Helping readers think beyond print through self-questioning. *Middle School Journal, 17*(1), 26–27.

De Bono, E. (1989). The direct teaching of thinking in education and the CoRT method. In P. Davies & S. Maclure (Eds.), *Learning to think– Thinking to learn: Proceedings of the 1989 Organization for Economic Cooperation and Development Conference* (pp. 3–14). New York: Pergamon.

Deci, E. L., Vallerand, R. J., Pelletier, L. G., & Ryan, R. M. (1991). Motivation and education: The self-determination perspective. *Educational Psychologist, 26,* 325–346.

Deem, J. (1993). *Study skills in practice.* Boston, MA: Houghton Mifflin.

De Jong, P. C. M., & Robert-Jan Simons, R. P. (1992). Training metacognitive processes of self-regulated learning. In B. Y. L. Wong (Ed.), *Contemporary intervention research in learning disabilities: An international perspective* (pp. 115–133). New York: Springer-Verlag.

Deshler, D.D., Schumaker, J.B., & Lenz, D.K. (1984). Academic and cognitive intervention for LD adolescents: Part I. *Journal of Learning Disabilities, 17,* 108–117.

Downing, J.A., Moran, M.R., Myles, B.S., & Ormsbee, C.K. (1991). Using reinforcement in the classroom. *Intervention in School and Clinic, 27,* 85–90.

Dunn, L.M., & Dunn, L.M. (1981). *Peabody Picture Vocabulary Test–Revised (PPVT-R).* Circle Pines, MN: American Guidance Service.

Dunn, R., & Dunn, K. (1978). *Teaching students through their individual learning styles.* Englewood Cliffs, NJ: Prentice-Hall.

Eccles, J.S., & Midgely, C. (1989). Stage-environment fit: Developmentally appropriate classrooms for young adolescents. In C. Ames & R. Ames (Eds.), *Research on motivation in education* (Vol. 3, pp. 139–186). San Diego, CA: Academic.

Ellis, D. (1994). *Becoming a master student.* Rapid City, SD: Houghton Mifflin.

Ellis, E.S. (1993). Integrative strategy instruction: A potential model for teaching content area subjects to adolescents with learning disabilities. *Journal of Learning Disabilities, 26,* 358–383, 398.

Ellis, E.S., Deshler, D.D., Schumaker, J.B., & Alley, G.R. (1989). Effects of generalization instruction on the written language performance of adolescents with learning disabilities in the mainstream classroom. *Journal of Reading, Writing, and Learning Disabilities, 4,* 291–309.

Ellis, E.S., Deshler, D.D., Schumaker, J.B., Lenz, D.K., & Clark, F.L. (1991). An instructional model for teaching learning strategies. *Focus on Exceptional Children, 23,* 1–4.

Englert, C., Raphael, T., Fear, K., & Anderson, L. (1988). Students' meta-cognitive knowledge about how to write informational texts. *Learning Disabilities Quarterly, 11,* 18–46.

Fantuzzo, J.W., & Atkins, M. (1992). Applied behavior analysis for educators: Teacher centered and classroom based. *Journal of Applied Behavior Analysis, 25,* 37–42.

Fernald, G. (1943). *Remedial techniques in basic school subjects.* New York: McGraw-Hill.

Ferrett, S.K. (1994). *Peak performance.* Burr Ridge, IL: Irwin Mirror Press.

Fisher, R., Ury, W., & Patton, B. (1991). *Getting to yes: Negotiating agreement without giving in.* Boston: Houghton Mifflin.

Fox, L., Brody, L., & Tobin, D. (Eds.). (1983). *Learning disabled gifted children: Identification and programming.* Baltimore: University Park Press.

Frith, G. (1991). Facilitating homework through effective support systems. *Teaching Exceptional Children, 21,* 242–252.

Fry, E. (1977). Fry's Readability Graph: Clarifications, validity, and extension to Level 17. *Journal of Reading, 21,* 242–252.

Frymier, J. (1989). *A study of students at-risk: Collaborating to do research.* Bloomington, IN: Phi Delta Kappa.

Fuchs, L.S. (1994). *Connecting performance assessment to instruction.* Reston, VA: Council for Exceptional Children.

Gagne, R.M. (1985). *The conditions of learning and theory of instruction.* New York: Holt, Rinehart and Winston.

Gajar, A.H. (1989). A computer analysis of written language variables and a comparison of compositions written by university students with and without learning disabilities. *Journal of Learning Disabilities, 22,* 125–130.

Ganschow, L. (1984). Analysis of written language of a language learning disabled (dyslexic) college student and instructional implications. *Annals of Dyslexia, 34,* 271–284.

Garmston, R., & Linder, C.W. (1993). Reflections on cognitive coaching. *Educational Leadership, 51*(2), 57–61.

Gillingham, A., & Stillman, B.W. (1973). *Remedial training for children with specific disability in reading, speaking, and penmanship.* Cambridge, MA: Educators Publishing Service.

Girdano, D., & Everly, G. (1979). *Controlling stress and tension.* Englewood Cliffs, NJ: Prentice-Hall.

Goldstein, A.P. (1988). *The Prepare Curriculum: Teaching prosocial competencies.* Champaign, IL: Research Press.

Goyette, C.H., Conners, C.K., & Ulrich, R.F. (1978). Normative data on revised Conners' Parent and Teacher Rating Scales. *Journal of Abnormal Psychology, 6,* 221–236.

Graham, S., & Harris, K.R. (1992). Self-regulated strategy development: Programmatic research in writing. In B.Y.L. Wong (Ed.), *Contemporary intervention in learning disabilities: An international perspective* (pp. 47–64). New York: Springer-Verlag.

Graham, S., Harris, K.R., MacArthur, C.A., & Schwartz, S. (1991). Writing and writing instruction for students with learning disabilities: Review of research program. *Learning Disability Quarterly, 14,* 89–114.

Graham, S., MacArthur, C. A., Schwartz, S., & Page-Voth, V. (1992). Improving the compositions of students with learning disabilities using a strategy involving product and process goal setting. *Exceptional Children, 58,* 322–334.

Grayson, D. A., & Martin, M.D. (1985). *Teacher expectations of student achievement (TESA).* Downey, CA: Los Angeles County Office of Education.

Greenbaum, J. (1990a). An overview of parent involvement activities. *Equity Coalition: Programs for Educational Opportunity, 2,* 3, 21 [School Newsletter].

Greenbaum, J. (1990b). The Parent Involvement Checklist. *Equity Coalition: Programs for Educational Opportunity, 1,* 12–13 [School Newsletter].

Greenbaum, J., & Markel, G. (1992). Crisis prevention for parents of children with handicapping conditions. In H. Parad & L. Parad (Eds.), *Crisis intervention: Book 2* (pp. 359–385). Milwaukee: Family Service of America.

Greenbaum, L.A., & Schmerl, R.B. (1970). *Course X: A left field guide to freshman English.* Philadelphia: Lippincott.

Greenberg, L. M., & Waldman, J.W. (1993). Developmental normative data on Test of Variables of Attention (T.O.V.A.). *Journal of Child Psychology and Psychiatry, 34,* 1019–1030.

Hagen, J.W. (1984). Development of memory and attention. In M.D. Levine & P. Satz (Eds.), *Middle childhood: Development and dysfunction* (pp. 31–45). Baltimore: University Park Press.

Hagen, J.W., & Barclay, D.R. (1982). The development of memory skills in children: Portraying learning disabilities in terms of strategy and knowledge deficiencies. In W. Cruickshank (Ed.), *Coming of age: The best of ACLD* (Vol. 3, pp. 127–141). Syracuse, NY: Syracuse University Press.

Hall, R.J. (1980). Cognitive behavior modification and information processing skills of exceptional children. *Exceptional Children Quarterly, 1,* 9–16.

Hallahan, D.P., & Bryan, T.H. (1981). Learning disabilities. In J.M. Kauffman & D.P. Hallahan (Eds.), *Handbook of special education* (pp. 141–164). Englewood Cliffs, NJ: Prentice-Hall.

Hammill, D.D. (1995). Problems in written composition. In D.D. Hammill & N.R. Bartel (Eds.), *Teaching students with learning and behavior problems* (5th ed., pp. 179–217). Boston: Allyn & Bacon.

Hammill, D.D., Brown, V.L., Larsen, S.C., & Wiederholt, J.L. (1993). *Test of Adolescent Language: TOAL-3* (3rd ed.). Chicago: Riverside.

Hammill, D.D., & Larsen, S.C. (1988). *Test of Written Language: TOWL-2* (2nd ed.). Austin, TX: PRO-ED.

Harris, K.R., & Graham, S. (1988). Self-instructional strategy training: Improving writing skills among educationally handicapped students. *Teaching Exceptional Children, 20,* 35–37.

Hartley, J., & Marshall, S. (1974). On notes and note-taking. *Universities Quarterly, 4,* 225–235.

Hayes, J., & Flower, L. (1986). Writing research and the writer. *American Psychologist, 41,* 1106–1113.

Heacox, D. (1991). *Up from underachievement: How teachers, students, and parents can work together to promote student success.* Minneapolis: Free Spirit.

Helge, D. (1989a). Concerns regarding "at-risk" students. In *Hearing before the Subcommittee on the Handicapped of the Committee on Labor and Human Resources on the Reauthorization of the EHA Discretionary Programs* (pp. 237–238). Washington, DC: U.S. Government Printing Office.

Helge, D. (1989b). Rural "at-risk" students: Directions for policy and intervention. *Rural Special Education Quarterly, 10*(1), 3–16.

Hendrickson, J. (1992). Assessing the student-instructional setting interface using an eco-behavioral observation system. *Preventing School Failure, 36*(3), 2–8.

Herman, J.L. (1992). What research tells us about good assessment. *Educational Leadership, 49*(8), 74–78.

Herman, J.L., Aschbacker, P.R., & Winters, L.A. (1992). *A practical guide to alternative assessment.* Alexandria, VA: Association for Supervision and Curriculum Development.

Hipp, E. (1995). *Fighting invisible tigers: A stress management guide for teens.* Minneapolis: Free Spirit.

Homme, L., Csanyi, A.P., Gonzales, M.A., & Rechs, J.R. (1970). *How to use contingency contracting in the classroom.* Champaign, IL: Research Press.

Horowitz, J. (1986). Controlling impulsiveness: Self-awareness exercises. *Academic Therapy, 21,* 275–282.

Hudson, P., Lignugaris-Kraft, B., & Miller, T. (1993). Using content enhancements to improve the performance of adolescents with learning disabilities in content classes. *Learning Disabilities Research & Practice, 8*(2), 106–126.

Hughes, C.A., & Smith, J.O. (1990). Cognitive and academic performance of college students with learning disabilities: A synthesis of the literature. *Learning Disabilities Quarterly, 13,* 66–79.

Humes, A. (1983). Research on the composing process. *Review of Educational Research, 53,* 201–216.

Jones, B.F., Palincsar, A.S., Ogle, D.S., & Carr, E.G. (1987). *Strategic teaching and learning: Cognitive instruction in the content areas.* Alexandria, VA: Association for Supervision and Curriculum Development.

Kahle, A.L., & Kelley, M.L. (1994). Children's homework problems: A comparison of goal setting and parent training. *Behavior Therapy, 25,* 275–290.

Karlsen, B., Madden, R., & Gardner, E. (1977). *Stanford Diagnostic Reading Test.* Orlando, FL: Harcourt Brace Jovanovich.

Kaufman, A.S. (1979). *Intelligent testing with the WISC–III.* New York: Wiley.

Kaufman, A.S., & Kaufman, N.L. (1985). *Kaufman Test of Educational Achievement.* Circle Pines, MN: American Guidance Service.

Keeney, R.L., & Raiffa, H. (1976). *Decisions with multiple objectives: Preferences and value tradeoffs.* New York: Wiley.

Kerman, S., Kimball, T., & Martin, M.D. (1980). *Teacher Expectations and Student Achievement (TESA).* Bloomington, IN: Phi Delta Kappa.

Kern, L., Childs, K.E., Dunlap, G., Clarke, S., & Falk, G.D. (1994). Using assessment-based curricular intervention to improve the classroom behavior of a student with emotional and behavioral challenges. *Journal of Applied Behavior Analysis, 27,* 7–19.

Kiewra, K.A. (1984). Implications for notetaking based on relationships between notetaking variables and achievement measures. *Reading Improvement, 21,* 145–149.

King, W.L.K., & Jarrow, J.E. (1990). *Testing accommodations for students with disabilities.* Washington, DC: Association on Higher Education and Disabilities.

Knapczyk, D.R., & Livingston, G. (1972). Self-recording and student-teacher supervision variables within a token economy structure. *Journal of Applied Behavior Analysis, 5,* 293–309.

Kolb, D.A. (1976). *The Learning Style Inventory.* Boston: McBer.

Krumboltz, J.D., & Thoresen, C.E. (1969). *Behavioral counseling: Cases and techniques.* New York: Holt, Rinehart and Winston.

Lazear, D. (1991). *Seven ways of teaching: The artistry of teaching with multiple intelligences.* Palatine, IL: Skylight.

Lenz, D.K., Bulgren, J., & Hudson, P.J. (1990). Content enhancement: A model for promoting the acquisition of content by individuals with learning disabilities. In T. Scruggs & B.Y.L. Wong (Eds.), *Intervention research in learning disabilities* (pp. 122–165). New York: Springer-Verlag.

Levine, E.K., Zigmond, N., & Birch, J.W. (1983, April). *A follow-up study of 52 learning disabled adolescents.* Paper presented at the meeting of the American Educational Research Association, Montreal.

Levine, M.D. (1986). *The ANSER* system: Aggregate Neurobehavioral Student Health and Educational Review.* Cambridge, MA: Educators Publishing Service.

Levine, M.D. (1987). *Developmental variations and learning disorders.* Cambridge, MA: Educators Publishing Service.

Levine, M.D. (1990). *Keeping a head in school.* Cambridge, MA: Educators Publishing Service.

Levine, M.D. (1993). *All kinds of minds.* Cambridge, MA: Educators Publishing Service.

Lindsley, O.R. (1992). Precision teaching: Discoveries and effects. *Journal of Applied Behavior Analysis, 25,* 51–57.

Maag, J.W., & Reid, R. (1994). Attention Deficit Hyperactivity Disorder—A functional approach to assessment and treatment. *Behavior Disorders, 20,* 5–23.

Madraso, J. (1993). Proofreading: The skill we've neglected to teach. *English Journal, 82*(2), 32–39.

Malnar, K. (1993). Toward an analysis of assessment: Current practice and beyond. *Michigan Association for Supervision and Curriculum Development, 15*(1), 7–13.

Margulies, N. (1991). *Mapping inner space: Learning and teaching mind mapping.* Tucson: Zephyr.

Markel, G. (1981a). Improving test-taking skills of LD adolescents. *Academic Therapy, 16,* 333–342.

Markel, G. (1981b). Self-management in the classroom. In Percy Bates National Support Systems Project (Ed.), *Mainstreaming: Our current knowledge base* (pp. 161–183). Minneapolis: University of Minnesota, School of Education.

Markel, G., & Greenbaum, J. (1985). *Parents are to be seen and heard: Assertiveness in educational planning for handicapped children.* Ann Arbor: G & M Associates.

Mason, L.J. (1980). *A different kind of classroom: Techniques and dimensions of learning.* Alexandria, VA: Association for Supervision and Curriculum Development.

McCarney, S.B. (1989). *Attention deficit disorders intervention manual.* Columbia, MO: Hawthorne Educational Services.

McCarthy, B. (1990). Using the 4MAT system to bring learning styles to schools. *Educational Leadership, 48*(2), 31–37.

McWhorter, K.T. (1980). *College reading and study skills.* Rapid City, SD: Little, Brown.

Meichenbaum, D.H. (1977). *Cognitive behavior modification.* New York: Plenum.

Meichenbaum, D.H., & Goodman, J. (1971). Training impulsive children to talk to themselves: A means of developing self-control. *Journal of Abnormal Psychology, 77,* 115–126.

Menke, D.J., & Davey, B. (1994). Teachers' views of textbooks and text reading instruction: Experience matters. *Journal of Reading, 37,* 464–470.

Menke, D.J., & Pressley, M. (1994). Elaborative interrogation: Using "why" questions to enhance learning from text. *Journal of Reading, 37,* 642–645.

Mercer, C.D., & Mercer, A.R. (1993). *Teaching students with learning problems* (4th ed.). Columbus, OH: Merrill.

Miholic, V. (1994). An inventory to pique students' metacognitive awareness of reading strategies. *Journal of Reading, 38,* 84–86.

Miller, D.L., & Kelley, M.L. (1994). The use of goal setting and contingency contracting for improving children's homework performance. *Journal of Applied Behavior Analysis, 27,* 73–84.

Morgan, M. (1987). Self-monitoring and goal setting in private study. *Contemporary Educational Psychology, 12,* 1–6.

National Joint Committee on Learning Disabilities. (1987). A position paper. *Journal of Learning Disabilities, 20,* 107–108.

Naughton, V.M. (1993/1994). Creative mapping for content reading. *Journal of Reading, 37,* 324–326.

O'Leary, S.G., & Dubey, D.R. (1979). Applications of self-control procedures by children: A review. *Journal of Applied Behavior Analysis, 12,* 449–465.

Olympia, D.E., Sheridan, S.M., Jenson, W.A., & Andrews, D. (1994). Using self-managed interventions to increase homework completion and accuracy. *Journal of Applied Behavior Analysis, 27,* 85–99.

Palincsar, A.S., & Brown, A.L. (1984). Reciprocal teaching of comprehension fostering and comprehension monitoring activities. *Cognition and Instruction, 2,* 117–175.

Palincsar, A.S., Brown, A.L., & Martin, S. (1987). Peer interaction in reading comprehension instruction. *Educational Psychologist, 22,* 231–253.

Palincsar, A.S., & David, Y.M. (1992). Classroom-based literacy instruction: The development of one program of intervention research. In B.Y.L. Wong (Ed.), *Contemporary intervention research in learning disabilities: An international perspective* (pp. 65–80). New York: Springer-Verlag.

Palkes, H., Stewart, W., & Kahana, B. (1968). Porteus maze performance of hyperactive boys after training in self-directed verbal commands. *Child Development, 39,* 817–826.

Paris, S.G., Lipson, M.Y., & Wixson, K.K. (1983). Becoming a strategic reader. *Contemporary Educational Psychology, 8,* 293–316.

Paris, S.G., & Newman, R.S. (1990). Developmental aspects of self-regulated learning. *Educational Psychologist, 25,* 87–102.

Parker, H. (1990). *Listen, look, and think: A self-regulation program for children.* Plantation, FL: Impact.

Peck, K.L., & Hannafin, M.J. (1983). The effects of notetaking pretraining on the recording of notes and retention of aural instruction. *Journal of Educational Research, 77,* 100–117.

Pintrich, P.R., & Schrauben, B. (1992). *Students' motivational beliefs and their cognitive engagement in the classroom.* Hillsdale, NJ: Erlbaum.

Pressley, M., & Rankin, J. (1994). More about whole language methods of reading instruction for students at risk for early reading failure. *Learning Disabilities Practices, 9,* 157–168.

Quinn, E. (1988). *Rational management: Mastering the paradoxes and competing demands of high performance.* San Francisco: Jossey-Bass.

Radencich, M.C., & Schumm, J.S. (1988). *How to help your child with homework.* Minneapolis: Free Spirit.

Rankin, E.P., Jr. (1959). Uses of the cloze procedure in the reading clinic. In J.A. Figurel (Ed.), *International Reading Association conference proceedings: Reading in a changing society* (Vol. 4, pp. 228–232). New York. Scholastic.

Reid, D.K. (1988). *Teaching the learning disabled: A cognitive developmental approach.* Boston: Allyn & Bacon.

Reynolds, M., Wang, M.C., & Walberg, H.J. (1987). The necessary restructuring of special and regular education. *Exceptional Children, 53,* 391–397.

Rhode, G., Morgan, D. P., & Young, K.R. (1983). Generalization and maintenance of treatment gains for behaviorally disordered students from resource rooms to regular classrooms using self-evaluation procedures. *Journal of Applied Behavior Analysis, 16,* 171–188.

Rief, S. (1993). *How to reach and teach ADD/ADHD children: Practical techniques, strategies, and interventions for helping children with attention problems and hyperactivity.* West Nyack, NY: Center for Applied Research in Education.

Roberts, G.C., & Guttormson, L. (1990). *You and stress: A survival guide for adolescence.* Minneapolis: Free Spirit.

Robin, A.L. (1990). Training families with ADHD adolescents. In R. Barkley, *Attention Deficit Hyperactivity Disorder: A handbook for diagnosis and treatment* (pp. 462–497). New York: Guilford.

Robinson, A. (1993). *What smart students know.* New York: Crown.

Robinson, F. (1941). *Effective study.* New York: Harper & Row.

Rose, M.C., Cundick, B.P., & Higbee, K.L. (1983). Verbal rehearsal and visual imagery: Mnemonic aids for learning disabled children. *Journal of Learning Disabilities, 16,* 352–354.

Rosenbery, M.S. (1989). The effects of daily homework assignments on acquisition of basic skills by students with learning disabilities. *Journal of Learning Disabilities, 22,* 314–323.

Rosenshine, B., & Meister, C. (1992). The use of scaffolding for teaching higher level cognitive strategies. *Educational Leadership, 49*(8), 26–33.

Rosenthal, R., & Jacobson, L. (1968). *Pygmalion in the classroom: Teacher expectations and pupils' intellectual development.* New York: Holt, Rinehart and Winston.

Ruhl, K.L., Hughes, C.A., & Gajar, A.H. (1990). Efficacy of the pause procedure for enhancing learning disabled and nondisabled college students' long- and short-term recall of facts presented through lecture. *Learning Disabilities Quarterly, 13,* 55–64.

Salvia, J.E., & Ysseldyke, J.E. (1991). *Assessment in special and remedial education* (4th ed.). Boston: Houghton Mifflin.

Saski, J., Swicegood, P., & Carter, J. (1983). Notetaking formats for learning disabled adolescents. *Learning Disabilities Quarterly, 6,* 265–272.

Sattler, J.M. (1988). *Assessment of children.* San Diego: Author.

Scardamalia, M., & Bereiter, C. (1986). Research on written composition. In M. Wittrock (Ed.), *Handbook of research and teaching* (Vol. 3, pp. 778–803). New York: Macmillan.

Schumaker, J.B., & Deshler, D.D. (1992). Validation of learning strategy interventions for students with learning disabilities: Results of a programmatic research effort. In B.Y.L. Wong (Ed.), *Contemporary intervention research in learning disabilities: An international perspective* (pp. 22–46). New York: Springer-Verlag.

Schumm, J.S., & Radencich, M. (1992). *School power: Strategies for success in school.* Minneapolis: Free Spirit.

Schunk, D.H. (1990). Goal setting and self-efficacy during self-regulated learning. *Educational Psychologist, 25,* 71–86.

Schunk, D.H. (1991). Self-efficacy and academic motivation. *Educational Psychologist, 26,* 207–231.

Schunk, D.H., & Rice, J.M. (1987). Enhancing comprehension skill and self-efficacy with strategy value information. *Journal of Reading Behavior, 19,* 285–302.

Schunk, D.H., & Zimmerman, B.J. (1994). *Self-regulation of learning and performance: Issues and educational applications.* Hillsdale, NJ: Erlbaum.

Schwartz, S.S., & MacArthur, C.A. (1990). They all have something to say: Helping learning disabled students to write. *Academic Therapy, 25,* 459–472.

Scruggs, T., & Mastropieri, M. (1993). Special education for the twenty-first century: Integrating learning strategies and thinking skills. *Journal of Learning Disabilities, 26,* 392–398.

Semel, E., Wiig, E.H., & Secord, W. (1987). *Clinical Evaluation of Language Fundamentals–Revised (CELF-R).* San Antonio: Psychological Corporation.

Shapiro, E.S. (1989). Teaching self-management skills to learning disabled adolescents. *Learning Disabilities Quarterly, 12,* 275–287.

Short, E.J., & Weissberg-Benchell, J.A. (1989). The triple alliance for learning: Cognition, metacognition, and motivation. In C.B. McCormick, G.E. Miller, and M. Pressley (Eds.), *Cognitive strategy research: Implications for the curriculum from basic research to educational applications* (pp. 33–63). New York: Springer-Verlag.

Silver, L.B. (1992). *Attention Deficit Hyperactivity Disorder: A clinical guide to diagnosis and treatment.* Washington, DC: American Psychiatric Press.

Silverman, L.K. (1989). Invisible gifts, invisible handicaps. *Roper Review, 12,* 37–42.

Smith, D.E.P. (Ed.). (1961). *Learning to learn.* New York: Harcourt Brace Jovanovich.

Smith, D. J., Young, R., West, R. P., Morgan, D. P., & Rhode, G. (1988). Reducing the disruptive behavior of junior high school students: A classroom self-management procedure. *Behavior Disorders, 13,* 231–239.

Smith, J. C. (1985). *Relaxation dynamics: Nine world approaches to self-relaxation.* Champaign, IL: Research Press.

Sprick, R. M., Sprick, M., & Garrison, M. (1993). *Interventions: Collaborative planning for students at risk.* Longmont, CO: Sopris West.

Suinn, R. M. (1990). *Anxiety management training.* New York: Plenum.

Sulzer-Azaroff, B., & Mayer, G. R. (1986). *Achieving educational excellence using behavioral strategies.* New York: Holt, Rinehart and Winston.

Suritsky, S. K., & Hughes, C. A. (1991). Benefits of notetaking: Implications for secondary and postsecondary students with learning disabilities. *Learning Disabilities Quarterly, 14,* 7–17.

Suter, D. P., & Wolf, J. S. (1987). Issues in the identification and programming of the gifted/learning disabled child. *Journal for the Education of the Gifted, 10,* 227–237.

Taylor, R. (1989). *Assessment of exceptional students: Educational and psychological procedure.* Englewood Cliffs, NJ: Prentice-Hall.

Torgensen, J. K., & Houck, D. G. (1980). Processing deficiencies of learning disabled children who perform poorly on the Digit Span Test. *Journal of Educational Psychology, 72,* 141–160.

Tucker, J., Stevens, L. J., & Ysseldyke, J. E. (1983). Learning disabilities: The experts speak out. *Journal of Learning Disabilities, 16,* 6–14.

Ullman, R. K., Sleator, E. K., & Sprague, R. L. (1991). *ADD-H: Comprehensive Teacher's Rating Scale (ACTeRS)* (2nd ed.). Chicago: Riverside.

Vernon, A. (1989). *Thinking, feeling, behaving: An emotional education curriculum for adolescents.* Champaign, IL: Research Press.

Walter, T., & Siebert, A. (1992). *Student success: How to be a better student and still have time for your friends.* New York: Holt, Rinehart and Winston.

Weber, A. M. (1988). A new clinical measure of attention: The Attentional Capacity Test. *Neuropsychology, 2,* 59–71.

Wechsler, D. (1981). *Wechsler Adult Intelligence Scale–Revised (WAIS-R).* San Antonio: Psychological Corporation.

Wechsler, D. (1991). *Wechsler Intelligence Scale for Children–Third Edition (WISC-III).* San Antonio: Psychological Corporation.

Weinstein, C.E., Schulte, A.C., & Palmer, D.R. (1987). *LASSI: Learning and Study Strategies Inventory.* Clearwater, FL: H & H Publishing Company.

Welch, M., & Link, D.P. (1992). The PLEASE strategy: A metacognitive learning strategy for improving the paragraph writing of students with mild learning disabilities. *Learning Disabilities Quarterly, 15,* 119–128.

White-Blackburn, G., Semb, S., & Semb, G. (1977). The effects of good behavior contracts on the classroom behavior of sixth-grade students. *Journal of Applied Behavior Analysis, 10,* 310–312.

Whitmore, J. (1980). *Giftedness, conflict, and underachievement.* Boston, MA: Allyn & Bacon.

Wiederholt, J.L., & Bryant, B.R. (1992). *Gray Oral Reading Test (GORT-3)* (3rd ed.). Chicago: Riverside.

Wiens, J. (1983). Metacognition and the adolescent passive learner. *Journal of Learning Disabilities, 16,* 144–149.

Wiggins, G.P. (1993). *Assessing student performance: Exploring the problems and limits of testing.* San Francisco: Jossey-Bass.

Wilkinson, G.S. (1993). *Wide Range Achievement Test (WRAT-3).* Wilmington, DE: Jastak.

Will, M.C. (1986). Educating children with learning problems: A shared responsibility. *Exceptional Children, 52,* 411–415.

Williams, R.A. (1972). A table for rapid determination of revised Dale-Chall readability scores. *The Reading Teacher, 26,* 158–165.

Wittrock, M.C. (Ed.). (1983). *Handbook of research and testing.* New York: Macmillan.

Wong, B.Y.L. (Ed.). (1992). *Contemporary intervention research in learning disabilities: An international perspective.* New York: Springer-Verlag.

Wong, B.Y.L. (1993). Pursuing an elusive goal: Molding strategic teachers and learners. *Journal of Learning Disabilities, 26,* 354–357.

Wong, B.Y.L., & Jones, W. (1982). Increasing metacomprehension in learning disabled and normally achieving students through self-questioning training. *Learning Disabilities Quarterly, 5,* 228–240.

Wood, J. (1992). *Adapting instruction for mainstream and at-risk students.* New York: Merrill.

Wood, R., & Bandura, A. (1989). Impact of conceptions of ability on self-regulatory mechanisms and complex decision-making. *Journal of Personality and Social Psychology, 56,* 407–415.

Woodcock, R.W. (1987). *Woodcock Reading Mastery Tests.* Circle Pines, MN: American Guidance Service.

Woodcock, R.W., & Johnson, M.B. (1989). *Woodcock-Johnson Psycho-Educational Battery–Revised: Parts I and II.* Allen, TX: Developmental Learning Materials.

Zieffle, T.H., & Romney, D.M. (1985). Comparison of self-instruction and relaxation training in reducing impulsive and inattentive behavior of learning disabled children on cognitive tasks. *Psychological Reports, 57,* 271–274.

Zimmerman, B.J. (1989). Models of self-regulated learning and academic achievement. In B.J. Zimmerman & D.H. Schunk (Eds.), *Self-regulated learning and academic achievement: Theory, research, and practice.* New York: Springer-Verlag.

Zimmerman, B.J., Greenberg, D., & Weinstein, C.E. (1994). Self-regulating academic study time: A strategy approach. In B.J. Zimmerman & D.H. Schunk (Eds.), *Self-regulation of learning and performance: Issues and educational applications.* Hillsdale, NJ: Erlbaum.

Author Index

Subject Index

Academic writing.
    See Writing skills
ACT
    American College Test, 178
    Attentional Capacity Test, 91
ACTeRS (ADD-H:
    Comprehensive Teacher's
    Rating Scale), 91
Active listening, 188–189, 194
ADD. *See* Attention Deficit
    Disorder (ADD)
ADD-H: Comprehensive
    Teacher's Rating Scale
    (ACTeRS), 91
Adolescence, 13–15
All Kinds of Minds (Levine), 101
American College Test (ACT), 178
Anxiety
    about assessments, 92, 100
    about reading, 176
    about tests, 212, 217, 235
    and stress management,
        151–153
Assessment. *See also* Feedback;
    Testing; Tests; Test-taking
    skills
    analyzing and interpreting
        results of, 96–98
    of behavioral functioning,
        90–91
    collecting and reporting infor-
        mation in, 95–96
    components of, 83–91
    discussing results of, 98–101
    fairness of, 96
    monitoring progress, 37,
        181–182

of outcomes, 41
and periodic reviews, 103
pretesting and collecting
    information, 33–34,
    176–178, 200, 224–225,
    250–251, 270
process of, 92–103
program planning recommen-
    dations based on, 101–102,
    116–118
psychometric, 87–90
purpose of, 82, 91
referrals for, 82–83
selection of methods for, 123
student and family involvement
    in, 92–95, 148
team approach to, 91–92
Attention, focus and maintenance
    of, 10, 31, 139–141, 176,
    193, 211, 241
Attention Deficit Disorder (ADD)
    definition of, 6
    diagnosis of, 11–12
    and drop-out rate, 15
    impact on learning, 12–13
    symptomatic behaviors of,
        9–11
Attention Deficit Disorders
    Evaluation Scale, 91
Attention Deficit/Hyperactivity
    Disorder, 6
Attention problems
    definition of, 6
    impact on learning, 12–13
    incidence of, 6
Attentional Capacity Test
    (ACT), 91

About the Authors

Geraldine Markel, Ph.D., directs college and adult services at the Reading and Learning Skills Center at the University of Michigan. She is also a consultant with the Instructional Development Workshop at the Executive Education Center of the Graduate School of Business Administration, also at the University of Michigan. She earned her doctorate in educational psychology and master's degree in reading from that university and has held faculty and research positions in both the School of Education and the School of Dentistry there.

The author of numerous articles and instructional materials, she is coauthor, with Dr. Judith Greenbaum, of *Parents Are to Be Seen and Heard: Assertiveness in Educational Planning for Parents of Handicapped Children* (G & M Associates, 1985) and a book chapter entitled "Crisis Prevention for Parents of Children with Handicapping Conditions" (Family Service of America, 1992). With Linda Bizer, Ph.D., she coauthored *The ABCs of the SAT: A Parent's Guide to College Entrance Examinations* (ARCO, 1983).

Dr. Markel has taught students with learning disabilities, attention deficit disorders, emotional impairments, and physical disabilities in both secondary and postsecondary settings. She is a popular speaker and trainer and consults widely in the areas of systems analysis and performance enhancement.

Judith Greenbaum received her Ph.D. from the University of Michigan with a focus on special education. Her extensive experience with students with special needs ranges from preschool (Head Start) through postsecondary settings (Washtenaw Community College).

At the University of Michgan and as an educational consultant in private practice, Dr. Greenbaum has worked with parents and schools in order to design appropriate educational programs for students with learning and attention problems.

Dr. Greenbaum has developed multimedia training materials such as the award-winning videotapes *Science Abled: Return on Equity* (University of Michigan, School of Dentistry, 1987) and a package on diversity and pluralism for the Michigan Metro Girl Scout Council. In addition, she has conducted numerous workshops for teachers and parents on topics such as underachievement, homework, and parent-teacher collaboration.